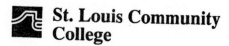

From Slavery to Freetown

From Slavery to Freetown

Black Loyalists After the American Revolution

by
MARY LOUISE CLIFFORD

McFarland & Company, Inc., Publishers
Jefferson, North Carolina, and London

British Library Cataloguing-in-Publication data are available

Library of Congress Cataloguing-in-Publication Data

Clifford, Mary Louise.
    From slavery to Freetown : Black Loyalists after the American
Revolution / by Mary Louise Clifford.
      p.   cm.
    Includes bibiographical references and index.
    ISBN 0-7864-0615-1 (library binding : 50# alkaline paper) ∞
    1. Sierra Leone—History—To 1896.   2. Nova Scotia—His-
tory—1763–1867.   3. Afro-American loyalists—Sierrra Leone.
4. Afro-American loyalists—Nova Scotia.   5. Afro-Americans—
Colonization—Sierra Leone—History—18th century.   6. Afro-
Americans—Colonization—Nova Scotia—History—18th century.
7. Freetown (Sierra Leone)—History—18th century.   8. Afro-
American loyalists—Sierra Leone—Freetown.   9. Afro-Americans—Colonization—Sierra Leone—Freetown—History—18th
century.   I. Title.
DT516.7.C57   1999
966.4—dc21   99-21345
                                                          CIP

Manufactured in the United States of America

McFarland & Company, Inc., Publishers
  Box 611, Jefferson, North Carolina 28640

To the Wren Writers—Lillian Barrett, Miriam Cardi,
Julie Hotchkiss, Charlotte Kelly, Joanne Kennedy,
Maggie Rastetter, Thea Seats, Ann Stubbs, and Lorna Trauth:
sincere thanks for patiently listening to this tale and
offering useful suggestions and abundant nourishment.

Thanks also to Candace Clifford and
Carter Cowles for their helpful insights.

Contents

Part III. The Province of Freedom

Part IV. Freetown

Introduction

Freetown is the capital of Sierra Leone on the coast of West Africa. If you were to go into a tired-looking bookshop on a busy downtown street (as I did while living there in 1964), you might find on a dusty shelf a few old issues of a small, gray paperback series called *Sierra Leone Studies*, published by the Crown Law Office. The issue of March 1927 (no. 8) caught my eye because it was the diary of Lieutenant John Clarkson, R.N., who was governor in 1792. Clarkson described in vivid detail the first year that he governed the tiny pioneer settlement of Freetown, naming the many residents, black and white, who struggled to establish a precarious foothold on the green mountain slopes and crags beside one of the world's most magnificent harbors. On an otherwise wave-swept coast, the estuary of the Rokel River had been a major entrepôt for the European slave trade since the Portuguese first penetrated that coast in the mid-fifteenth century. The site of Freetown's origins was blessed with a freshwater spring, and passing ships regularly stopped to take on potable water.

Anyone who stays in Freetown very long takes a river boat upstream to Bunce Island, the principal English slave factory in the river, where eighteenth century cannons still sit on their mounts, pointing defensively downstream. The solid stone fortress behind them, now empty and deserted, broods close to the shore amidst lush vegetation, its interior rooms very dark, very damp and very dirty.

The first settlers of Freetown were 1,200 former slaves, freed from

1

their American masters by the British during the American Revolution. The outlook of this group was very much shaped by their allegiance to charismatic black preachers who had led their exodus from Nova Scotia. Some of the black settlers left memoirs that detail their backgrounds and their long struggle to be free. The prominent figures appear regularly in all these accounts, and they are the particular focus of this book. Governor Zachary Macaulay also kept a diary, and much can be gleaned from the Thomas Clarkson papers and the records of the Sierra Leone Company, which sponsored the settlement. Official records in London tell the story after Freetown became a Crown colony in 1807.

Several excellent books have been written detailing and documenting all that is known of the black loyalists and the early history of Freetown. The bibliography lists these titles and other sources of information about the Revolutionary period. Much can be learned about the black loyalists in New York from the Sir Guy Carleton papers in the New York Public Library and from official government records in London. Official records in Halifax, Nova Scotia, where the freed blacks spent nine years, tell much of the later story.

As I learned more about the founding of Freetown, my attention gradually focused on several specific individuals from Virginia and the Carolinas. My narrative attempts to recreate their lives in the period of 1776 to 1813, when the last of them left the scene. The turbulent events of that time gain substance when seen through their eyes, coloring all the decades that followed.

After 1800 the original settlers' ranks were expanded by 500 Maroons from Jamaica—also freed, but rebellious slaves—and several thousand Africans liberated from slave ships by Britain in the early nineteenth century. The British felt obligated to provide schools and pastors for all these immigrants in order to teach them basic English and the principles of Christianity. A church dominates every village on the Freetown peninsula even today.

Over the years, these Freetown immigrants—all of them trans-

Opposite page: Freetown in 1798 as drawn by William Augustus Bowles, a visiting Creek Indian leader. Used as a frontispiece for Dr. Thomas Winterbottom's book, *An Account of the Native Africans of Sierra Leone,* published in 1803, and reprinted in 1969 by Frank Cass Publishers. Courtesy of Frank Cass Publishers.

planted and retransplanted Africans—developed a unique language and culture. They spoke a *lingua franca* based on the black English learned on southern plantations, mixed with vocabulary from dialects spoken by the Africans liberated from slave ships, along with bits of German, French,[1] and Portuguese.[2] This cozy dialect predominated in daily life and commerce for decades (and evolved gradually into the rich language today known as Krio). In addition to this dialect, those early Freetown settlers who went to school read and wrote the King's English, learned primarily from the King James Bible.

Any foreigner in Freetown today quickly becomes aware of the Krios. Their churches are grand, and the quaint formal attire they wear to services catches the eye. Their language is encountered everywhere (all the servants and market people speak it), and their musical intonations are infectious. The cotton tree under which their ancestors gathered to hold their first Thanksgiving service in 1792 still rises over a prominent intersection in Pademba Road, reminding the Krios of their remarkable ancestry.

Sierra Leone is a relatively new nation, having received its independence from Britain only in 1961. Its geographic boundaries were established in 1898, when the British created a protectorate over the hinterland. In both the eighteenth and nineteenth centuries the upcountry regions were racked with continuous petty struggles among the migrating and competing indigenous tribes—the source of the slaves shipped to the coast for sale in the seventeenth and eighteenth centuries. In the nineteenth century those tribal conflicts interfered with British trade; frequent expeditions were launched to put down tribal squabbling.

Today, much of Freetown is in ruins, the result of air and artillery bombardment and fierce gun battles raging through the city as different ethnic leaders in Sierra Leone have fought each other for control. Neither civilian nor military governments have been able to reconcile these age-old tribal differences.

The Krios of Freetown and the peninsula villages have seen history pass them by while they attended their schools and churches and worked as government clerks, teachers, and other minor functionaries. They watched power pass into the hands of the indigenous Africans when the British left. Today they probably observe the mayhem among those indigenous Africans with much the same frustration that the first immigrant settlers felt in 1792.

The saga of those first 1,200 settlers is heroic in many ways. In the pages that follow you will meet my favorites as they make their escape from their colonial masters. The American Revolution gave them the opportunity, but their aspirations to be free, land-owning citizens who took part in their own government were repeatedly thwarted in America. They finally returned to the continent of their origin, but even there they continued their struggle against foreign rule. Their descendants today remember their courage and determination with pride.

Mary Louise Clifford
Williamsburg, Virginia, 1999

PART I

The War for Independence

Chapter 1

Mary Perth of Norfolk, Virginia

Mary Perth was born around 1740 as the property of John Willoughby of Norfolk, Virginia, who owned 90 slaves.[1] She left no record of her own, but some of the events that mattered most to her were recorded in later years by others. Mary had learned to read in Virginia—an extraordinary fact at a time when most slaveholders feared that education would cause their slaves to question the reasons for their bondage. Mrs. Willoughby, however, admired Mary's initiative and gave her a New Testament, which she cherished throughout her long, dramatic life.

Mary not only learned to read and find solace in the Gospels, but while she lived in Norfolk, she was intent on spreading her message of hope for the downtrodden and Jesus's promise of heavenly mansions for all God's children—white or black. One night each week, after her master and mistress were in bed, she would tie her baby on her back (the name of the man who fathered her child, Patience, is not known, for Mary's own name was not recorded until after she married Caesar Perth some time before 1783) and walk ten miles to a secret meeting place in the country where other slaves assembled in a barn to hear her read God's message. After the lesson, Mary plodded the ten miles home before her owners awoke and the next day's labor began. She continued her teaching until the group was large enough to have its own preacher.

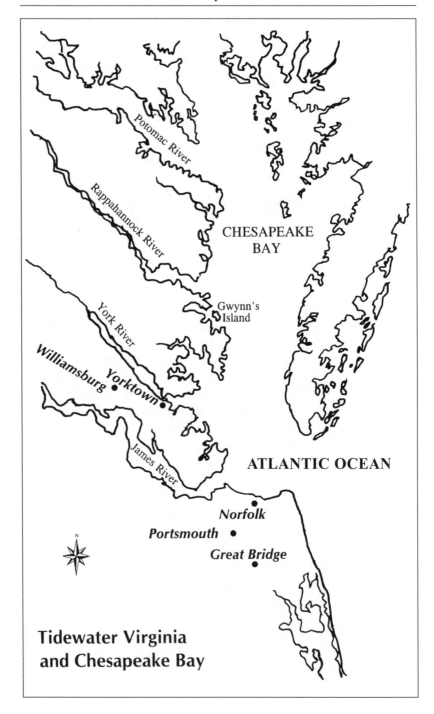

Tidewater Virginia
and Chesapeake Bay

During her bondage in Norfolk, Mary certainly never imagined that in 1775 events in the colonial capital of Virginia would change her life forever. John Murray, Earl of Dunmore, was the English governor, living in a palace in Williamsburg. He had dissolved the Virginia House of Burgesses for denouncing the closing of the port of Boston after the Boston Tea Party. The Burgesses promptly met elsewhere and activated their Committee of Correspondence[2] to coordinate a convention of all the colonies; their purpose was to oppose British taxation by imposing sanctions against the export and import of all goods to and from Great Britain. The Virginia convention met in St. John's Church in Richmond in March 1775 and decided to form a militia to defend themselves.[3]

Alarmed by this move, Dunmore imposed martial law and ordered British sailors to empty the powder magazine in Williamsburg in the dead of night. In April, the first shots were fired against the British at Lexington and Concord in Massachusetts. When Dunmore learned that the Virginia militia was about to gather in Williamsburg, he fled from his palace to the British man-of-war *Fowey*, and sailed to Norfolk; he felt safer among the Tory merchants dominating that port.

Dunmore was anxious about his ability to control the rebels[4] for he had only 600 regular troops and perhaps 60 able-bodied Tories at his command. As he cast about for some other way to increase his military force, he was inspired to issue a proclamation promising freedom to any slaves of rebel masters who would come to his side and fight the colonists. Obviously, the British intended to win any future conflict in the colonies and could reward such freed men with unlimited land on the frontier.

Mary Perth may not have understood the import of Dunmore's November 1775 proclamation, but word must have spread like wildfire through the slave quarters that some in the area were slipping away from their masters to join Dunmore's Ethiopia Corps. Within a week, over 300 black men were given shirts with "Liberty to slaves" emblazoned across the front and were taught to march and fire muskets. They saw their first military action in a minor skirmish at Kempsville in Princess Anne County, when they went out to intercept North Carolina rebels coming to join the Virginians. Dunmore won an easy victory over the disorganized colonials. In fact, the colonel leading the rebels was captured in a swamp by two of the slaves fighting for the British. The news must have electrified the black community. At the same time, the threat of a slave insurrection infuriated the colonists.

Flushed with his easy victory, Dunmore decided to attack the rebels at Great Bridge.[5] A slave belonging to Thomas Marshall (the father of John Marshall, later chief justice of the Supreme Court) crossed into the British lines and misled the British into thinking that Great Bridge was an easy target. Instead, the American sharpshooters were ready for battle this time, entrenched behind stout breastworks and waiting for their opponents to come within range. At fifty yards they opened fire and decimated the attacking force.

The British fell back in disorder and fled to their ships. The Tories in Norfolk saw themselves in peril, particularly when Dunmore threatened to bombard the city. All available civilian shipping, to which the Tories fled, hastened to join his fleet. British vessels actually opened fire on January 1, 1776, as British sailors rowed ashore and set fire to the warehouses along the Norfolk waterfront. The rebels finished the job by razing the rest of the city so that nothing would be left to any returning Tories.

John Willoughby was among the Tories who joined Dunmore, doubtless taking many of his slaves with him, among them Mary Perth and her daughter, Patience.

Dunmore's fleet anchored first at Portsmouth with the idea of attacking the Americans once spring came. But smallpox and jail fever broke out on board the ships, and the Americans brought up cannons to fire on the fleet. Dunmore weighed anchor and headed north for Gwynn's Island at the mouth of the Piankatank River, where he expected support from the predominantly Tory white population.

The sick and dying were put ashore there. Did Mary Perth see this as an opportunity to slip away from her master? She may have gone ashore with her daughter to nurse a sick comrade and care for her two bewildered children, Zilpah and Hannah Cevils.[6]

What a dreadful scene that must have been. Tenders rowing back and forth from ships to shore, ferrying the sick and dying along with barrels of water, rum, and hard biscuits for their sustenance. (The dead were simply dumped overboard.) Sailors heaved inert bodies onto the shining strip of sand along the east shore of the island. Dark, inhospitable forest stretched away behind them. Almost nothing was available in the way of care or medicine to alleviate the suffering—no shelter, no beds, no nurses, no kitchen. Moans and desperate cries rose from those who had no one to help them.

It was early spring, and biting winds swirled in off Chesapeake Bay, battering the shore. The nights were damp and cold. Those who could crawl crept into the shelter of the trees, fleeing the icy blasts of wind. In those grim weeks, disease cut down more of the blacks fleeing with Dunmore than battle ever did; at least 500 are believed to have died of typhus or smallpox. Captain Thomas Posey, who was among the American liberators of Gwynn's Island, described what the British left behind:

> I cannot help but observeing, that I never saw more distress in my life, than what I found among some of the poor deluded negroes which the [British] could not take time, or did not chuse to cary off with them, they being sick.... Those that I saw, some were dying, and many calling out for help; and throughout the whole Island we found them strew'd about, many of them torn to pieces by wild beasts—great numbers of the bodies haveing never been buried.[7]

In July 1776 the Americans brought up cannons on the mainland under shelter of darkness and began bombarding Dunmore's ships. Once again, the English governor weighed anchor and sailed away. If Mary Perth was abandoned on Gwynn's Island with Patience and two other young girls whose mother died there, they somehow made their way to New York, which was in British hands after General William Howe captured it in September 1776.

Escape might not have been as difficult as caring for the sick on Gwynn's Island, for British warships prowled the Chesapeake Bay and its tributary rivers—the James, York, Rappahannock, and Potomac. The rebellious Americans had no navy when the war began, and although the hidden militia battery guarded Gwynn's Island to prevent Dunmore's return, by September they were needed elsewhere. The Americans were hard put to fend off well-armed British warships hunting for rebels. Loyalists, both black and white, were doubtless picked up along the many miles of Chesapeake shoreline and taken to the safety of New York.

In any case, at some point after leaving Norfolk, Mary Perth gave

Willoughby the slip. She was completely on her own, undoubtedly, for the first time in her life. She must have been tremulous with hope that she and her daughter and her two extra charges might finally make their way to that promised land she had read about in her Bible. The fact that Mary named her daughter Patience Freeman tells us something about her character and her way of coping with the humiliation of slavery. Before she married Caesar Perth, [7] she may have called herself Mary Freeman in a gritty effort to elude Willoughby. When she arrived in New York, she would certainly have sought out other blacks from Virginia (750 of them were sheltering there by the time the war ended) with whom she could worship and share memories of their former home in the warm southland.

Chapter 2

Moses Wilkinson of Nansemond County, Virginia

Handicapped Moses Wilkinson was the slave of Miles Wilkinson of Nansemond County, Virginia. He was probably in his twenties when he escaped in 1776, doubtless guided by other slaves who fled in response to Dunmore's proclamation.[1] Unable to see or walk unaided, Moses had busied his mind with learning by heart a great deal of scripture—enough to feel called to spread the gospel among his fellows.

Biblical promises of salvation and redemption resonated among the blacks as solace against oppression and the indignities of slavery. Those who had come directly from Africa remembered well the rites of passage led by their medicine men and shamans. All the black slaves witnessed or participated in the preparations for the christenings, weddings, and funerals of their white masters. They watched Anglican clergy read the Christian liturgy for these rites from the Bible and the *Book of Common Prayer*. The ability to read must have seemed an awesome mystery. Those few blacks who managed to learn how would have been blessed with extraordinary powers in the eyes of their brethren. Learning scripture, whether by reading or by rote, also conferred great respect.

Moses Wilkinson must have truly been an inspiration to his comrades, for they provided whatever assistance he needed in the perilous escape from the plantations south of the James River. No written record exists to tell us how he reached the safety of New York. Once there, Moses would have reassured his companions by reciting scriptures and preaching faith and optimism during the long years of privation within the British lines. Mary Perth also would have joined such assemblies, listening and joining her voice in praising the Lord. She and Moses exemplified a new kind of fervent Christian, born in slavery, with the audacity and confidence to inspire the refugees in New York with hope for their future.

Their faith was born in a wave of evangelical Christianity that swept the American colonies in the second half of the eighteenth century. White Protestant revivalists traveled to farms and plantations, to villages and towns to preach the infectious idea that every man and woman had a God-given right to salvation, and they could address their petitions directly to the creator, not needing the intercession of trained clergy. Mary Perth had certainly heard such preachers and had been motivated herself to teach Bible classes back in Norfolk.

Reverend George Whitefield was the first evangelist to travel from England to the colonies; he returned seven times before 1769, and his fiery message electrified his listeners.[2] The itinerant white Methodist and Baptist evangelists who spread the doctrine of individual worth from Maine to Georgia often had little formal education and were seldom trained for the ministry. But they learned their scripture and preached their message to both blacks and whites with a conviction and eloquence that enraptured congregations.

Blacks enthralled by the revivalist message began to preach as early as 1743.[3] Needless to say, their influence spread quickly among their fellow slaves. Moses Wilkinson must have absorbed those exuberant words of hope as a very young man.

The revival meetings were a vivid contrast to the official Church of England, which permitted only trained clergy in its pulpits following sedate set texts. Anglican clergymen in the colonies often owned slaves. Blacks were very aware that slaveholders dominated the Anglican Church and sat on the local vestries. They may have been somewhat mystified when missionaries from the Anglican Society for the Propagation of the Gospel in Foreign Parts sought out blacks and native Americans and tried to convert them. Heated arguments ensued as to whether their version of the Christian faith would create obedient workers or instill invidious ideas of freedom. Southern slaveholders had no doubts on this score, fearing that reading the Bible and encouraging baptism would lead their slaves to rebel or try to escape. The slaveholders saw to it that their colonial legislatures passed laws making education for slaves illegal.[4]

Nevertheless, the religious enthusiasm that swept the American colonies in the decades before the Declaration of Independence was signed certainly influenced the black population in America, although their emancipation was never part of the colonists' demand for liberty. A few prominent white voices did condemn as hypocrites slaveholders who professed their love of freedom. Granville Sharp, the leading British abolitionist of the time, sympathized with the American colonists who had declared their independence, but pointed out that "toleration of domestic Slavery in the Colonies greatly weakens the claim or *natural Right* of our American Brethren to Liberty. Let them put away the *accursed thing* ... before they presume to implore the interposition of divine justice."[5] Thomas Paine, shortly after emigrating to the colonies, asked his readers to consider "with what consistency, or decency they complain so loudly of attempts to enslave them, while they hold so many hundred thousands in slavery; and annually enslave many thousands more."[6]

As a group, the Quakers were strongly against slavery, suggesting as early as 1713 that slaves should be sent back to Africa. The first anti-slavery society in America was founded in Philadelphia by a mostly Quaker group just five days before the battle of Lexington. During the American Revolution, the Quakers were condemning slavery, freeing their own slaves, and admitting blacks to their services and schools. In both Virginia and North Carolina they sought the legal right to manumit slaves and protect their free status. The Quakers were, however, concentrated in the North and had contact with only small numbers of blacks.

In the 1760s and 1770s a number of slaves in New England petitioned the courts, claiming that the royal charters granted to the colonies made all subjects residing there free. Although the legislators paid little attention, black freemen joined the New England colonial militias in the hope of improving their status. White patriots could also hire substitutes to serve in those militias, and some put their black slaves into uniform. Several states purchased or hired slaves for military duty; they fought with the minutemen at Lexington, Concord, Bunker Hill, Valley Forge, White Plains, and beyond.

In a total population of two and a half million in the colonies when Moses Wilkinson began preaching, 500,000 were black slaves. The concentration of slaves in large numbers, however, was in the South— 446,000 in Maryland, Virginia, the Carolinas, and Georgia. In Virginia they were 40 percent of the population; in the Carolinas and Georgia, they represented more than half. Any voices of protest against slavery in the South were muted by the simple economic fact that the plantation economy depended on black labor for profitability. Many, including Thomas Jefferson, blamed Britain for the slave trade in Africans and the establishment of slavery in the colonies, but they saw no way that tobacco and cotton plantations could survive without slaves.

Moses Wilkinson came of age inspired by dissidents who railed against the evils of subjugation, and he took that message so much to heart that he spent his entire life urging his fellows to stand tall and demand their rights.

Chapter 3

David George of Essex County, Virginia

David George was born around 1743 on a Nottoway River plantation in Essex County, Virginia, the property of a Mr. Chapel. David was one of nine children of parents named John and Judith (both of whom had been transported from Africa). His story is told in a memoir related to fellow Baptists during a visit to England in 1793.[1]

Memories of his childhood reverberated with the brutality he had witnessed and suffered. He recalled many years later that as a boy he had fetched water, carded cotton, and labored in the corn and tobacco fields. He told of beatings when he was flogged until the blood ran over his waistband. His sister Patty was whipped until her back was "all corruption," as though it would rot. His brother Dick ran away and was captured.

Southern plantation owners did not treat runaways lightly, for slaves were valuable property. A skilled craftsman was worth £150, a domestic servant £50–100, field hands £60–75, a child £15–20. Their owners called out their neighbors and formed armed posses to search the highways and rivers for runaways. Those who were captured were punished; some of them were banished to the back country, sold to the West Indies, or hanged.

The second time Dick ran away he was hunted with dogs and horses; when they brought him back, he was dangled by his arms from a cherry tree with his legs tied tightly together. A pole was thrust between his legs, and Chapel's two sons sat on either end of it to keep him down. After 500 lashes, they washed his back with salt water and whipped it in. Then Dick was sent back to work in the field.

David George's mother was Chapel's cook. Whenever her master was angry with her, he stripped her and lashed her. The trauma of seeing her on her knees, begging for mercy, haunted her son all his life.

David had from time to time attended the English church eight miles away, but he felt no religious conviction. When he was about 19 and his mother was dying, he ran away and spent five years as a fugitive, hunted by his master the whole time. Keeping track of their slaves was a top priority with slaveholders. If they heard that a British army was approaching, they hid their slaves. In fact, the British found it easier to win battles in the South than in the North, because the Southerners were more concerned with keeping track of their work force than with winning the war.[2]

David crossed the Roanoke River into North Carolina and found work there. Within a month he heard that a reward of 30 guineas was offered for his return. His employer advised him to head for the Savannah River. He worked for about two years there for a John Green before the searchers caught up with him again.

Then he escaped into Creek tribal territory in central Georgia and was captured by Native Americans. They kept him busy making fences, plowing, and planting corn. Chapel's son caught up with him there and paid the tribe chief with "rum, linnen, and a gun" for his return. Before he was taken out of Creek country, David escaped again and found sanctuary with a Natchez chief who put him to work mending deerskins and taking care of horses. Then he persuaded a Native American trader to introduce him to George Galphin of Silver Bluff, on the Savannah River south of Augusta. Galphin was an Irish immigrant who built a lively frontier trading town and acted as the Indian Agent during the American Revolution. He was generous with his family and servants, allowing his slaves to meet in his mill. He gave George work as a house servant.

About 1770, David married a woman named Phillis (who was possibly half Native American) and had a child. He also began attending prayer meetings led by a black man named Cyrus from Charleston.

There, he met a figure from his boyhood—George Liele (now owned by Henry Sharp of Burke County, Georgia), who was a Baptist deacon. Liele had been converted and baptized and had begun preaching to the other slaves along the Savannah River who were permitted to attend his meetings. He converted David and Phillis George and six others. They became the nucleus of the Silver Bluff Baptist Church, the first black church in America, founded sometime before December 1777.[3]

George soon experienced his first compulsion to preach and was encouraged to begin by praying with his friends and singing hymns from Watts's *Psalms and Hymns*.[4] He became an elder of his church. Then war broke out, and traveling preachers were denied access to slaves. George began conducting services for his fellows.

Galphin employed a schoolmaster, but it was illegal in Georgia to teach a slave to read. David obtained a spelling book and asked the children in the schoolmaster's class to repeat their lessons to him. Thus, he learned to read the Bible.

By the time the American Revolution began, George's little congregation had grown to 30 members. The trading post at Silver Bluff was stockaded and renamed Fort Galphin. When the British neared Galphin's plantation, he fled, leaving his slaves on their own. David, his wife and two children, and more than 50 others immediately set out for Savannah in search of their old leader, George Liele.[5]

The British took Savannah in 1779 in a surprise attack guided by an aged slave named Quamino Dolly. British commander-in-chief Henry Clinton repeated in his Philipsburg Proclamation the same offer of freedom to rebel slaves that Lord Dunmore had made four years earlier in Virginia and was reavowed by General Howe after New York was captured in 1776. In the siege that followed, Major General Augustine Prevest armed 250 blacks who fought valiantly. Hundreds of others toiled on the fortifications that permitted the British to hold the town until 1782, when the British surrender at Yorktown led to the abandonment of Southern seaports.

The black Baptists thrived in this period as free blacks, supporting themselves with odd jobs. Phillis George did General Clinton's laundry during his short stay there in 1780. David ran a butcher's stall supplied by his brother-in-law in the country. They rented a house with a garden and a field. George carried a pass signed by the town adjutant certifying that he was "a good Subject to King George" and a "Free Negro Man."

After the war, the British evacuated thousands of loyalists from Savannah (July 1782), including 5,000 blacks, most of whom were sent to east Florida and Jamaica into continued slavery. David and Phillis had meanwhile escaped to Charleston, from which the British evacuated 6,000 loyalists in November 1782.

Charleston was choked with refugees who had to be fed. Many fell sick in the crowded conditions. The British, using slave labor, attempted to keep captured rebel estates functioning in order to produce food. When the war ended, the British lost the countryside. Loyalists were demanding compensation for their property losses and were hardly satisfied with promises that confiscated rebel property could be sold to pay their claims. Nor were the Americans enthusiastic about the idea of their confiscated property being sold to compensate loyalists.

And what was to be done with the captured slaves? Some had been formed into a brigade under the command of Lieutenant Colonel James Moncrief. Southern rebels saw Moncrief as a rapacious rogue who sent hundreds of stolen slaves to his east Florida plantations.[6] Some British officers became attached to their black servants and wanted to keep them. The blacks in turn believed that life would be easier staying with them than being set loose to scavenge on their own.

When the war ended, the British evacuated all the loyalists from Charleston between August and December 1782. During this time, David George was befriended by Major General James Paterson, who was ordered in August 1782 to take over the Halifax military district in Nova Scotia. George and his family sailed with General Paterson in November.

Chapter 4

Four Men from Charleston: Boston King, Isaac Anderson, Cato Perkins, John Kizell

Boston King was born about 1760 on the plantation of Richard Waring, 28 miles from Charleston. His father had been kidnapped from Africa and was a driver on the plantation. His mother was a seamstress and nurse and also knew Native American herbal lore. Both were favorites of their master. Boston's father had been converted to Christianity in the 1740s, but missionary work among the blacks was halted after several lenient masters were poisoned by their slaves. Boston recalled that his family prayed together every night, and his father went into the woods on Sundays to pray.

Boston was put to work as a house servant at age six, and by age nine he was tending cattle. A dream when he was twelve made an enormous impression on him:

> At mid-day, when the cattle went under the shade of the trees, I dreamt that the world was on fire, and that I saw the supreme Judge descend on his great white Throne! I saw millions of souls; some of whom ascended up to heaven; while others were rejected, and fell into the greatest confusion and despair. This dream made such an impression upon my mind, that I refrained from swearing and bad company,

and from that time acknowledged that there was a GOD; but how to serve GOD I knew not.[1]

At age sixteen, Boston was apprenticed to a carpenter in Charleston and became a craftsman, a skill that contributed to his survival in later years. When the British captured Charleston in 1780, he was working as a carpenter several miles away. When his master, Richard Waring, was captured by the British, Boston immediately offered his services to the British. He soon came down with smallpox and was quarantined a mile from the British camp. "We lay sometimes a whole day without any thing to eat or drink; but Providence sent a man, who belonged to the York volunteers whom I was acquainted with, to my relief. He brought me such things as I stood in need of; and by the blessing of the Lord I began to recover."[2]

When he had recovered, Boston marched with the army to Major General Charles Cornwallis's headquarters at Camden, South Carolina, where he served as an orderly to English Captain Grey. He was off fishing when the British were attacked and abandoned their camp. Finding them gone, Boston walked 24 miles to find Captain Grey.

When the British found themselves outnumbered, Boston was given dispatches to carry through the American lines, successfully bringing reinforcements. King later made his way to Charleston harbor, where he waded out to a British man-of-war headed for New York.

Isaac Anderson was born a free man in Charleston, South Carolina. He worked as a carpenter until the British captured Charleston during the American Revolution. He then found it expedient to offer his skills to the British army, and must have been evacuated to New York, and thence to Nova Scotia.

Anderson doubtless knew Cato Perkins, also from Charleston, South Carolina, who in Nova Scotia would become a Methodist preacher of the Countess of Huntingdon's Connection. Anderson and Perkins would be fatally linked together years later in Freetown.

John Kizell was born the son and nephew of African chiefs in Sherbro country of Sierra Leone. At age twelve he had been seized in an attack on his uncle's village and transported across the Atlantic to

Charleston. He, too, joined the British when they captured Charleston and was with the guerrilla leader Major Patrick Ferguson when Ferguson was killed at the battle of King's Mountain in 1780. From there, Kizell made his way to New York.

The names of these four men from Charleston would reverberate a quarter of a century later in Freetown, Sierra Leone.

Chapter 5

Thomas Peters of Wilmington, North Carolina

His descendants now living in Freetown claim that Thomas Peters was of royal birth, kidnapped from the Yoruba coast of Africa in the 1760s, and sold into slavery. American accounts place his birth at about 1738 on the plantation of William Campbell of Wilmington, North Carolina. He certainly belonged to Campbell on the eve of the American Revolution. In 1776 he slipped away, made his way to New York, and joined a Black Pioneers company of the British regiment of Guides and Pioneers, formed that year with a promise of freedom after the war. The unit varied from 60 to 70 men. All of the officers were white; however, Peters became one of three black sergeants (along with Mingo Leslie and Murphy Steele), and some of the corporals were black. Peters was wounded twice and proved to be a man of outstanding determination and ability.

Black residents of the countryside in which the British were fighting would have been invaluable because they had intimate knowledge of the landscape and its hazards, the trails and shortcuts, the streams and marshes, and the hiding places and dangers. Many black slaves distinguished themselves by making their way through enemy lines, carrying messages, spying on enemy positions, and leading sorties that captured rebels.

The Black Pioneers left New York with British forces in September

1777 to capture Philadelphia, where the Continental Congress[15] was sitting. They probably departed amid great excitement and rejoicing, for the British surely spread word that the capture of the headquarters of the rebellious colonists would end the rebellion. In the largely illiterate black community of the time, there were few sources of accurate information—no daily newspapers or radio news broadcasts. News spread by word of mouth with amazing speed, embroidered with rumor on its way and often distorted by misunderstanding. The freed slaves would have waited eagerly for news of the successful Battle of Brandywine and the flight of the Continental Congress to Baltimore. When it came, there was surely dancing and singing in the streets of Manhattan. Soon the war would be over, and every freed slave would become a prosperous farmer.

Their simple belief that the British could emancipate them with a single stroke of the pen must have been crushed by harsh reality as the months dragged by. They hardly understood how in 1777 General John Burgoyne was ordered to move down the Hudson from Canada to link up with General Howe's army in Pennsylvania, cutting the colonies in half so they could no longer aid each other. Then word of Howe's defeat at the Battle of Princeton in January 1777 would have filtered back to the puzzled blacks, followed months later by Burgoyne's surrender to the Americans at Saratoga in October 1777. All of New York would have buzzed with endless discussions and speculation as to what it all meant.

A year later who could have understood that the whole character of the war changed when the rebellious Americans won French support in their struggle for independence? In October 1778, before a French fleet could reach the Delaware River and cut them off, British forces abandoned Philadelphia and returned to New York. Thomas Peters was among them.

Hope would have soared again when the British captured Savannah in December 1778 and Charleston in May 1780. But jubilation again turned to bitter disappointment in 1781 when word came that Cornwallis had surrendered at Yorktown. Indeed, the whole progress of the war must have seemed erratic and incomprehensible to the black refugees when joyous promises of assured victory gave way months later to inexplicable failures.

In the end, of course, their hopes were completely dashed. The British had capitulated. The freed black men and women shielded by a British Army on Manhattan Island must have worried and speculated endlessly as to what would become of them.

Chapter 6

Refuge in British New York

However circuitous their escape routes, all of them—Mary (not yet married to Caesar), Caesar Perth, Moses Wilkinson, David George, Boston King, Thomas Peters, and the four men from Charleston—eventually ended up in New York, the city held longest by the British at the end of the American Revolution.

The British had captured New York in September 1776 and used it as a central base from which to patrol the Atlantic coast. The population of the city had been concentrated in the mile at the southern tip of Manhattan below Chambers Street, protected by Fort George, with a barracks for 200 men, two powder magazines, a battery of 120 cannons frowning over the harbor, and the skeleton of a governor's house, which had burned several years earlier. The waterfront beyond the battery was lined with wharves and warehouses. To the north of the fort were Bowling Green and the Broad Way, which was lined with a double row of shade trees and the stately homes of leading citizens. Old Trinity Church sat on Wall Street. The Bowery was still a rural lane, green with the vegetation that had inspired its name.

Before the revolution, the city was dominated by merchants, shopkeepers, tradesmen, and artisans. Those who wanted greater economic independence from Great Britain to increase their success had sided with the patriots and fled the city when Howe occupied New York. As many as 15,000 may have departed, leaving perhaps 5,000 loyalists behind. Refugee white loyalists quickly swarmed into the homes abandoned by patriots and were given pensions, free fuel, and candles.

Some of the refugees arrived as early as Dunmore's fleet, which, after it left Gwynn's Island, marked time until New York was safely in British hands, then transported the white loyalists from Norfolk and the black survivors of his Ethiopia Corps to that central city, where they could be attached to other units. Then the hapless Virginia governor sailed back to England, probably taking many white loyalists with him.

Shortly before the first refugees arrived, two raging fires had swept through New York, destroying a quarter of the houses and public buildings. No one knew for sure whether they were started by accident or by rebellious colonists. Little of the city was rebuilt, for construction materials were hard to come by.[1]

When Dunmore's fleet arrived a few weeks later, his black loyalists competed with swarms of other refugees and camp followers for shelter from the elements. Autumn was well along, with crisp, chilly nights giving warning of the coming winter. Sailcloth was hastily stretched between skeletal walls and chimney stacks. Temporary huts were erected of whatever building material could be scavenged from the streets and alleys. Laborers were packed tightly into crowded barracks and issued one pint of oil or one pound of candles per room per week. "The commerce on which a great part of the population relied for its existence was for the moment at an end; the great warehouses deserted; and the wharves empty save for ships of war, supply, and transports."[2]

Moses Wilkinson surely held regular prayer meetings for his followers in one of those deserted warehouses. Other refugees would soon flock to his services for the solace and companionship they found there. Mary Perth was probably among them.

Buoyed by her vision of freedom, Mary must have struggled to find shelter and sustain herself and the three children in her care (ages three, seven, and ten when they reached New York). Work was hard to find; food was extremely expensive because all of it was imported by sea. Orphans, indigents, and the elderly were aided by overseers of the poor, who collected rents, license fees, fines, lottery proceeds, and charitable contributions. The able-bodied poor scrounged for subsistence.

Hundreds of black refugees worked for the British military departments. Mary Perth competed with others for jobs as domestic servants, seamstresses, laundresses, or artisans, accepting whatever meager wages they could get. Laborers sought day jobs of any sort—driving wagons, delivering wood and coal, carrying lumber, pulling down fences for firewood, stripping churches, and converting King's College to be used as barracks or hospitals. Many resorted to begging and thievery, and the jails were full. Those convicted of robbery were deported to the West Indies.

Mary Perth and her girls shivered through six winters with more snow than they had ever seen before. In 1779 the snow began to fall in November and accumulated to a depth of four feet by March. The harbor was frozen solid for over a month, and no ships could be docked. The rivers around Manhattan were no longer a protective barrier against the enemy, for cannons could easily be pulled across the ice.

When the war ended in 1781, loyalist civilians and soldiers, white and black, were evacuated from Philadelphia, Savannah, and Charleston to New York, swelling the refugee population to 40,000—all of them expecting Britain to provide them with some sort of future haven.[3] The wealthy lost much property, for there was no way to carry all their possessions away from the colonies. All of them, rich or poor, slave or free, faced severing ties with family and friends and evacuation to some unknown destination.

Chapter 7

Peace Treaty Terms

When the British surrendered at Yorktown and word reached New York that they had lost the war, consternation swept through the black refugee community. Hundreds of freed blacks were sheltering behind British military lines. Would the bold promises of freedom made by British commanders be kept? How was rightful ownership of slaves to be sorted out? The burden was so great that the British were forced to close their lines to any more fleeing blacks.

The blacks under British protection had to compete with thousands of white loyalists who were clamoring for compensation for property they lost in the colonies and were also demanding transportation to safety—away from the victorious American colonists. The victors—the patriot Americans—were determined to win back property (including slaves) the British had seized in the course of the war.

The black loyalists learned in 1782 that peace negotiations were going on in Paris; Moses Wilkinson's prayer meetings surely witnessed endless debates as to why it was taking so long. Then they learned of the arrival of Sir Guy Carleton in New York to succeed Clinton, but had only a vague understanding of his mission. His orders were to remove all British forces and salvageable property from Savannah, Charleston, and New York and divert them to the West Indies for use against France and Spain—a monumental task. Months passed with no clear explanation of his plans.

He sent word to British commanders in Savannah and Charleston to remove all loyalists there to New York. Communications between New York and the two southern cities was by sailing ship. Brigadier General Alexander Leslie, who was in charge in Charleston, worked out a plan for a commission of British and Americans to hear appeals from both owners and slaves before they were evacuated. The two sides agreed that blacks who had served the British would remain free, their worth to be paid to any master who could prove previous ownership. The blacks so freed—among them David and Phillis George, Boston and Violet King, Isaac Anderson, Cato Perkins, and John Kizell—would be removed to some other part of the British empire. All other blacks, sequestered or captured as prizes, would be returned to their owners.

To make certain that no rebel slaves got away, departing vessels were to be inspected jointly. That practice broke down when a British armed party sent out to forage for food met with armed resistance. The redcoats were attacked by an American contingent led by Colonel John Laurens, son of Henry Laurens, a wealthy South Carolina planter.[1] The colonel was killed in the skirmish, and three British soldiers were taken prisoner. The Americans refused to give up their hostages, giving Leslie an excuse to proceed with his evacuation without American inspection.

The provisional peace treaty was concluded in December 1782.[2] An armistice followed, along with more months of uncertainty. The terms of the peace treaty ending the war were finally published in New York in March 1783, and they were received with joy and elation until the freed blacks learned of Article VII, promising the return of all confiscated property to its rightful owners. White loyalists were scathing in their denunciation of the British negotiators for agreeing to Article VII, for they thought the artful Americans had outwitted the British. When rumor spread that all escaped slaves must go back to their former masters, a tidal wave of fear swept through the black community.

Boston King wrote of the inexpressible anguish and terror when his people encountered slave owners from Virginia, the Carolinas, and Georgia, now permitted to enter New York to search for their slaves. "Many of the slaves had very cruel masters, so that the thoughts of returning home with them embittered life to us. For some days we lost our appetite for food, and sleep departed from our eyes."[3]

Boston had no way of knowing that the terms of Article VII of the peace treaty were worked out by two wily slave merchants—an American and an Englishman who had both made fortunes in buying and selling captured Africans. Henry Laurens, father of the Colonel John Laurens killed in the skirmish outside Charleston, joined the peace negotiations in Paris in November, a month before their conclusion. He was both a wealthy plantation owner[4] and a prominent political leader in the American colonies. He had been captured at sea on a diplomatic mission and spent nearly two years in the Tower of London, until he was exchanged for Cornwallis in 1781. Bail for Laurens's release was provided by a close English friend, Richard Oswald.

The new U.S. Congress then directed Laurens to Paris in November 1782 to join the talks working out a peace treaty. The chief British negotiator was that same friend of Laurens—Oswald—a wealthy merchant and army contractor who had owned for years the main British slave factory on Bunce Island in the Rokel River in Sierra Leone. When Oswald shipped slaves from Africa to Charleston, Laurens received a 10 percent commission for handling the cargo at his end.

Laurens knew that the British had already successfully evacuated Charleston, taking away hundreds of blacks whom the Americans expected to be given up. He was also grieving the death of his son in that minor skirmish with the British. He suggested that a stipulation be added to the peace treaty stating that the British troops should carry off no Negroes or other American property. Oswald agreed, and Article VII was born. It read in part:

> all Hostilities both by Sea and Land shall from henceforth cease; all prisoners on both sides shall be set at Liberty and His Britannic Majesty shall, with all convenient Speed and without Causing any destruction or carrying away any Negroes or other Property of the American Inhabitants, withdraw all his Armies, Garrisons, and Fleets, from the said United States.[5]

In New York, General Carleton knew perfectly well that Article VII contravened the pledge of freedom made by three successive commanders to those blacks who came over to the British side. With his strong sense of honor and obligation, Carleton never believed for a moment that his government intended to break its promise to the fugitives. He interpreted Article VII to apply only to those blacks who were *not* free. Those blacks already within the British lines before November 1782 were free; thus, they could no longer be considered American property. He therefore told all black loyalists who had been in New York for the preceding year or longer to present themselves to General Samuel Birch, who would issue certificates stating that they were free. When he informed the king's prime minister in London of his action, he received support.

Carleton turned away further deserters by declaring that only refugees who had spent a year within British lines would qualify for Birch's certificate indicating their free status. To Caesar and Mary Perth, Boston and Violet King, Moses Wilkinson, and Thomas Peters, those certificates must have seemed more precious than gold.

Chapter 8

Evacuation from
New York

In the two years between Cornwallis's surrender at Yorktown and the armistice, displaced blacks in the colonies were in extreme peril. British, Hessian, French, and American troops alike sought last minute booty of every sort. Colonists loyal to the British crown tried desperately to hold onto their slaves, find those who had strayed, and get them out of the country with the rest of their goods. American slaveholders insisted they should be allowed to go behind British lines to track down the fugitives. Few of them were successful, but their demand for compensation for their lost property plagued British-American relations for the next half a century.[1]

In New York, the last British post to be evacuated, Carleton insisted on precise procedures to settle claims to disputed property. Although directed by London to depart as swiftly as possible, limitations in shipping made this impossible, so Carleton dealt with the weakest spots first, leaving New York until last. He was determined to evacuate all the loyalists before the military pulled out, but the chaos took weeks to sort out. Some 40,000 loyalists were waiting for transport, agonizing over which of their possessions could be taken with them, auctioning off what could not be accommodated. The victorious Americans seethed as 81 loaded vessels shuttled between New York and Nova Scotia from April to December.

Members of the new U.S. Congress heard from their furious constituents who felt the British had tricked them; they demanded that the British evacuation of former slaves be stopped. Governor Benjamin Harrison of Virginia proposed that British prisoners of war be held until the slave issue was resolved. Others saw the opportunity for repudiating debts owed to loyalists. Protests were lodged with Carleton and in London, but the British government stood behind Carleton.[2] Strong pressure was put on General George Washington to protest.[3] The new president, preoccupied with devising some form of suitable and acceptable government for the victorious colonists, met with Carleton in May 1783 and argued that the treaty promised return of all patriot property. Carleton would not budge. Eventually, Washington had no alternative but to accept Carleton's promise that all evacuees would be recorded and compensation paid for legitimate American claims. The "Book of Negroes" contains the information recorded to keep that promise:

Mary Perth	Age 43	Stout Wench
Zilpah Cevils	Age 15	Likely Girl
Hannah Cevils	Age 10	Ditto
Patience Freeman	Age 18	Ditto
Violet King	Age 35	Stout Wench
Boston King	Age 23	Stout Fellow

Between April and November of 1783 the British lined up 3,000 black evacuees to be recorded: name, details of escape or other claim to freedom, military record, name of former master, and the name, commander, and destination of the vessel in which each was to remove. Two-thirds were black loyalists who had escaped from the South. Some 14 percent of them claimed to have been born free, to have been freed, or to have purchased their freedom. The rest claimed to have escaped from patriot owners, who would be compensated on the basis of information recorded in the "Book of Negroes." The ledger said these traveled "on their own bottoms"—a British phrase indicating that they had been freed in return for service to the Crown. Ship's captains could carry no one whose name was not on the roll.[4]

In the confusion of preparations to relinquish New York, Tory slaveholders came, seeking to establish that some of these refugees were their property and had no right to leave. Disputed claims over ownership of blacks were heard by a joint board of Americans and British who met each Wednesday at Fraunces Tavern. If the owner was a loyalist, the blacks had no chance of winning their freedom because no British subject could be divested of his property without his own consent.

How tremulous those who had dreamed of freedom must have felt as the days slipped by. Those refugees who had formed close ties in New York must have worried about their friends. Mary Perth surely knew Judith Jackson, who was also from Norfolk, having been a slave there of loyalist John McLean. Before he fled to Britain, McLean sold Judith to Jonathan Eilbeck. When McLean left the country, however, Judith considered herself free and went over to the British army, where she washed and ironed clothes for Dunmore and other officers. She had her certificate stating that she had served the British, signed by Birch, and was about to embark for Nova Scotia when Eilbeck arrived in New York and claimed her. The inspectors separated her roughly from the others and locked her up in a nearby shed until the next hearing was scheduled. Eilbeck meanwhile sent her clothes, the money she had saved, and her child back to Virginia. The board ruled in Eilbeck's favor. Mary Perth never saw Judith again.

The date when Mary married Caesar Perth and assumed his name is unknown. The name of her husband does not appear next to hers in the "Book of Negroes" because he was a war veteran and captain of the company to which she belonged. The 1,800 black men and their families were organized into "Black Companies" to aid in food distribution and relieve the British of the myriad details of the evacuation. Caesar Perth had belonged to Hardy Weller, also of Norfolk, but had not deserted his master until 1779, when he was about 33 years old. Mary may have known him in Norfolk or found him among the slaves from Virginia who helped each other survive in New York.

When providing information for the "Book of Negroes," Mary Perth gave her daughter's name as Patience Freeman. Had she not married Caesar Perth after she escaped from John Willoughby, would she have called herself Mary Freeman when she lined up to be recorded in the "Book of Negroes"? Many of the other black fugitives probably lied about their names and origins in the hope that their former owners would be unable to track them down.

John Willoughby appeared in New York in 1783 after the armistice, searching for his 90 lost slaves—among them Mary and Patience, and probably Hannah and Zilpah Cevils as well. Had Willoughby tracked them down, their brief taste of freedom would have ended. Certainly Mary would have learned through the grapevine that her former master was tramping angrily up and down the streets of New York, demanding the return of his lost property.

She must have held her breath as British soldiers lined up her company on the docks, and the British inspectors questioned each black claiming freedom. Would her married name be enough to shelter her from Willoughby? Patience, Zilpah, and Hannah must have watched the enrollment with dry mouths and rapidly beating hearts, knowing what was at stake, although they were old enough to stand tall and expressionless through the hours of waiting in line for the entries to be written in the "Book of Negroes." Mary and Caesar probably sweated and held the three girls close to them through that long ordeal, aware that they would never be safe until the British ship that was to evacuate them weighed anchor and sailed away from New York.[5]

Mary and Caesar knew absolutely nothing about Nova Scotia, but they were trusting that it was to be the promised land about which Moses Wilkinson preached and they praised in the songs the evangelists had taught them. Their faith in a promised land was the dream that had sustained Mary through those six long, difficult years in New York.

The Perth family—Caesar, Mary, Patience, Zilpah, and Hannah— sailed from New York on *L'Abondance* on July 31, 1783. *L'Abondance* carried 409 blacks, more than any other single ship making the trip to Nova Scotia.[7] Crippled Moses Wilkinson was on board as well. Surely every morning he was carried on deck to recite scripture, say prayers, and preach heartwarming sermons to the eager passengers gathered around him. His courage and determination would have been an inspiration to them all.

PART II
Nova Scotia

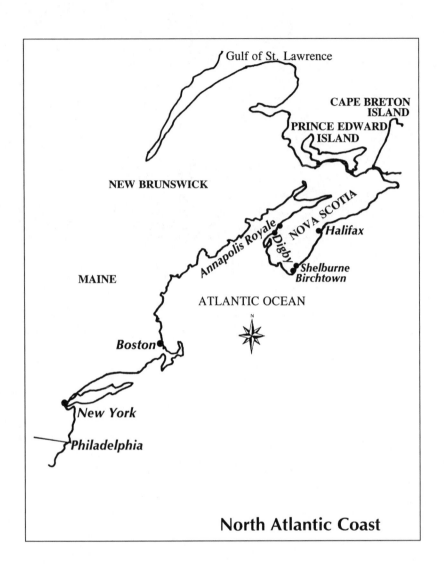

Gulf of St. Lawrence

CAPE BRETON
ISLAND

PRINCE EDWARD
ISLAND

NEW BRUNSWICK

Annapolis Royale

NOVA SCOTIA

Digby

Halifax

Shelburne
Birchtown

MAINE

ATLANTIC OCEAN

N

Boston

New York

Philadelphia

North Atlantic Coast

Chapter 9

The Founding of Birchtown

L'Abondance weighed anchor in a fine natural harbor on the southern coast of Nova Scotia.[1] Nova Scotia had been chosen by the British as a place of refuge because it was nearby and thinly populated. Halifax, its capital, was barely 600 miles from New York. A town named Port Roseway (renamed Shelburne in July 1784 to honor William Petty, second earl of Shelburne, the British secretary of state who had supervised the peace negotiations) had already been established by white loyalists and their slaves[2] and servants on the northeast side of the heart-shaped bay.

The governor in Halifax, Lieutenant Colonel John Parr, was a career soldier, an assertive man who cared a great deal about his own status and reputation. He knew instinctively that more was to be gained in pleasing prosperous white refugees than in catering to a rabble of emancipated, penniless blacks. He assured General Carleton in New York that land would be set aside for the refugees and all available necessities would be provided, but he worried privately about the cost of the influx and the British Treasury's willingness to pay for the resettlement. He also warned Carleton that "there is not any Houses or Cover to put them under Shelter; this Town [Halifax] is already so crowded. ... And when I add the Scarcity and difficulty of providing fuel, and lumber for building which is still greater, the many inconveniences and great distress these people must suffer, if any of them come into this Province this Winter, will sufficiently appear."[3]

The governor's apprehensions were well founded. The black loyalists brought very little with them, save what they had been issued before leaving New York—a spade and an ax, two yards of woolen cloth, seven yards of linen, two pairs of stockings, one pair of mitts, and one pair of shoes.[4] Hardly the equipment needed to hack a town from the Nova Scotian wilderness. No saws, hoes, hammers, nails, hinges, fireplace tools, buckets, cooking pots, or furniture. Of course, shopkeepers in Shelburne were very willing to sell them all these necessities, but few of the refugees carried any savings with them to their new home—probably only those who had found steady work in New York.

Because Shelburne was already bursting at the seams,[5] the free black loyalists on *L'Abondance* were told to start a new town three miles away on the northwest side of the bay. The newcomers must have borne their lame preacher, Moses Wilkinson, ashore to lead them in prayer and thanksgiving on the beach of what they believed was their promised land. Brother Wilkinson would have been eager to designate a spot on which a meeting house could be built so that he could hold proper worship services for his shipmates. The company captains were told that one Benjamin Marston, an impoverished merchant from Massachusetts whose influential cousin had arranged his appointment as deputy surveyor for Shelburne, would lay out town and farm plots. They probably would not have been told that Marston had no experience in surveying.[6] The day following the arrival of *L'Abondance*, Marston conducted Caesar Perth, John Cuthbert, Robert Nicholson, William O'Neil, James Reid, Nathaniel Snowball,[7] and the other company captains over the suggested site for their town. They returned to the ship to tell Wilkinson and the others of the luxuriant growth of forest along the shore and the potential for hunting and fishing. They happily agreed to the site chosen for them, and in a general discussion among the ship's passengers decided to call their settlement Birchtown, in honor of the English general who had signed their certificates of freedom in New York. They could not foresee that rock outcroppings lay just below the surface, that forest and swamps would be a formidable barrier to clearing farms, that the shallow, sandy soil along the south coast produced only scanty crops, and that the harbor froze over in the winter.

They waited eagerly for the surveying to be completed so they could go ashore and begin clearing their town plots. Barely two weeks later they heard that white loyalists were claiming the area adjacent to Shelburne and wanted the surveying stopped. Then in September, ships bearing 5,000 more unexpected white refugees arrived, pulling the surveyors away to mark out more town plots in Shelburne for them. White claims always took priority over those of the free blacks—a reward for Tory loyalty during the war and compensation for losses in the colonies they had left. By the end of the year, Shelburne had 800 houses finished, 600 more under construction, and several hundred begun. Governor Parr estimated its population at 12,000, with 100 vessels anchored in "the finest and best Harbour in the World."[8] But none of this benefited Moses Wilkinson and his flock, who spent that winter on board the ship or under tents on shore. Fortunately, the winter of 1783–84 was mild.

Mary Perth was pregnant with her second child when the Perth family arrived in Birchtown; she was 43 years old. Her daughter Susan was born before the year ended, so the task of felling trees and burning brush on their town lot would have been beyond Mary's capabilities. None of the freed blacks had horses or equipment with which to do this heavy work. Think of chopping through huge tree trunks with just an ax. The men must have worked together in teams to cut down the virgin spruce and maple trees and uproot or burn their stumps. Mary Perth's daughter Patience at age 18 was probably sturdy and strong and could work beside her step-father in clearing a plot for their cabin. Zilpah and Hannah Cevils were 15 and 10—old enough to tackle lighter tasks such as burning brush and gathering firewood.

The first tentative dwellings built on the town lots were very crude. Some of the refugees were experienced carpenters who knew how to cut lumber, and they may have had a few handsaws. But they could produce only rough, unseasoned boards, which would certainly warp in the damp months ahead. They could caulk the cracks adequately with mud during the summer, but in winter the wind and snow must have penetrated all the chinks.

The other men had only the spade and ax issued to them in New York. The rough, one-room cabins they threw up had a small window or two to admit light and shutters to close against the wind and snow. A fireplace would have been essential for heat and cooking; it was constructed of local stone because no one had money to buy bricks. Perhaps a loft was added above as a sleeping place for the children and a drying place under the roof for herbs and vegetables. They carried water from a nearby stream or spring and relieved themselves behind a bush or a tree. Picture this in a blizzard with the wind howling down out of the Arctic. Free pork and corn meal were distributed to the 21 company captains in Birchtown, but parceling out rations in large quantities was often delayed, for refugees arrived in unexpected numbers and distribution was cumbersome. All loyalists were to receive full rations for their first year, two-thirds rations for the second year, and one-third the third year, by which time they should have been able to support themselves on their cleared and planted farms. This theory never worked out in practice; few loyalists along the south coast, white or black, were able to grow sufficient food for their own needs. Many of them remained dependent on government rations for several years. In fact, food production in Nova Scotia fell so far short that a temporary law was passed in 1788 permitting the importation of food, livestock, and lumber from the United States. All of British North America suffered a severe famine in 1789 and sought food elsewhere through the next four years.[9]

An Englishman named William Dyott visited Birchtown in 1788 and wrote the following description:

> The place is beyond description wretched, situated on the coast in the middle of barren rocks, and partly surrounded by thick impenetrable wood. Their huts miserable to guard against the inclemency of a Nova Scotia winter, and their existence almost depending on what they could lay up in summer. I think I never saw such wretchedness and poverty so strongly perceptible in the garb and countenance of the human species as these miserable outcasts.[10]

Every town plot was to have yard space for growing fruits and vegetables. Even if Caesar Perth and his family had succeeded in clearing virgin forest and laying out a garden with only a spade and an ax, they arrived too late in that first fall to plant. They had no livestock, no ammunition or guns for hunting, and no finished lumber for building houses. Nor did any of them have any capital or credit with which to buy these essentials or start a business.

Even the government rations they had been promised were not

always distributed. English officials in charge of the food often had agendas of their own. Freed blacks were required to give six days of unpaid labor each year on public works. Withholding rations was one way to force the black refugees to perform public service. The discussions at Moses Wilkinson's evening prayer meetings must have been heated. Caesar Perth, Nathaniel Snowball, and James Reid surely complained loudly that they were being exploited, forced to work without pay before they had received any farm allotments.

Consider, too, how difficult it must have been for them to clearly articulate their grievances and reason out solutions to ameliorate them. They spoke no common language brought from Africa, for they and their ancestors came from an array of African tribes, each of which had its own dialect. They spoke black English, and each would have learned his limited English in a different setting. The vocabulary they shared in common derived from the workings of southern plantations and did not encompass their quest for legal title to wilderness land in Nova Scotia or arguments with white government officials as to whether they should be forced to labor for their promised food rations. Nothing had prepared them to deal with the dilemma they faced. Caesar Perth probably would have come home after a hard day on a road gang and complained bitterly. Mary Perth would surely have responded with sympathetic murmurs and a relaxing back rub. She probably also urged him not to lose faith and trust in the Lord, reminding him of their precious freedom.

As the fall slid into winter and surveying was halted by snows, freedom must have seemed more and more ephemeral. Many of the freed blacks had little choice but to seek paid work to put a roof over their heads and food in their stomachs. The white loyalists, long accustomed to slaves working as servants and field hands, regarded the blacks as a reservoir of cheap labor. And labor was both needed and scarce in Nova Scotia because of the great surge in building houses, clearing land for new farms, and the commercial needs of a huge population influx.

A few black refugees were fortunate. Luke Jordan, Thomas Godfrey, and John Thomas found berths on merchant ships, for they had navigational skills that commanded fair wages.[11] Some of the black Guides and Pioneers who had building or masonry skills found full-time jobs building barracks, storehouses, wharves, and roads. Other black loyalists were not so lucky. Many whites were contemptuous of the blacks' claims to equality; others sought to make the most of the plight of the freed slaves, who were forced into the labor market because they lacked land or another means of support. Pittance wages were paid for occasional work. Free blacks hired to clear and plant white property as tenant farmers would have barely enough money left to buy seed for the next planting after the proprietor took his percentage of the harvest.

As the long winter weeks crept by, Patience Freeman may have left her mother and stepfather to hike around the bay to Shelburne and knock on doors until she found a family in need of a servant. She could have indentured herself for a year's service for perhaps one English pound a month plus room and board.

If she received her small wage promptly and was released at the end of her indenture, she was luckier than many. Those who hired themselves out or accepted indentures were often exploited. When Henry McGregor indentured himself to Alphea Palmer for a year at £50, a disagreement after eight months led to his dismissal without pay. Thomas London, a cooper, also worked for Palmer, who collected London's food ration for eight months, but gave him only a quarter of the ration. Cyrus Williams indentured himself to Palmer for a year for £50, but was charged 12 shillings a week for what should have been free provisions.[12] If servants left the master with whom they were registered, they lost their government food issue.

Some free blacks went to work for masters who then claimed they were slaves. Proving their free status was difficult and uncertain, for any loyalist claim to black property was valid in the British courts and was upheld when the white loyalist presented reasonable evidence of ownership. Court decisions in such cases were made by English judges; the blacks targeted thus could not demand a jury trial by their peers.

Patience Freeman would always have been in fear of ruthless individuals who went so far as to kidnap free blacks to sell back to the United States or the West Indies. The white loyalist refugees from the American colonies brought an estimated 1,232 slaves to Nova Scotia with them.[13] Many of them settled in Shelburne on the south coast. When times were hard, white slave-owners were known to rent their slaves out or turn them loose to fend for themselves, knowing that they could reclaim them at will.

The arrival of so many freed blacks, however, complicated the situation for slaveholders because they could no longer tell who was in bondage and who was free. And the presence of hundreds of free blacks in Nova Scotia made those still belonging to loyalists question their bondage. Birchtown became a haven to which slaves fled from all over the province, knowing that the free blacks would hide them from their masters. Still, all the free blacks lived in fear that some master with a prior claim on them would appear and convince the court to deprive them of their freedom.

Chapter 10

Education Mattered

A substantial number of loyalists, white and black, appear briefly in the records in Nova Scotia and then pass off the scene.

One Captain Hamilton, for example, claimed that he had owned four black veterans ten years before in North Carolina, even though they had documents and witnesses to support their service to the Crown. The court in Halifax sided with Hamilton, granting him a warrant to seize them and sell them in the Bahamas. When their ship put into Shelburne, the four managed to get word to the court there that they were being held without a hearing. They were unusually fortunate in that Presiding Judge Isaac Wilkins ruled that Hamilton's claim was too old to be valid and freed the four.

Mary Postill, probably a neighbor of Caesar and Mary Perth, was less fortunate. Although she had been a slave of a rebel officer and had a certificate signed by Birch in New York, a white loyalist named Jesse Gray claimed her and her children and brought her to court. A black couple who came to court to testify on her behalf returned home to find their house on fire and one of their children dead. The judge granted Gray a year to prove his ownership.[1]

Punishment for breaking the law varied from county to county, but was always more severe for blacks. Whites paid fines when convicted of theft, slander, prostitution, assault, or even rioting. Blacks, on the other hand, were imprisoned or whipped. Impoverished blacks who could find no work sold their meager belongings to buy scarce food, then resorted to begging or died of starvation and exposure. A man named Prince Frederick received 78 lashes and a month's hard labor for stealing a pair of shoes. A black woman named Diana, convicted on two counts of petty larceny, received 200 lashes for the first offense and 150 for the second. Alicia Wiggins received 39 lashes for theft and was hanged for a second offense. A black man in Halifax was hanged for stealing a bag of potatoes.

A free black from Barbados, Stephen Blucke, was far more fortunate than his contemporaries in making a place for himself in Shelburne. The response of the black company captains to official demands depended, of course, on the ability and personality of the individuals involved. Officials in Nova Scotia particularly liked to deal with Blucke because he was a churchgoing Anglican who was prosperous enough to pay the pew fee (20 shillings a year) at Christ Church in Shelburne. He had received some formal education in Barbados, and, unlike the black slaves, he spoke with proper grammar and an English accent. Why he left his native Barbados and how he reached New York is unknown, but he volunteered to serve the loyalist forces, believing his future would be more secure with the British than with the Americans.

In the 1783 evacuation from New York, Blucke was recorded in the "Book of Negroes" as being 31 years old, a "stout fellow," born free in Barbados. With him was his wife, Margaret, age 40, who had purchased her freedom from the New York family into which she was born in slavery. They were accompanied by 21-year-old Isabel Gibbons (who was possibly Margaret's daughter) whom Margaret had bought from her former mistress and freed.

Described as "a mulatto of good reputation," Blucke was initially put in charge of organizing a black corps to work on the construction of public works in Shelburne as well as building a town for freed blacks across the bay (Birchtown). His facility for dealing with white officials in Nova Scotia obviously earned him respect and authority and may be why he was always called Colonel Blucke. There is no record of his having actually seen military service in the American Revolution, but he was given a lieutenant colonel's rank in the black militia in the Shelburne district,[2] serving under white Major Stephen Skinner.

Few in Birchtown had the advantages of Stephen Blucke in Shelburne, whose education made him seem more worthy than his fellows

51

to the British. He received 200 acres of farmland in 1786,[3] although his application had apparently not included the other members of his company. In the meantime, the Anglican Society for the Propagation of the Gospel (SPG) appointed Blucke to run their charity school in Birchtown, paying him 12 shillings per pupil per year. He augmented that income by running a small fishing smack.

A letter he wrote to the SPG before Christmas 1787, requesting clothes for his 38 pupils, spelled out the harsh conditions encountered by the freed blacks and solicited aid for them:

> The innumerable hardships that this new country abounds with, and the very few Opportunities that the poor blacks enjoy bereaves them of the means for Obtaining more than a scanty pittance of food, and in some families hardly that, which Occasions the poor little objects to be in the pityfull situation they now endure, and must experience still more, if some relief is not handed them; ... I apply for this relief humbly beseeching that your charity, may cover them, with a suit of clothes, a pair of Shoes and a Blanket....[4]

Fortunately, the Anglicans in London sent boxes of blankets, clothing, and shoes to both Birchtown and Digby on the west coast in 1787 and 1789.

Chapter 11

Black Preachers Offer Hope

David George arrived in Halifax early in 1784. He spent the spring there, aided by his white mentor, General James Paterson. In July he was given six months' rations by Governor Parr, but received no further supplies. He wanted to continue his preaching, but Halifax was an official town with a more than adequate number of Anglican clergymen in residence and 31 more newly arrived from the colonies. All of them would have been offended had the Halifax blacks gone off by themselves to listen to a black evangelist. Because St. Paul's Church in Halifax had too little space in the balcony to accommodate the large numbers of blacks who wanted to attend services, they were sent off to private homes with lay readers appointed to instruct them in the Bible and the Prayer Book.

Finding Halifax unwelcoming, David George headed for Shelburne in June and immediately began holding Baptist meetings there. The response thrilled him:

> The Black people came far and near, it was so new to them: I kept on so every night in the week, and appointed a meeting for the first Lord's day in a valley between two hills, close by the river; and a great number of White and Black people came, and I was so overjoyed with having an opportunity once more of preaching the word of God, that after I had given out the hymn, I could not speak for tears.[1]

David George was one of a number of black preachers who offered the black population of Nova Scotia a new sense of dignity and identity. The freed blacks were expected to look after themselves in their new home, a daunting reality for which they had few qualifications and little experience. No one else was really very concerned about what happened to them. Their dreams of owning prosperous farms seemed as ephemeral as ever. Job opportunities were meager and uncertain, and the winters were colder and more bitter than any they had ever known. A gospel meeting where one of their own promised them that God loved them and would take care of them seemed the only hope in the wilderness surrounding them. Just coming together with their fellows to share their misery and fear rallied their spirits and gave them courage to struggle on.

Nova Scotia had only recently experienced an invasion of the Great Awakening that had swept New England in the 1740s. New Lights chapels were established in every part of the province by Henry Alline, a revivalist Congregational preacher from Rhode Island who went to Nova Scotia in 1776. He returned regularly to preach his fiery message until his death in 1784. Alline founded chapels to free men from the authority and ritual of the ordained Anglican clergy and turn them to direct communication with God. He denied that the state had any right to interfere in spiritual matters, a stand that enraged Anglican clergy. They regarded the Church of England as a force conducive to loyalty and submission to duly constituted authority; any dissident denomination must be guilty of conspiracy against both God and the English government.

The free blacks in Shelburne and Birchtown must have been elated that they could now freely attend worship services, for this privilege had been strictly regulated or forbidden by their former masters in the colonies. Moses Wilkinson had set to work immediately, inspiring his flock to put up a crude Methodist chapel in which to worship. Not only could the blacks attend divine services but after David George's arrival, they could choose between a Methodist and Baptist preacher addressing them—both promising redemption and salvation.

The Anglicans living in Shelburne were aghast at the emotion and fervor expressed in David George's gospel meetings. Traditional Anglican services were very staid, led by a preacher reading familiar texts from the *Book of Common Prayer* and requiring only decorous spoken or sung responses from the congregation. The enthusiastic singing of rhythmic Negro spirituals and the stamping and shouting at revival meetings offended the Anglican sense of propriety. They had already been disturbed by Alline and by the Reverend William Black, a Methodist evangelist from Yorkshire who had been traveling through the province and moving his audiences to a frenzy with "lips ... touched with holy fire." Anglican hecklers came to his meetings to yell oaths and throw stones. Rather than intimidating the congregation, "this disturbance brought many more to hear."[2]

Now a black man set himself up in Shelburne as a missionary, preaching dissent and encouraging noisy, public affirmation of strong emotions. The Anglicans were furious at such display and wanted to send David George and other exuberant blacks packing. They talked the magistrates in Shelburne into restricting the movement of evangelists and distributed handbills "forbidding Negro dances, and Negro Frolicks in this Town." Offending blacks were charged with "riotous behaviour," hauled into court, and sent to the house of correction. A second offense could deprive them of their homes.[3]

The controversy was not solely religious, nor was opposition confined only to the Anglicans; class differences aggravated the religious turmoil. Disbanded soldiers rioted because desperate free blacks would work for lower than the going wages, depriving them of jobs.[4] They saw the evangelists stirring up trouble by telling their congregations to make their own decisions and not rely on local authorities to take care of them. David George wrote in his memoir that "40 to 50 disbanded soldiers ... came with the tackle of ships, and turned my dwelling house, and every one of [my free black neighbors' houses] quite over." Later they came armed with heavy sticks and "stood before the pulpit and swore how they would treat me if I preached again" before they drove him into a swamp. He and other blacks sought refuge in Birchtown, but even there incursions of angry veterans continued for a month. Governor Parr was summoned from Halifax to deal with the unrest. Without any investigation, he blamed the surveyors, fired Marston, and returned to Halifax.

A white settler Brother George had known in Savannah offered him a town lot in Shelburne, where he quickly put together a hut of poles and bark. He held outdoor meetings by this makeshift dwelling every evening, and the people flocked to him "as though they had come for their supper."

David George's wife and children joined him in July, making him eligible for his own town lot and provisions for six more months. Just before Christmas, he baptized his first four converts in the creek running by his plot. When snowfalls put an end to his outdoor meetings, he began to construct a meeting house. Although George never received a farm allotment, his preaching talents rewarded him sufficiently over the next few years to purchase four additional town lots and a 50-acre farm.[5]

The indefatigable efforts of inspired men like Moses Wilkinson, David George, and a dozen others led eventually to the establishment in the new black settlements of several black chapels, whose members cherished a close-knit sense of identity with the group to which they belonged. Congregations looked after their own, sharing food and misery, providing care and comfort in adversity and hope in the face of privation. Years later, their ties were so strong that whole congregations banded together to move to a new home in Africa.

Violet King was Moses Wilkinson's first convert in Nova Scotia. Her husband, Boston, was soon moved as well, so intensely that he immediately began to preach and assist in Wilkinson's chapel.

Boston King earned a living as a carpenter through his first winter in Nova Scotia. Like most of the other refugees, he did not receive his farm until years later—in his case, in the harsh winter of 1789. King's memoirs recount the dire circumstances of his fellows in the meantime:

> Many of the poor people were compelled to sell their best gowns for five pounds of flour, in order to support life. When they had parted with all their clothes, even to their blankets, several of them fell down dead in the streets through hunger. Some killed and eat their dogs and cats; and poverty and distress prevailed on every side.

Hired by a Shelburne man to build a chest, King carried it from Birchtown to the man's house through three feet of snow, only to have it rejected. "On my way home, being pinched with hunger and cold, I fell down several times, thro' weakness, and expected to die on the spot." When he struggled back to Shelburne with a second chest, he was paid in cornmeal. The rejected chest he managed to sell for 25 cents, then sold his saw as well for a quarter of what he had paid for it—thankful for a "reprieve from the dreadful anguish of perishing by famine."

Later, King got orders to build several flat-bottomed boats for salmon fishing for £1 each. The same employer gave him work fishing for salmon and herring from June to October. At the end of the season, he received £15 and two barrels of fish. He bought clothes for Violet and himself, a barrel of flour, three bushels of corn, and nine gallons of treacle. Violet had used the seed potatoes given them by a Mr. and Mrs. William Taylor, white loyalists from London, to grow 20 bushels of potatoes, permitting them to enjoy "the best winter they ever saw in Burchtown."[6]

Others were far less fortunate as the years ground slowly by. Those who suffered sickness or injuries fared badly. Andrew Ross withheld four months' rations from Thomas Plumm when he was injured by a "piece of Timber falling on his head & fractured his Skull." Samuel Wiley developed rheumatism while he was bound to work three years at £40 a year for Daniel McLeod and was turned away at the end of one year. Dr. Kendrick hired John Primus at £4 a month and his wife at £2 a month, but paid them no wages in the year they lived with him.[7]

Faced with such devastating adversity, these wretched free men and women turned to the chapels, seeking solace and sustenance. They had no glass to weatherproof their windows, no lamps to light their sanctuary, and no stove to keep them warm. Even on the coldest days of winter, when the meeting house shutters were kept closed against the bitter wind and a few feeble candles flickered wildly in the drafts, the warmth of the bodies crowded together in the dim half-light brought comfort to the faithful. The black preachers who promised them God's love and redemption became the natural leaders of the anguished men and women struggling to survive in Nova Scotia

Chapter 12

Farms for White Loyalists

In return for their pledge of allegiance to the British Crown, the refugees were promised farms—100 acres for each civilian household head and 50 acres for each additional person in the family—surveyed without cost, and the quitrent suspended for ten years.[1] Frederick North, King George III's prime minister in London, authorized Governor Parr to increase the size of grants up to an extra 1,000 acres to those who demonstrated the ability to cultivate it. Whether these promises were to apply equally to both whites and blacks was a matter of continuous dispute and confusion within both groups.

Certainly the white refugees had a much better understanding of how to apply the pressure that would guarantee that their needs were quickly met. They expected to receive better treatment than poverty-stricken blacks who had just escaped slavery. The same feelings of class superiority led English officials in Nova Scotia to take care of the whites' needs as soon as possible after their arrival, postponing blacks' claims until after the whites were settled.

Communications were cumbersome and slow, but well-to-do whites could travel to Halifax to lobby English officials, with whom they felt a comfortable kinship. They knew whom to see and what to say to ensure that their land allotments were surveyed speedily. Indeed, they hired agents to check out the best locations, exerted pressure until the surveyors marked their boundaries, and insisted that no blacks be allowed to infringe on the spots they had selected.

As a result, the surveyors were regularly snatched away from the black settlements to lay out plots for newly arrived whites, or they were told to halt black surveys in mid-course because the land had been promised for other purposes. Everything was supposed to be free, but white loyalists had know-how, money, and clout to get what they wanted. The blacks had no experience whatsoever in dealing with government officials. They had no funds to travel or to hire agents, and they had no idea how to compete for what they had been promised. They had no right to vote or to a jury trial and little understanding of the law. They were not even aware of how their lack of experience would hamper their progress in their new land.

Indeed, the very process of applying for their land allotments must have seemed impossibly complicated to the largely illiterate blacks. Each company captain was supposed to petition the governor for allotments for all the members of his company. If the governor judged the petition worthy, he sent a warrant to the surveyor-general requesting the survey. When the survey was completed, the survey plan was returned to the governor, and a report was submitted to the surveyor-general of the King's Woods, who decided whether timber stands on the land were needed by the Royal Navy. If not, he issued a certificate, and the two documents were sent to the provincial secretary. He in turn drew up a draft grant for the attorney-general to sign. Only then was the actual grant written out and signed by the governor.[2]

As thousands of loyalist immigrants arrived in late 1783, the Nova Scotian administration was simply overwhelmed by the influx. When winter overtook the surveyors, snow fell and blew into drifts three or four feet deep, halting all surveying until spring came again. In spite of the logjam, Governor Parr reported a year later (August 1784) that 4,882 grants—enough to situate approximately 20,000 people—had been finalized.[3]

This was a substantial accomplishment, but it would have been little comfort to the 10,000 refugees (including 3,000 freed slaves) still without land. With few voices raised on their behalf in government circles, the blacks were fortunate if they received even the barest necessities. To make ends meet, many of them sought employment in the towns and ports; a very few managed to save a little money with which to buy land that they were unable to obtain otherwise.

When a special board was established in Shelburne to process land applications, the hopes of the Birchtown settlers soared again. During the two years the board operated, most of the white loyalists were settled. But when word came of its dissolution in 1786, the 649 families in Birchtown still had not received any farm land.[4] Not until December 1787 was a farm survey done for the residents of Birchtown. In February 1788, Caesar Perth and 183 other men in Birchtown received land grants of about 34 acres each.[5] The others were left permanently landless, except for perhaps a hundred industrious men who managed to save meager wages earned in Shelburne to purchase small farms in more fertile locations.

When Caesar went to examine his farm plot and start clearing it, his elation quickly faded. Tales told of the excellent agriculture in the province were misleading. On the south coast sturdy virgin forests grew around rocky outcroppings and in wetlands that were not suitable for crops. The recently emancipated men had no idea how to clear the trees alone or drain the swamps. Some of them found their parcels located some distance away from their town plots, requiring long daily hikes back and forth to work on the land.

They grumbled and wrung their hands and complained to each other, and soon they noticed that even the white refugees were having great difficulty farming in the area around Shelburne. The land simply was not very productive, and the whites turned quickly to fishing, lumbering, boatbuilding, storekeeping, and trading as better ways to make a living. Blacks and whites alike abandoned unproductive land grants to search for other occupations.

Chapter 13

Thomas Peters
in Annapolis County

Thomas Peters sailed from New York in November of 1783 on the *Joseph James*. He was then about 45, older than many of his fellow emigrants. He carried a passport directed "to all Commanders" from Lieutenant Colonel Alan Stewart attesting to faithful, honest service that had "gained the good wishes of his officers and Comrades." Accompanying him were his wife Sally, age 30, and two children, Clairy, age 12, and John, 18 months. The ship was blown off course by gales and spent the winter in Bermuda. The Peters family reached Annapolis Royal on the north coast of Nova Scotia in May 1784.[1]

Thomas Peters knew nothing of the problems in Shelburne and Birchtown when he arrived in Annapolis County along the banks of the Annapolis River. By the autumn of 1784 over 4,000 loyalist refugees had disembarked there. All existing public and private buildings were needed to shelter them—churches, courthouse, stores, and dwellings. Over 200 of them were free blacks; Peters and 68 others were Black Pioneers veterans with their families.

Peters had distinguished himself as one of only two blacks who reached the rank of sergeant in the Black Pioneers. He was placed in charge of the 76 blacks settling in Digby, near Annapolis Royal, where a single-acre town lot was made available to each family.[2] Some 65 additional families of free blacks established their own community of

61

Brindley Town, about a mile from Digby, and eventually received farm allotments nearby.[3]

Peters and his company waited impatiently for their allotments. The four agents appointed by Governor Parr to plot land grants in Annapolis County seem to have been either negligent or corrupt in parceling out the 20,000 acres available for the refugees who settled in Digby. When impatient refugees moved onto unassigned land and refused to leave until their allotments were granted, a commission was appointed to investigate their complaints. No accurate plan of surveys in Digby could be found, so officials in Halifax had to authorize additional funds to resurvey the area.

While they waited, the blacks were dependent on government food rations. In December 1784, 12,098 pounds of flour and 9,352 pounds of pork—80 days' worth of full rations for 160 black adults and 26 children—was issued to the Reverend Edward Brudenell, one of the Digby government agents, for Peters's black company. Brudenell stored the rations and gave them out only to those blacks who worked on the township roads—a labor requirement not imposed on white refugees. That shipment was all the food that the Digby blacks ever received, although they had been promised three years' worth of rations.[4]

In August 1784, Thomas Peters and Murphy Still (the other Black Pioneers sergeant) submitted a petition for farmland for their fellow veterans, citing the promises that had been made to them when they enlisted. Although Governor Parr wrote the surveyor to meet their request as quickly as possible, snowfalls ended the surveying with only their town lots laid out. Peters and Still submitted two more petitions; in June 1785 land on a peninsula across the Annapolis River from Brindley Town was finally assigned, about 20 acres each, to 23 black veterans. No sooner had they started work clearing, however, when word came that the tract was reserved for an Anglican school, and the blacks were told to move back to their one-acre town plots.[5]

Shortly thereafter, the government in Halifax discontinued the pay of deputy surveyors and informed them that any further surveys would have to be paid for by the petitioners. In October 1788, after receiving another request for land from Peters and Still, Governor Parr wrote the head surveyor, Charles Morris, to locate some land in the area for the black veterans. His deputy misunderstood the order and went ahead with a survey of 147 lots of 50 acres each in Clements Township. Morris had no funds to pay for the survey. In September 1789 the black veterans signed their approval of the tract, but no final grant was ever issued. They cleared a road to their tract themselves, but without a legal title to it, they never cleared the land or moved onto it.

Peters and a number of other veterans, frustrated in their search for land in Annapolis County and required to do road work before their rations were given to them, moved to New Brunswick (which was part of Nova Scotia until 1784) and petitioned for land there. How did they make that long journey? They had no horses to ride. There may have been a stagecoach or ferry, but where would they find money for such a journey? Sally Peters had a child and a toddler; did they remain in Digby while Thomas went hunting for work?

The 121 plots laid out for them in New Brunswick were, in Peters's own words, "so far distant from their Town Lots (being 16 or 18 Miles back) as to be entirely useless to them and indeed worthless in itself from its remote situation."[6] The blacks had always lived, both in Africa and on southern plantations, in groups close together with constant contact and interaction. Nothing in their experience would motivate a family to go off by themselves and homestead all alone in the wilderness. Only five black families occupied those remote farms. The other 116 lots were escheated and reassigned to whites. Elsewhere, although most of the white loyalists were quickly resettled, the freed blacks remained landless unless they occupied unclaimed land without any legal title or saved enough to buy land for themselves.[7]

Of the estimated 3,550 black loyalists transported to Nova Scotia, 385 are recorded as having received legal title to land. Of those, 184 received a total of 6,382 acres in Birchtown; 76 received one acre each in Brindley Town; 74 received a total of 3,000 acres in Little Tracadie; and 51 received a total of 2,557.5 in Preston. Another 350 may have received some 5,900 acres in Chedabucto (the records are confused on this point).[8]

Peters was not one to sit around and wait for things to happen. He had demonstrated his ability and leadership qualities in the Black Pioneers, and he felt that the local officials were recalcitrant in carrying out the Crown's instructions. He complained to the governor about the Reverend Brudenell withholding rations to make the refugees work on roads, but when questioned, the local officials claimed he had gone off to New Brunswick to avoid public service.[9] When he received no land in New Brunswick, Peters found work as a millwright and did his best to keep white men from selling his fellows back into slavery by petitioning Governor Thomas Carleton (brother of the New York general) of New Brunswick and the justice and mayor of Fredericton, all without avail.

Nor did the authorities in Nova Scotia ever concede that red tape and official stalling contributed to the discontent of Peters and his companions. Instead, they blamed all the black dissent on dislike of public labor and the harsh climate. Peters, on the other hand, concluded that the provincial authorities had unjustly rejected his three petitions for land and that their action was contrary to the intentions of the British government.

Then, in 1790, six years after his arrival in Nova Scotia, Thomas Peters heard about the Province of Freedom in Sierra Leone.

PART III
The Province of Freedom

*Thomas Peters knew nothing of the background of the
Province of Freedom, but some understanding of
events in England is needed to make sense of the confusion faced by the blacks who later emigrated from
Nova Scotia to Sierra Leone. The plans made in London for a settlement in Sierra Leone for blacks living
in poverty in England were a prior step in the founding of Freetown by the Nova Scotian blacks. Their exodus followed the aborted first attempt described in the
following pages.*

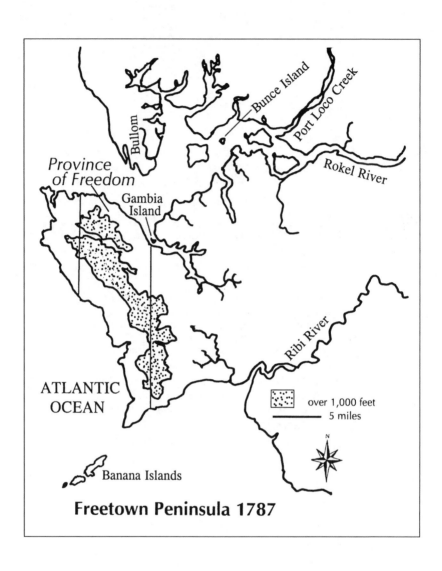

Province
of Freedom

Gambia
Island

Bullom

Bunce Island

Port Loco Creek

Rokel River

Ribi River

ATLANTIC
OCEAN

over 1,000 feet

5 miles

N

Banana Islands

Freetown Peninsula 1787

Chapter 14

Refuge in London

Englishmen first purchased Africans for labor in tobacco fields in the Virginia colony in 1619. And to England's empire were added Bermuda (1609), Saint Kitts (1623), Barbados (1625), Nevis, Antigua, and Montserrat. After the capture of Jamaica from Spain in 1655 (breaking the Spanish monopoly on West African trade), the need for laborers on sugar plantations in the West Indies colonies brought England very actively into the slave trade.[1]

The Royal African Company was organized in 1672 as an official sponsor of a lucrative triangular maritime exchange in African slaves, West Indies raw materials, and English manufactured goods. In 1698 the Royal African Company lost its monopoly, and any Englishman was free to trade in blacks. Black domestic slaves had become very fashionable in noble households in England during the reign of King James I. West Indies planters often brought home slaves to carry sedan chairs and serve as domestic servants.

Thereafter, blacks were brought to England for many reasons.[2] The largest number were simply servants. Many came as seamen in the navy or merchant marine, some as trumpeters and drummers in the army. Some were sent for training as interpreters by slave traders and missionaries. Children of African chiefs were sent as a guarantee of continuing friendly relations with slave trader sponsors. Many worked on the construction of public buildings and as street sweepers. Some were migrant workers, others were actors, buskers, or street entertainers. Some hoped to settle and find a new life away from racial prejudice. A few came as missionaries or to raise church funds; a small number came because they wanted to live in peace with a white wife. After the American Revolution, hundreds of black loyalists went from the colonies to England as refugees; many of them were discharged seamen. Some of them found intermittent work on ships. Some had been servants for British officers and stayed with them; others were attached to regiments demobilized in England. Few had any possessions or provisions.[3]

Some of the refugees petitioned the British government for compensation for their wartime losses. If they were successful, they received far less than white loyalists. Shadrack Furman, for example, received a pension for £18 a year for providing information and food to the British, the most generous settlement any of the black claimants ever received. He had been captured by Americans, who flogged him, leaving him blind and crippled. He played a fiddle in the streets of London.[4] Those who had no trade or assistance often ended up begging in the streets or stealing when opportunity arose.

"Benjamin Whitecuff, the British spy who had narrowly escaped death by hanging, set himself up as a saddler and chair bottom maker on his £4-a-year pension and a small dowry from his English wife, Sarah." John Provey, who had served in the Black Pioneers, stated that he was "an entire Stranger in this Country illeterate and unacquainted with the Laws thereof."[5] In 1788 London had a total population of around 780,000,[6] of whom at least 5,000 were free and mostly destitute blacks.[7] Big cities were a haven for runaways from British masters and from West Indian planters (many of whom maintained homes in London and lobbied in opposition to the abolitionists and in support of the slave trade).[8]

The numbers of freed black men were beyond the means of charity to support. The law in England at that time left the support of paupers to their parish of origin. Because the blacks were "born in other lands," the Poor Law authorities in English parishes had no legal responsibility for them. Many of the blacks had served the British faithfully during the American Revolution, but they found no employment and little help in England. Peter Anderson was a typical example. He had been a woodcutter in Virginia when he was press-ganged by one of Dunmore's officers and taken prisoner by the Americans at Great Bridge. He later escaped and joined the British forces voluntarily. In his petition for government assistance he wrote, "I endeavor'd to get Work but cannot get Any. I am Thirty Nine Years of Age & am ready & willing to serve His Britinack Majesty While I am Able, But I am realy starvin about the Streets, Having Nobody to give me A Morsel of bread & dare not go home to my Own Country again."[9] He was awarded £10 for his wartime service.

Many Englishmen felt strongly about the plight of the freed blacks. Prominent among them was Granville Sharp, who resigned his position in the Ordnance Office to protest the British laws that sparked the war in the American colonies. A man with a compelling sense of right and wrong, Sharp worked tirelessly, after rescuing a mistreated slave in 1765, to make slavery in Britain illegal.[10] In 1772 he brought a case before the lord chief justice to determine whether an escaped slave named James Somerset, brought to England from Virginia, could be seized by his master and forced to board ship for sale in Jamaica. The decision in Somerset's favor was the first step in the long road to the abolition of slavery in Britain.[11] After that, all the major cities in England attracted freed blacks because of a widely held belief that Britain was a haven from prejudice and discrimination.

The second legal decision that greatly aroused public opinion involved a slave-ship captain who had thrown his cargo of 132 slaves overboard because they were sick and dying and would bring him no profits. The court ruled that the captain could collect the insurance on his lost cargo, but the implications of such inhumanity reverberated across Britain.

The winter of 1786 in Britain was severe enough to cause scores of people to perish on the streets. A private Committee for the Relief of the Black Poor was organized in London that year, chaired by Jonas Hanway and made up of bankers, merchants, and politicians.[12] They raised money for clothes, job searches, and a small sickhouse for the blacks.

Because the numbers of blacks in England were so large, an alternate haven was sought. Some advocated sending the poor blacks in London to the maritime provinces in America, but the resettlement problems in Nova Scotia were already more than the government could handle. Another possibility was to send them back to Africa—certainly not a new idea. Quakers in America had discussed that possibility for decades. By 1763 Quaker meetings excluded from membership anyone "concerned in the unchristian traffic in negroes."[13]

In 1773 a Congregational preacher in Newport, Rhode Island, Reverend Samuel Hopkins, suggested from his pulpit that negroes in America be returned to their place of origin. His church was the first to forbid its members to own slaves; blacks were even welcomed to special services held on Sunday evening. Because white Americans were prejudiced against blacks, Hopkins believed that slaves should be freed, trained as missionaries, and sent back to Africa for their own welfare and to spread Christianity.[14] Three men were chosen to be trained at Princeton as missionaries, but the American Revolution intervened.

English Quakers crusaded against slavery to such an extent that ordinances were passed on the English sugar islands in the West Indies forbidding Quaker meetings and prohibiting any Quakers from landing.

An eminent English Quaker doctor and abolitionist, Dr. John Fothergill, actually sent Henry Smeathman, a botanist, to Sierra Leone[15] in 1771 to examine the possibility of establishing plantations there using black labor from England. Smeathman spent four years collecting specimens, and another four years in the West Indies studying tropical agriculture. He was convinced that he could pay his debts and make his fortune by promoting a settlement for loyal blacks in Africa.[16]

Smeathman proposed to Granville Sharp[17] and the Quakers working against the slave trade that he personally conduct free blacks to Sierra Leone and run their colony—for a fee, of course. He praised the balmy climate and ease of growing food. He was certain that, "by moderate labour, of the most comfortable livelihood, [settlers] will find a certain and secure retreat from their former sufferings."[18]

The burden of caring for the poor in London had become too great for individual philanthropists; the Committee for the Relief of the Black Poor welcomed Smeathman's idea and began raising funds. They convinced the government to contribute £12 per pauper to emigrate and engaged Smeathman to oversee their transport and settlement. A handbill was also published for distribution:

> It having been very maturely and humanely considered, by what means a support might be given to the Blacks, who seek the protection of this government; it is found that no place is so fit and proper, as the Grain Coast of Africa; where the necessaries of life may be supplied, by the force of industry and moderate labour, and life rendered very comfortable. ...

The Committee for the Black Poor, accordingly, recommended Henry Smeathman, Esq. who is acquainted with this part of the coast of Africa, to take charge of all the said persons, who are desirous of going with him; and to give them all fit and proper encouragement, agreeable to the humanity of the British Government.

By desire of the Committee,
Jonas Hanway, Chairman

Boston's Coffee-house
17th May, 1786

Those who are desirous of profiting by this opportunity, of settling in one of the most pleasant and fertile countries in the known world, may apply for further information to Mr. Smeathman, the Author of the Plan, and Agent for the Settlement, at the Office for Free Africans, No. 14, Canon-street.[19]

As volunteers signed up, the committee organized them into companies of 12, each headed by a corporal, all of whom could read and two of whom could write as well. They were to be responsible for administrative matters, maintain order in their company, and hand out allowances.[20] White wives of two of the black colonists were sent to the London Lying-In Hospital to be trained as midwives. An ordained clergyman, Patrick Fraser, was recruited and given instructions that all emigrants were to be baptized before departure.[21] The expedition also included about 20 artisans, a town major to build fortifications, five doctors, and a sexton.[22]

The blacks requested 400 guns and a supply of ball and powder with which to hunt game, constables' staves, stationery, and two movable forges. They also wanted documentation to protect them from slavers whose business was centered in Sierra Leone. Each potential settler received a parchment "passport" in a twopenny tin box, bearing the royal coat of arms and a statement that the bearer was a loyal British subject, and signed by a naval official.[23] This contained, however, no promise of protection for the settlers, which would have required an English garrison.

In July 1786, when 400 colonists were committed to sail, Smeathman died. The committee appointed his clerk, Joseph Irwin, to succeed him, but Irwin had never been to Africa. Hanway and his fellow committee members had misgivings and suggested the whole group go to Nova Scotia or New Brunswick instead.[24] Few were willing to do so or to consider the Bahamas or Gambia as alternatives. Those who withdrew had their shore allowances stopped, and they were threatened with prison if they were found begging. The public controversy that developed between the blacks and their sponsors at this time led to accusations that the Sierra Leone settlers were banished from London against their will.

By coincidence, the Committee for the Black Poor was seeking a home for the black loyalists at the same time that the English government was planning to dispose of the convicts filling the country's jails. A colony in West Africa was discussed.[25] The committee lobbied against using Sierra Leone for that purpose; Botany Bay in Australia became the convict destination instead. The two enterprises moved forward in tandem in the same harbor at Spithead, just below Portsmouth, however, which led to considerable confusion and distortion in the sensationalist press and in the minds of the emigrant blacks as to who was being sent where and why.[26]

Chapter 15

The Founding
of Granville Town

Chairman Hanway (of the Committee for the Relief of the Black Poor) died in September, and he was replaced by Samuel Hoare, a Quaker banker in whom the blacks had far less confidence. With Smeathman and Hanway dead, the project had "lost its visionaries."[1] By October Joseph Irwin had 675 men, women, and children signed up.[2] Irwin and the committee were to provide clothing and provisions; the British government paid their passage.

A remarkable black man named Gustavus Vassa was appointed commissary of supplies.[3] Unfortunately, the duties of the agent and the commissary overlapped in a way that made complete cooperation essential. Vassa soon charged that Irwin was mishandling funds and supplies, and complained vigorously to Captain Thomas Boulden Thompson, who was to escort the convoy to Africa. Thompson also had his doubts about Irwin, but Vassa's forthright championing of black rights seemed more dangerous to him. Thompson told the committee chair, Hoare, that Vassa was a seditious malcontent, indicating as well some doubt about Irwin's sincerity. Hoare sided with Irwin, and Vassa was dismissed. Thus, an opportunity was lost to have one talented black involved in this innovative project who understood the importance of training and guiding the freed blacks to assume responsibility for their own welfare. The only other black man with unusual survival skills was

Abraham Elliott Griffith, a London servant who had been taught to read and write at Sharp's expense. He was appointed one of three deputies to represent the blacks. (He would use his talents to escape the colony before it disintegrated.)

In December 1786, three transport ships set out, accompanied by the HMS *Nautilus*.[4] A severe gale in the English Channel damaged the ships before they were out of sight of land and delayed them by six months for repairs, during which time controversies over and among their spokesmen and fear that they were heading for a slaving center led scores to change their minds and quit the expedition. Those who stayed on board were cold, uncomfortable, and poorly fed. Typhus broke out on one of the ships; 50 people died before the voyage began.

As the months went by, British Treasury officials were increasingly concerned by the mounting cost of the expedition. Matters were exacerbated when early December newspaper reports claimed that the police were to round up all blacks found begging, with the implication that they would also be sent to the new colony in Africa.

The final roster when the ships were to sail in February listed 459 passengers: 344 blacks and 115 whites (mostly wives of blacks or of white artisans—sawyers, carpenters, surveyors, and so on—who bound themselves to stay at least four months in Sierra Leone). Even then, another month slid by while repairs were made to one of the vessels.

The fleet of three ships and one naval sloop for protection finally sailed on April 9, 1787.[5] Captain Thompson of the *Nautilus* was a capable and experienced naval officer, acting under government orders. He carried supplies for eight months, 3,000 yards of canvas for tents and ropes to construct them, and orders to purchase land from the Temne people inhabiting the Sierra Leone peninsula and supervise the new settlement, providing provisions until the first crop was harvested. After that, the settlers would be on their own.[6] None of the organizers of the expedition foresaw how poorly equipped these former slaves were to make decisions and assume responsibility for their own well-being.

At that time only a handful of small villages dotted the Sierra Leone peninsula—tiny brown clearings studded with thatched huts. The peninsula is actually the remains of an ancient volcano, thrust up 2,500 feet above sea level long ago in some violent cataclysm, cut off from the mainland by a swath of mangrove swamps and a network of deep ravines that made it almost an island.[7] The northern slopes of the volcano are generally too steep for farming, and even small gardens erode rapidly in the deluges that pound the landscape every rainy season.[8] The southern slopes are gentler, but require constant vigilance against the fierce encroachment of tangled jungle that grows almost overnight and blankets the landscape.

The peninsula forms the southern shore of the Rokel River, where its many branches and tributaries open into a wide estuary and fresh water meets the sea—4,000 acres of sheltered mooring, eight to fourteen fathoms deep, with a bottom of good holding ground for anchors—one of the finest harbors in the world.[9] By 1787 the local Temne people, whose area stretched northward up the river for a hundred miles, were very accustomed to European merchant ships regularly calling there to take on fresh water and to trade in camwood, ivory, and slaves.

On the slopes above the many coves and bays along the estuary, several local chiefs lived in small villages. The excellent freshwater spring used by all passing ships was within the area of Chief Tombo, whom the English called King Tom. King Jemmy (Jimmy) reigned a little further south along the shore. Halfway up the steep slopes that overlook Freetown was the village of Pa Demba.[10] Around the base of the mountain, still further to the east, was Foro Bay,[11] where the reigning chief was a Portuguese-African who called himself Signor Domingo and claimed to be Christian. These chiefs regularly took fees from British and French traders, permitting them to take on fresh water and establish trading factories.

They were minor chiefs, however. The paramount Temne chief under whose much broader jurisdiction they lived was King Naimbana, whose headquarters was upstream at Robana. One of his predecessors had rented Bunce Island in the Rokel River to the English as early as 1664 to use as a slave factory (where captured Africans were held by European factors, awaiting the arrival of slave ships to buy them). There the nephews of Richard Oswald (the prominent English slave merchant mentioned earlier who participated in the negotiations in Paris to end the American Revolution) still held and shipped slaves from a triple-bastioned stone fortress with loopholes from which 50 cannon muzzles protruded. The French ran another factory on Gambia Island, not far away. The local chiefs acted as landlords, collecting the slaves brought down the rivers for sale, enforcing the rules of trade, and settling prices and any disputes with the European traders. Many of the local Africans worked for the slave traders and were so used to English ships stopping there that some of them knew rudimentary English and could serve as interpreters.

Captain Thompson was ignorant of the power arrangements among the Africans. His orders were to land his immigrants in the area with access to the freshwater spring ruled by Chief Tombo on the Sierra Leone peninsula, so he negotiated only with him. King Tom happily accepted Captain Thompson's £60 worth of muskets, powder and ball, lead and iron bars, laced hats, rum, tobacco, cloth, and beads as rent for the use of a 20-square-mile piece of land bordering the harbor.[12] On June 11, 1787, King Tom put his mark on an agreement that he "for ever quit claim to a certain district of land for the settling of the said free community to be theirs, their Heirs and successors for ever."[13] The boundaries were vague, and King Tom couldn't read the agreement. Neither he nor his interpreters had any idea that Thompson thought he was buying permanent title to the land, for no land was owned individually in black Africa. Its occupants had only the right to use the land as decided by their chiefs, who considered themselves more as landlords, receiving periodic rent from any foreigners who received permission to occupy some parcel of it.

The new arrivals from England called their land grant the Province of Freedom and their settlement Granville Town. The settlers were to govern themselves through elections as outlined in Sharp's *Short Sketch of Temporary Regulations (Until Better Shall Be Proposed)*. Sharp was a visionary with an unshakable belief in individual rights and racial equality. Slavery was an abomination in his eyes, and the blacks cast adrift during the American Revolution offered a divine opportunity to prove that men freed of their shackles would prosper and govern themselves responsibly as soon as they adopted sound Christian principles. His *Temporary Regulations* read in part that every ten households would elect a tithingman; every hundred households would choose a hundredor. They would meet in a council, much like a town meeting, and pass any laws they needed, as long as they were not inconsistent with British law. Householders would serve as militiamen. Each man over age 16 was entitled to a one-acre town plot and a small farm. Each day's community work would be worth a set amount of paper currency issued by the council, redeemable for goods from the store. Each man would pay his taxes by working 62 days a year on community projects. Refusal to work would be taxed. White settlers could join on the same terms as the black settlers.

Reality proved to be far different from Sharp's naive vision. The long delay in England brought the fleet to Sierra Leone at the worst time of year. The annual torrential rains began shortly after the arrival of the English ships on May 9. The peninsula is pounded by 144 inches of rain annually, all within a six-month period between May and November. In June and July, water streams off the mountains in raging torrents. These deluges promote devastating disease, for cleared ground turns to a morass of mud, nothing dries out, food and clothing mildew and rot, nights are raw, and the landscape steams whenever the sun comes out. Mosquitoes breed furiously; malaria is endemic. The new settlers were unable to plant gardens, and the old canvas provided by the navy for tents collapsed in the downpours. When the rains finally slackened, the seeds brought from England were ravaged by ants and yielded little. Soon the settlers were trading their tools and clothes for native food.

They tried to set up some form of community government, electing first Richard Weaver and then James Reid governor. Each tried vainly to deal with the overwhelming confusion and distress. By July Irwin was dead, and the chaplain, James Fraser, was ill with tuberculosis. By September, 122 of the settlers had been buried. Only six of the white artisans were still alive, and they soon left Granville Town for better prospects on Bunce Island.

Without an established and stable government, Captain Thompson found it impossible to maintain order in Granville Town. Many of the settlers were industrious and determined to earn a living, but some of the more desperate settlers resorted to cheating or robbing the local Africans and slave traders passing through. This lawless element led Thompson to conclude that "the major part of them were a worthless, lawless, vicious, drunken set of people." In September he gave a final gift to King Tom and set sail, leaving the settlers on their own.[14] The venture under his command had cost the English government £15,679, ten times Smeathman's estimate of £4 per person.[15]

As for Sharp's dream of the glorious harmony that would result when men were given the privilege of governing themselves, Elliott Griffith praised the idea, but was soon disgusted with the confusion that prevailed in Granville Town. He wrote his benefactor, Granville Sharp, that "this country does not agree with us at all; and, without a sudden change, I do not think there will be one of us left at the end of a twelve-month."[16] Griffith soon realized that he could prosper more in King Naimbana's town at Robana. He left Granville Town to work as a scribe and interpreter for the king, eventually marrying his daughter.

The English slave traders on Bunce Island were openly hostile to their new neighbors, whom they perceived as a threat to their lucrative trade. Once the settlers had arrived, the Bunce Island factor was annoyed that they had "intermixed with the Natives and have by telling them a number of Falsehoods given them a great many bad Notions of White Men in general that has made them more saucy and troublesome than ever they were known before."[17] The agent, James Bowie, offered arms to some of the local chiefs to oppose the settlement.

A showdown came after five Granville Town residents robbed the store at Bunce Island. They were arrested by the elected constables and turned over to the Bunce Island factor to stand trial. Although their sentence was banishment, Bowie sold the five to a French slaver leaving for the West Indies. His employer, Alexander Anderson, supported Bowie's action, claiming there was no other way to carry out the sentence.[18]

In spite of the tension between the settlers and the factors on Bunce Island, supporters back in London clung to the hope that the freed men in Granville Town would somehow put a brake on the sale of Africans into slavery. Sharp particularly was encouraged when Griffith wrote him that the Temne King Naimbana was a kindly father figure with a sincere interest in learning about Christianity. He was delighted that Griffith was tutoring Naimbana's children, and he helped arrange for the eldest son to be sent to England to be educated.[19]

The harsh reality was that within a year of their arrival in the Province of Freedom, half the settlers were dead or had deserted. Word was slow getting back to England, but as soon as it did, Sharp scraped together a fund, much of it his own money, to finance a relief expedition. The brig *Myro* sailed in June 1788 with 33 new settlers (fewer than the 50 hoped for) and supplies of bread, spruce beer, and live pigs to slaughter en route. The captain was to buy cattle, poultry, goats, sheep, and swine at the Cape Verde Islands, along with other supplies and seeds. The arrival of 20 new settlers (13 had died on the way) and supplies attracted some of the scattered residents back to Granville Town.

King Tom had died, however. His overlord, King Naimbana, who had not been consulted about the original grant, insisted on a new treaty. Captain Taylor negotiated a new agreement, signed by King Naimbana and King Jemmy. Sharp received letters soon after from the settlers pleading for some sort of arrangement that would provide them with credit to purchase provisions until they had crops to sell. Sharp's financial situation was not up to supplying this on his own, nor could any individual afford to assume responsibility for such an undertaking without the protection of incorporation. Sharp adjusted his naive dreams of a pastoral society in the Province of Freedom and sought the assistance of a few respectable English merchants and gentlemen to form a company to trade in Africa. Sharp and his two brothers joined Henry Thornton (a prominent 31-year-old banker), Samuel Whitbread, Joseph Hardcastle, and William Wilberforce (at age 32 a leading abolitionist) in setting up the St. George's Bay Company (which would later become the Sierra Leone Company) in 1790, and asked Parliament for an act of incorporation.[20]

Scarcely had they purchased a small cutter (suitable for coastal trading) and applied for a charter when word arrived that Granville Town had been attacked by King Jemmy and his Temne warboys and the residents scattered. While the company directors in England waited for their act of incorporation to relieve them of individual liability, several of them took up a collection to send £150 worth of supplies on the cutter *Lapwing*, the sale of which should buy African produce. The *Lapwing* reached Sierra Leone with inadequate food and clothing, but an abundance of trade goods—tools and a "prodigious number" of children's half-penny knives and scissors.[21] Clearly Granville Sharp's dream of a utopia in the Province of Freedom needed a more practical foundation if it was to be rejuvenated.

Chapter 16

Thomas Peters Travels to London

Now we return to Thomas Peters in Nova Scotia in 1790 and his anger at being denied land there. He found out about the Province of Freedom by accident:

> one day, some company at dinner happened to be conversing on the projected scheme of the Sierra Leone colony, and mentioned Mr. Grenville [*sic*] Sharp, a name revered among the negroes, as the patron of the plan. A sensible black, who waited at table, heard the accounts with eagerness, and took the first opportunity of spreading them among his countrymen. The hope of relief animated them, and they resolved to send over their agent, one Thomas Peters, a respectable, intelligent African, to wait upon the [St. George's Bay] company, and learn if they might expect encouragement to go to the new colony. ... Never did ambassador from a sovereign power prosecute with more zeal the object of his mission than did Thomas Peters the cause of his distressed countrymen.[1]

Thomas Peters's £17 fare was raised either by Peters himself or by his sponsors—100 black families in St. John and 102 families in Annapolis County. Ignoring the very real possibility that an unscrupulous ship captain might conspire to seize him and sell him into slavery again, he traveled to Halifax and took ship to England, carrying a petition that said that he had been deputed "to procure for himself and his Fellow Sufferers some Establishment where they may obtain a competent Settlement for themselves and be enabled by their industrious Exertions to become useful Subjects to his Majesty." Government assistance was imperative "as the poor friendless Slaves have no more Protection by the Laws of the Colony (as they are at present misunderstood) than the mere Cattel or brute Beasts ... the free People of Colour who cannot conceive that it is really the Intention of the British Government to favour Injustice, or tolerate Slavery in Nova Scotia." The petition went on to say that "some Part of the said Black People are earnestly desirous of obtaining their due Allotment of Land and remaining in America but others are ready and willing to go wherever the Wisdom of Government may think proper to provide for them as free Subjects of the British Empire."[2]

In London, Peters looked up his old commander, Captain George Martin, who passed him on to General Henry Clinton, who recommended Peters to the proper authorities. Peters also met former slaves living in London, some of whom were so poor they were begging in the streets. They introduced him to their benefactor, Granville Sharp, a determined abolitionist at a time when ending the slave trade had become the crusade of the hour.[3]

Sharp was also a member of the Associates of Dr. Thomas Bray, who had organized and provided materials for schools in Nova Scotia, so he was aware of the situation there. He immediately took up Thomas Peters's cause (perhaps helping polish his petition) and arranged for the document to be presented to the British Secretary of State, Henry Dundas. He also introduced Peters to some of the directors, including Henry Thornton, the chairman of the St. George's Bay/Sierra Leone Company, then being organized to take charge of foundering Granville Town in Sierra Leone and run it on a sound commercial footing.

The Sierra Leone Company began as Sharp had intended—as a philanthropic enterprise to oversee a homeland for free blacks and discourage the slave trade. Profits from trade in materials other than slaves were to demonstrate to the Africans the superiority of a Christian way of life. A gradual switch in emphasis, however, from philanthropy to profitable trade in the years that followed would lead to continual friction between the black settlers, who believed they would govern themselves, and the English officials charged with running the company as a business.[4]

Thomas Peters arrived in London in 1790 as the plans for the Sierra Leone Company were taking shape. The abolitionists he met there were still talking in terms of philanthropy and a self-governing home for the freed blacks, although their dream was being eroded by security problems in Sierra Leone. The local chiefs were unhappy when they realized that the freshwater spring used by both Africans and visiting ships was within the Province of Freedom. To compensate, they demanded more tribute, but they were refused.

Then an American slave ship kidnapped some members of King Jemmy's tribe, who lived nearby. Jemmy's people attacked the next slave ship headed upstream, killing three crewmen, seizing the cargo of rum, and selling the boat to the French slave factory. The Granville Town settlers went to Captain Henry Savage of the *HMS Pomona*, anchored in the harbor, and asked him to mediate. He ordered King Jemmy to come on board, which he refused to do. Savage sent a party of marines to Jemmy's town, where a fire, perhaps accidental, destroyed all the thatch huts. When Jemmy's men threatened crew members working on shore to bury the dead and load supplies, Captain Savage shelled the beach and nearby bush, then sailed away.

King Jemmy could not retaliate against a warship, but nearby Granville Town was an easy target. Jemmy was not a signatory to the 1787 agreement with Captain Thompson and King Tom that established the Province of Freedom. Furious that his authority had been challenged by Captain Savage, he gave notice in December 1789 that he would destroy Granville Town three days later. All its inhabitants fled upriver, save four old people, whom King Jemmy seized and sold into slavery.

The directors of the Sierra Leone Company did not learn about this disaster until April 1790, for the slave ship captains in the area refused to carry a message to them. An unnamed settler risked passage on a slaver by way of the West Indies to carry the report back to England.

Among those who had rallied in London to the Committee for the Relief of the Black Poor was a surgeon named Alexander Falconbridge, whose employment on four slave voyages had so horrified him that he published a searing indictment of the slave traffic in 1788. The directors immediately engaged Falconbridge, whose strong abolitionist sentiments matched theirs, to go to Sierra Leone and gather the scattered residents of Granville Town together in a new settlement. He found 56 of the settlers, who had stuck together on their own in a swamp above Bunce Island, in spite of the slave traders' efforts to disperse them. The refugees wanted to return to the original site of Granville Town, despite its closeness to King Jemmy's village. King Naimbana arranged a palaver with the local chiefs, which lasted five days. Falconbridge persuaded them to accept £30 in exchange for reoccupation of the original tract.[5]

By April 1791, some 64 of the original settlers were back occupying abandoned African huts by Fora Bay and working industriously to complete houses before the rains started.[6] Fish, game, and poultry were plentiful, but Falconbridge sensed how fragile this small settlement was. He distributed tools and arms, but he also sent frantic letters to London begging for an armed ship to protect them. The company directors in London realized that a more substantial population would be needed to support a permanent settlement.

In the ten months that Thomas Peters from Nova Scotia spent in Britain, the Sierra Leone Company was being formed. He would hardly have been privy, however, to the many debates about the provisions to be included in the parliamentary act establishing the company, nor to the private correspondence between the company directors and Falconbridge in Sierra Leone. Peters's concern was to obtain help for his people in Nova Scotia. If he heard disquieting rumors about troubles in the Province of Freedom, they scarcely dampened his hopes.

In response to Peters's petition, Secretary of State Dundas immediately ordered an inquiry in Nova Scotia and promised to have land made available to the free blacks, either in the maritime provinces in America or in Sierra Leone. Dundas instructed Thomas Peters to issue an invitation offering free passage to the blacks in Nova Scotia who might want to go to Sierra Leone, and promised to send an English agent to Halifax to recruit settlers. Thomas Peters went back to Nova Scotia euphoric. He could tell his people that Sierra Leone, in the homeland of their ancestors, was to be their long-sought promised land.

Chapter 17

An Emissary from the
Sierra Leone Company

Thomas Clarkson and his younger brother, John, were both members of William Wilberforce's Committee for Effecting the Abolition of the Slave Trade in England, which was trying to get an act through Parliament to make trade in slaves illegal. Both were well known in Parliament and government circles.

John Clarkson had been sent into the Royal Navy at age 11, and received his lieutenant's commission while serving in the West Indies during the American Revolution. A clergyman's son, he had investigated the French slave trade at Le Havre in 1788. His convictions led him to believe that slavery was an abomination, and that fighting wars was indefensible. He was 27 years old when he heard of Thomas Peters's mission in London on behalf of the Nova Scotia blacks. He was so touched by their plight that even though he was engaged to be married, he volunteered to go to Nova Scotia himself to set the Sierra Leone plan in motion and make sure it was not sabotaged by local officials.[1]

If the Sierra Leone Company acted with undue haste in dispatching John Clarkson to Nova Scotia before their plans for the colony were solidified, they must have been impelled by an urgent sense that the Granville Town settlers needed speedy reinforcement before the local Africans could take advantage of their thin ranks and disperse them again.

Their sense of urgency was reinforced by members of the Abolition

Committee, who also felt frustrated by Parliament's rejection of a bill to end the slave trade. They saw the Sierra Leone colony as a humane alternative that might help maintain public interest in abolition. Only two of the company directors, however, had any colonial experience, and Granville Sharp's plans for organizing the Province of Freedom had proven quite impractical. English experience with colonization had heretofore relied on sending Englishmen out to rule the natives. Never before had indigenous people been sent back to their country of origin to rule themselves, so the Sierra Leone Company directors had no precedents to follow. None of them foresaw the anger and bitterness that would result from revising the ambiguous promises of land and self-government that John Clarkson carried to Nova Scotia.

John Clarkson may have suspected that, contrary to his public statements, even Secretary of State Dundas was at best lukewarm in his support of the Sierra Leone project, for certainly powerful slave-trading interests in London and the West Indies were opposed, as were employers of freed blacks in the maritime provinces in America. But the influential Sierra Leone Company directors had enough personal clout in London to keep their scheme moving forward. John Clarkson left London in August and arrived in Halifax in October 1791. His promises included:

> That every Free Black (upon producing such a Certificate [of good character]) shall have a Grant of not less than TWENTY ACRES of LAND for himself, TEN for his WIFE, and FIVE for every Child, upon such terms and subject to such charges and obligations, (with a view to the general prosperity of the Company,) as shall hereafter be settled by the Company, in respect to the Grants of Land to be made by them to all Settlers, whether *Black* or *White*.
>
> That for all Stores, Provisions, &c. supplied from the Company's Warehouses, the Company shall receive an equitable compensation, according to fixed rules, extending to Blacks and Whites indiscriminately.
>
> That the civil, military, personal, and commercial rights and duties of Blacks and Whites, shall be the same, and secured in the same manner.
>
> And, for the full assurance of personal protection from slavery to all such Black Settlers, the Company have subjoined a Copy of a Clause contained in the Act of Parliament whereby they are incorporated.[2]

These promises were, unfortunately, based on the scheme of utopian self-government that Sharp had devised in 1786 for the Province of Freedom in West Africa. Clarkson did not learn until he was in Nova Scotia that the settlers of Granville Town had been scattered in 1789, nor could he believe the report was true, for surely his brother and friends in London—who had learned of the disaster long before his departure—would have informed him about it. Even the packet that brought the news to Governor Parr carried no message from London to John Clarkson. He went so far as to argue with Parr that the report that Granville Town had been abandoned must be wrong, or he would have been informed. How and why John Clarkson's London associates kept the disaster from him is certainly an enigma; perhaps they feared he would not go to Nova Scotia if he knew of the fiasco in Sierra Leone. Certainly the terms of settlement the Sierra Leone Company directors sent to the Canadian provincial governors were ambiguous.

Secretary of State Dundas sent Governor Parr written instructions to conduct an investigation into Thomas Peters's claims, to assign land to any blacks who had received none, and to publicize the Sierra Leone opportunity as an alternative for those who did not wish to remain in Nova Scotia. In his first meeting with Governor Parr, Clarkson had misgivings. Parr could hardly refuse to receive Clarkson, as he had earlier refused to receive Thomas Peters on his return from England, but Parr was worried that his reputation would be clouded by a mass exodus of unhappy blacks from his province. "I could plainly see," Clarkson wrote, "that the Governor would rather I should not succeed in my business than otherwise, probably from the idea, that if the people were averse to leaving the province, it would be a good argument to prove that they were content, and their complaints were groundless."[3] When instructed to appoint agents to assist in the Sierra Leone recruitment, Parr chose men whose interests coincided with his own. With one exception, they did very little to inform the black population about the Sierra Leone project.

Undeterred, Clarkson began explaining his mission to the blacks in Halifax and then in nearby Preston, signing up 220 emigrants there in the first month. He was so impressed with the industriousness of the Preston residents in spite of their poverty and the poor soil on which they were settled that he decided to buy their poultry and garden produce for the Atlantic crossing.[4]

Then he sailed to Shelburne, where David George met him on the wharf. Clarkson decided to let Brother George spread the word among the Baptists, making himself available to answer questions. He traveled across the bay to Birchtown and attended a meeting of 300 or 400 blacks squeezed into Moses Wilkinson's Methodist chapel, where he explained the three options available—free land in Nova Scotia, land in Africa, or military service in the West Indies. He never spelled out what charges and obligations the company might impose on the land grants.

He promised that Governor Parr would issue land to all who wanted it, and he stressed the importance of assessing the danger and uncertainty of going to Africa. Those who were uncertain should not sign up now, for they could put their names down and wait for a later voyage.

> I desired them to weigh it well in their minds and not to suffer themselves to be led away on the one hand by exaggerated accounts of the fertility of the soil, and on the other by the representations of the badness of the climate—I cautioned them not to be influenced by the novelty of the thing and particularized the various difficulties which they might expect to experience in a newly established Colony, pointing out that if they were not determined to work and be industrious they would in all probability starve. ... I explained to them such expression in the Company's proposals as they did not comprehend and informed them that what was meant by the term, "Holding their lands subject to certain charges and obligations," was by no means to be considered as an annual rent, which idea had been industriously disseminated amongst them, but as a kind of tax.[5]

This promise was probably made in the enthusiasm of the moment, without Clarkson realizing what havoc it might cause at some future date.[6]

The enraptured assembly swept aside his caution and voted on the spot to go to Freetown. They had little faith in Parr's promises. Within the next three weeks some 600 blacks in Shelburne and Birchtown signed up. Realizing that sufficient shipping might be hard to find, Clarkson ceased recruiting and returned to Halifax.

He had intended to go on to Annapolis and Digby, but decided against it when he learned that his mission had greatly incensed the white population, some of whom were threatening violence against him. Many whites had come to depend on cheap black labor and the money they spent in local shops. They were fearful that Clarkson would recruit all the honest and industrious blacks, taking away their best employees and leaving behind the shiftless and objectionable who had no money to spend.

Instead of going to Annapolis and the St. John Valley, Clarkson relied instead on Thomas Peters to spread the news there. Peters received little support from Governor Carleton of New Brunswick, and he met angry opposition from the whites living there, but he managed to recruit 222 blacks in New Brunswick and 90 more in Annapolis.

Opposition to the departure of the blacks from Nova Scotia took many forms. Employers withheld salaries, and false debts were concocted through forged indenture agreements. Whites holding valid indenture agreements refused to release their servants, even though John Clarkson offered to pay a cash settlement for their release. Other white employers refused to write the character references emigrants needed to sign up. Some whites even offered bribes to their black employees to stay in Nova Scotia. In New Brunswick, free blacks were required to produce their certificates signed by General Birch, many of which had been lost or were so worn as to be illegible. Prevented by the New Brunswick authorities from boarding ship, Richard Crankapone and four companions walked over 300 miles from St. John to Halifax through thick wintry forests.[7]

All kinds of vicious rumors were circulated: The climate in Africa was devastating and had caused the deaths of all the settlers in Granville Town. The native Africans had attacked Granville Town and killed all the settlers (this was based on garbled rumors of the 1789 attack that reached Halifax while Clarkson was there). The Africans would prey on any new settlers and sell them into slavery. The Sierra Leone Company would charge the settlers annual rent for their land as well as exorbitant taxes. The company would sell free blacks into slavery once they reached Freetown. Thomas Peters was receiving a fee for each slave procured in this way. Inadequate shipping would strand the settlers in Halifax.

Even the terms used in describing the scheme resonated among the blacks. John Clarkson argued that the advertisement run in the *Royal*

Gazette in Halifax should use the word Africa rather than Guinea,[8] because "Guinea Coast" was a synonym in everyone's mind with "slave coast," and slave ships were commonly known as Guineamen. Although Parr promised Clarkson he would erase the word, it appeared in four weekly issues of the *Gazette*.

Furious letters protesting the Sierra Leone scheme were written to London by white loyalists. David George's life was threatened, as was the lives of blacks attending Clarkson's meetings. Word went out that John Clarkson would be killed if he went to Annapolis, as would Thomas Peters if he held meetings in Digby.

Chapter 18

Bonds Forged in
Nova Scotia
Congregations

Because the black congregations of the several Protestant denominations in Nova Scotia were all kept segregated by white prejudice or indifference, they soon developed a strong sense of unity and opposition to the authority and rigidities of the white churches and government. Their preachers persuaded them of the validity of their understanding of God's message and their right to follow their own path to redemption. As a result, their chapels became their guarantee of both spiritual and temporal security, the bulwark of their community. Their preachers were their natural leaders.

A few preachers who had land grants and reason to doubt the merits of the Sierra Leone scheme remained behind. The black Anglicans in Halifax and other white loyalist settlements reacted according to the welcome they had received from the church. The Anglican Church was the official Church of England. It had been the first church available to the black refugees and the first to solicit their membership. Many blacks joined soon after they arrived. To some, belonging to the church of their former masters seemed a logical step toward a better status. The increase in the number of Anglicans soon led to the appointment of a bishop for Nova Scotia and its dependencies.[1]

Anglican Bishop Charles Inglis recognized the importance of religious instruction and education for the free blacks, an opportunity they greeted with great enthusiasm. Eighteen of the refugee Anglican clergymen from the colonies received appointments as missionaries and were supported by the Anglican Society for the Propagation of the Gospel in Foreign Parts. The SPG paid Colonel Stephen Blucke, a free black from Barbados, to open a school in Shelburne. An English philanthropic organization known as the Associates of Dr. Bray opened four other schools, which employed black teachers of spelling, reading, and religion—Joseph Leonard in Brindley Town, Isaac Limerick in Birchtown, William Frumage in Halifax, and Thomas Brownspriggs at Little Tracadie—usually holding classes in their own homes. A black woman was engaged to teach the girls sewing and knitting—one of the few opportunities for black females to prepare for nondomestic employment. These blacks, by virtue of their ability to read and write, became leaders in their communities, and although the numbers of children who sat in their classrooms were only a small portion of the total, those few at least had the doors of literacy opened for them. Joseph Leonard would go to Freetown, in spite of owning a 100-acre farm, along with most of his congregation. So would Isaac Limerick and many of the Halifax blacks.

Bishop Inglis refused, however, to ordain Methodist[2] clergymen or to let them preach from Anglican pulpits. Nor did the Anglican churches or schools allow blacks to mingle with whites. This attitude led many blacks to link the Church of England with privilege and to mistrust white Anglicans in general and local authority in particular. They were aware that Governor Parr in Halifax headed the SPG corresponding board that controlled the provincial operations of the Anglican Church, making the church seem more like an arm of the government than a place of spiritual refuge.

In Halifax the balcony in St. Paul's Church was too small to hold the blacks who wished to attend. Instead, segregated services and instruction were held in private homes by Anglican laymen or clergymen. The black Anglicans in Preston, just outside Halifax, held meetings in the home of Adam and Catherine Abernathy. The Abernathys received a 50-acre farm, but sold it and led their congregation to Freetown, where Mrs. Abernathy opened a school a decade later.[3]

In Shelburne, few blacks could pay the high pew fees in St. George's Church, and so Anglican clergymen visited Birchtown periodically to preach and instruct. They even vied with each other for the loyalty of the black Anglicans there.

Blucke was the leading black Anglican in Shelburne; he was on good terms with white officials, and he was one of the few blacks to receive a land grant. He chose to stay in Nova Scotia rather than go to Sierra Leone—the only one of the black teachers to do so. A number of his fellow communicants followed his example. Blucke may have been much influenced by his superior officer in the provincial militia, Major Stephen Skinner, who understood how to work the system. Skinner had been an upper-class Tory in New Jersey, provincial treasurer, member of the royal council, and a judge. During the American Revolution, the patriots had jailed him and confiscated his property, valued at £24,000, for which he was compensated at no more than a fifth of its value. In reward for his military service he received an annual pension from the British of £140, but he was middle-aged and had ten children to support. He set up a business in Shelburne and was elected to the assembly, but never made a comfortable living.[4] The exodus of hundreds of free blacks to Sierra Leone threatened to crimp the local economy further.

Skinner shared Governor Parr's dislike of the whole emigration scheme. Because he had been ordered to appoint agents in each district to recruit emigrants for Sierra Leone, Parr chose Skinner as agent in Shelburne. John Clarkson's diary indicates that Skinner promised two years' free provisions to blacks who stayed in Nova Scotia. He also enlisted Blucke in a scheme to further their mutual interests. If some of the black loyalists were to have free transport to Africa, then those who remained in Nova Scotia should be rewarded as well. Skinner helped Blucke write a petition to the provincial government asking for a cow and two sheep for each black family that stayed, since they would not be using any British transport funds. Skinner supervised the signing of this document by Blucke, 49 other men, and 6 women, and then personally delivered it to Governor Parr. Skinner also forwarded a copy to the British Secretary of State, with an accompanying note saying that the blacks were being "flattered by imaginary prospects of happiness to leave a comfortable and decent maintenance. ... That they as well as numbers of the White Inhabitants have suffered, is notorious, but not more than might be reasonably expected, from the hardships and disappointments natural to the settling of all new Countries."[5] Skinner also urged Governor Parr to cut off further emigrant applications from Shelburne, forcing John Clarkson to argue at length with the governor and his council that this was contrary to instructions from London.

The Methodists, in contrast to the Anglican blacks, had no hesitation in responding. Moses Wilkinson had attracted into his fold the largest single Methodist congregation in Birchtown. He had adopted the Methodist faith before he ever left the colonies. His followers built a meeting house very soon after their arrival in Birchtown. When the Yorkshire evangelist William Black made his last visit to Nova Scotia in 1784 and heard Wilkinson preach, he wrote,

> It is truly wonderful to see what a work God hath been carrying on amongst these poor negroes. Upwards of sixty [in Birchtown] profess to have found the pearl of great price, within seven or eight months; and what is farther remarkable, the chief instrument whom God hath employed in this work is a poor negro, who can neither see, walk, nor stand. He is usually carried to the place of worship, where he sits and speaks, or kneels and prays with the people.[6]

The Methodist emigrants to Freetown outnumbered all the other denominations. Wilkinson's Birchtown congregation included two men who had been allotted 40 acres of land, but they decided to go with their congregation. John Gordon was born a Koranko tribesman about 130 miles inland from the Province of Freedom and sold from Bunce Island when he was about 15, then transported to Dorset County, Maryland, where he married and had two sons. Luke Jordon came from Nansemond County, Virginia, with a wife and five daughters. Other Methodist leaders who went to Freetown included Richard Ball from the Halifax area; Henry Beverhout, born free in St. Croix, who moved to St. John with Thomas Peters; and America Talbot, also from St. John. Mingo Jordan, from Isle of Wight County, Virginia, emigrated from Digby, even though he had a house lot and a 50-acre farm.

Boston King, after his conversion by Wilkinson, set out to preach in the other black settlements, and eventually supervised the black Wesleyan society at Dartmouth. His whole congregation, including his wife and six children, decided to emigrate. "It was not for the sake of the advantages I hoped to reap in Africa, which induced me to undertake the voyage, but from a desire that had long possessed my mind, of contributing to the best of my poor ability, in spreading the knowledge of Christianity in that country."[7]

In the same way that the black Anglicans were only occasionally supervised, the black Methodist congregations had very little white supervision and followed their own needs and interpretations of scripture. This was particularly true in Birchtown, where two local men had been ordained by the Reverend John Marrant,[8] who visited at the instigation of his brother, a Birchtown resident,[9] and assembled a Huntingdon[10] congregation of 40 members.

When Marrant rode the mission circuit, he left Cato Perkins and William Ash (both from Charleston, South Carolina) behind as preachers.[11] Both Perkins and Ash received 40-acre land grants, but Perkins never cleared his; he preferred to work as a carpenter and improved two town lots he had purchased with his wages. Nevertheless, he and Ash abandoned their property and led the Countess of Huntingdon Methodists in Nova Scotia to Sierra Leone.

Enthusiasm for emigration to West Africa depended very much on where the blacks lived in Nova Scotia and to which church they belonged.[12] Those Protestant preachers on the south coast of Nova Scotia who intended to go themselves had little difficulty in convincing all their followers to sign up for Freetown. They had not been delivered from one form of white bondage to submit to another. The communicants in many of the chapels not only chose to go together, but pooled their resources to pay debts and buy releases from indentures so that every member of their chapel could go.

The black Baptists in Nova Scotia went to Freetown en masse. David George's preaching in Shelburne and Birchtown had won many converts. Invitations soon came to preach in other towns. He made a tour of St. John, Horton, Preston, Halifax, Digby, and Liverpool, founding chapels in each location and appointing leaders to take charge. One of them—Hector Peters—became a famous preacher himself.

The rapid growth of the Baptist denomination among the blacks can be attributed to inspired preaching and their intense need for solace. Also, each chapel could be a self-originating, self-governing body, requiring no outside approval.[13] George dramatically extolled this kind of independence to his people, promising his followers complete freedom in seeking their redemption. Many of his white neighbors were far from enthusiastic about his popularity, and when he began baptizing white converts, their relatives rioted and called in the magistrates to put a stop to it. Angry with his success, other whites complained that he was preaching without a license. George then got in touch with a former officer he had known during the Revolution, now a supreme court judge in Nova Scotia, who arranged for him to receive a license from Governor Parr's office. This permitted him to preach only to black people in regular services. If whites wanted to hear him, they scheduled meetings held at other than regular times of worship.

By the time John Clarkson reached Shelburne with the Sierra Leone scheme, George was 48 years old and the father of six children. He headed two churches, although he listed his occupation as sawyer. He owned 50 acres of farmland and five town lots, but sold them to go to Sierra Leone.

In Annapolis County in the north, Brindley Town was a completely separate black community from white Annapolis Royal. Large numbers of its residents embraced the Anglican faith and were visited periodically by the rector from Cornwallis. In 1786 the Reverend Roger Viets was sent to head an Anglican parish in Digby, but again he only visited the black town periodically to "examine the People and preach a plain, practical Sermon."[14] Between visits, the blacks met in private homes and received instruction from one of their own—Joseph Leonard. When the Bishop visited in 1791, he was shocked to find Leonard baptizing converts and administering communion to some 60 black families, and he put a stop to it. The Huntingdonians had the same trouble with William Frumage, whom they dismissed and replaced with Isaac Limerick. Some of the black Anglican communicants in Annapolis County chose to stay in Nova Scotia, but both Leonard and Limerick went to Freetown.

In other, more remote areas a few of the blacks became Anglicans, but they were left largely on their own. The small numbers reflected a growing distrust of the official church; many converts drifted into Anglican offshoot sects such as the Huntingdonians and Methodists. Their chapels in Nova Scotia, however, became more and more independent of the Anglican church, particularly when the Countess of Huntingdon began ordaining men as preachers who had not taken Anglican orders.[15]

Recruitment for Sierra Leone was officially cut off when large numbers from the south coast and Annapolis signed up; word of the Sierra Leone scheme never reached the black families of Little Tracadie in the northern region of Nova Scotia. They lived 20 miles from the Anglican church in Manchester. Many of them made the trip there to baptize their children, but the rest of the time they made do with a local man, Thomas Brownspriggs, to instruct them, using the testaments, prayer books, and tracts the bishop sent from Halifax.

Chapter 19

Still Searching for Freedom and Security

When questions arose in Halifax as to why so many of the freed blacks were eager to leave, English officials sought to absolve themselves of any blame. They said that the blacks were unhappy with the severe Nova Scotia climate and that their experience in the colonies had hardly prepared them to look after themselves.[1] Both excuses may have contained a small kernel of truth, but not enough to dismiss their exodus so lightly. The petitions written and memoirs left by the Nova Scotia blacks seldom mentioned the cold climate, nor did more than a handful sign up for military service in the balmy West Indies. As for fending for themselves, John Clarkson expressed "surprise at their being able to support themselves upon such barren and stony land as they have done, which could never have been brought to the state their Lots are now in, but from great industry."[2]

Most of the free blacks called themselves farmers when they enrolled in 1791 to migrate to Africa, but in reality they worked whenever they could for wages as carpenters, sawyers, masons, blacksmiths, coopers, saddlers, barbers, tailors, shoemakers, weavers, and bakers. They lived on town lots in cabins or frame houses they had built themselves, tended a garden in the back, and tried to be self-sufficient. The women sewed and spun cloth. Many of the men fished to augment their food supply.

By signing up to go to Sierra Leone, the emigrants themselves expressed the same motivations that had led them to flee their masters in the American colonies. They wanted land and a future worth striving for. Those who had received no land in Nova Scotia were bitter and distrustful, and many of them were skeptical that Governor Parr would now see to their allotments. They had already waited eight or nine years. Even if Parr did assign land, where were they to get the tools and provisions needed to support them until they could make their farms productive?

Among those who had received land in Nova Scotia, some more pressing motivation must have caused them to sell or abandon it and go to Sierra Leone. Fear was part of it. In Nova Scotia they were constantly afraid of being seized by former American masters or tricked back into slavery. Their hope was to be secure in a black homeland in Africa. They felt an overwhelming need to be free of the caprices and avarices of white employers, who treated them not as equal citizens but as though they were still little better than slaves. Nova Scotia had taught them that independence in a white society was an illusion.

Clarkson did not encourage the Nova Scotia blacks to go to Sierra Leone without good reason. Indeed, he discouraged those who were relatively comfortable in Nova Scotia. He made some applicants take several days to consider their decision. He promised to use his influence to see that land grants were made to those who chose to remain. He turned down those who were lame or could not work for a living, unless they had a guarantor. Debtors were not allowed to sign up. Indentured servants were eligible only if someone paid off their indenture and their masters gave their consent. Clarkson required proof that each applicant would become a useful citizen in Africa, and he refused to accept applications from those who could not produce the required character references. Single or elderly women were not accepted unless they knew a man who would guarantee their maintenance.

While in Nova Scotia, Clarkson received no communications or instructions from the Sierra Leone Company directors in London—nothing to indicate any revision in plans. Clarkson must have believed that the land grants would be free, that taxes would be imposed only for the benefit of the settlers—to care for the poor and educate children. His understanding was that the settlers were to have full rights to participate in and govern the new colony.

Of course, communications by sailing ship between England, Nova Scotia, and Africa took months in the eighteenth century. The Sierra Leone Company was formally incorporated in mid–1791, and Clarkson was sent to Halifax in August of that year to recruit settlers and transport them, making promises based on what he had been told before he left England.

Governor Parr, meanwhile, was trying to convince his superiors that Thomas Peters was simply a troublemaker. In September, he wrote to Secretary of State Dundas in London: "Concerning the Complaint of Peters, I apprehend it to be a Misrepresentation.... I have at all times peculiarly attended to their Settlements [and] I think I may with safety say that these People were put on Lands and in a situation then much envied."[3] He also instituted an inquiry in Annapolis-Digby where Peters claimed he received no land. The commissioners concluded that the first tract was indeed laid out by mistake, but that Peters had left Annapolis before another could be surveyed or additional provisions issued. The fact that the second grant was never issued was ignored. As far as the governor was concerned, no further action need be taken. No wonder the blacks in Nova Scotia were skeptical that Parr would change his ways.

When Clarkson's list of potential emigrants reached 1,200, he returned to Halifax to arrange shipping for them, for this was a much larger group than had been expected. Time was needed to contract for 15 vessels. Prices were high, and the ships were often in such poor shape that Clarkson took Peters with him to inspect each one, ordering that decks be removed and ventilation holes cut so that the passengers would have sufficient space and air to travel comfortably. Berths were to be constructed for all the settlers and the ship holds smoked with tar and brimstone, then scrubbed out, aired, and washed with vinegar. He knew that a third of his charges had been brought to America on slave ships, and he understood the horrors of the Middle Passage, when men were confined in a dark space no bigger than a coffin.

One of the emigrants, John Kizell, could describe that horror from personal experience. He was the son and nephew of African chiefs, and he actually came from Sherbro country in Sierra Leone. He had been captured and sold into slavery at age 12, and he had vivid memories of his passage to Charleston, South Carolina. In Nova Scotia Kizell would call himself a farmer, but had no land and was forced to hire out to a white master for three years at $60. He learned to read and write in Nova Scotia and became an active Baptist. He was 28 when he joined the exodus to Sierra Leone, along with his wife Phillis and three children under age six.[4]

British officials seriously underestimated the costs of the emigration. The Treasury was prepared to spend £6,000 on the Nova Scotia exodus, but shipping expenses alone came to almost £10,000. To that was added demurrage for the two months the ships idled in Halifax harbor, the cost of accommodations for the blacks in Halifax before their departure, maintenance for the whole group ashore and during the voyage, and Clarkson's own expenses (a modest £287), bringing the total cost to the British government to almost £16,000.[5] Treasury officials in London were so appalled when they learned the size of the bill that they cut off all further support for transport from Nova Scotia. Those who still wanted to leave were offered only military service in the West Indies.

The migrants assembling in Halifax had sold or left behind nearly all of their belongings, except what few clothes they wore and packets of vegetable and flower seeds from their gardens. Weeks went by as they waited to depart. The storehouses in which they were billeted were crowded and not insulated against the cold winds of November and December. Many fell sick, and eight died of disease or exposure. It took time to collect the provisions needed to feed and clothe them.

Clarkson was overwhelmed with individual requests and complaints while he was trying to get ships in shape for the Atlantic crossing and buy and distribute food and clothing. He paid legitimate debts for those emigrants suddenly confronted with creditors, holding off until the last minute to avoid their taking advantage of this generosity. Last-minute debts totaling £50 were paid for eight, including such prominent leaders as Thomas Peters, Nathaniel Snowball, and William Ash. Clarkson was even asked to ordain black preachers and settle religious disputes.[6] The petition to Clarkson in December 1791 read:

> the humble petion of the Black pepel lying in mr wisdoms Store Called the anoplus [Annapolis] Compnay humbely bag that if it is Consent to your honer as it is the larst Christmas day that we ever shall see in the amaraca [America] that it may please your honer to grant us one days alowance of frish

Beef for a Christmas diner that if it is agreabel to you and
the rest of the Gentlemon to whom it may Consern
thomas Petus [Peters]
david Edmon [Edmonds][7]

Overwhelmed by the myriad details, Clarkson fell back on the old structure of companies headed by captains, usually preachers, to maintain order and relay information back to him. The captains were to act as constables, select juries, conduct trials, and punish minor offenses. Even so, the 27 captains brought so much petty business to him that Clarkson finally appointed Peters as his second-in-command, with David George and John Bull to assist as intermediaries between him and the emigrants.

With their help, Clarkson made out land certificates in the name of each settler, stating the number of acres he or she was to receive. These were ceremoniously presented by Clarkson to the passengers mustered on the deck of each ship during a tour of the fleet shortly before departure. At that same ceremony, Clarkson read his final instructions, advising the emigrants to be patient and soft-spoken, to avoid fraternizing with the white seamen, to help each other, to pay particular attention to divine worship and personal cleanliness, to guard against improper behavior, and to display their gratitude by accepting Clarkson's advice.[8] These instructions were read aloud, posted, and repeated weekly during the voyage.

If the instructions sounded paternal, they were, for the many requests and petty disputes dumped in his lap led Clarkson to view himself as the leader and protector of a large mass of simple children. Peters, 53 years old to Clarkson's 27, must have resented this attitude in a man half his age. After all, Peters had initiated the whole project and recruited over a third of the emigrants, so he felt his own views were valid in the arrangements for their departure. He and Clarkson struggled to find their way through heated disagreements as the weeks dragged by.

In October, while Clarkson was in Nova Scotia recruiting settlers, the Sierra Leone Company directors met in London and devised a new constitution for the West African colony, putting the government of the colony in the hands of a council of white Englishmen and giving the company a monopoly on trade. It was published in November and mailed to Clarkson in December—sent not to Nova Scotia but to Africa to await his arrival there.

The fleet's departure was delayed until January 15, 1792, so that it crossed the Atlantic in bitter winter weather. The ships were separated in storms; illness broke out on board. When the ships had all arrived in Africa in March 1792, Clarkson was astonished to find new orders from the company awaiting him, setting up a government without any black participation. Peters, who had set the exodus in motion, was totally unprepared on his arrival in Freetown to accept the idea that English officials sent from London were to run the new colony, not as a philanthropical settlement but as a viable commercial enterprise.

Part IV
Freetown

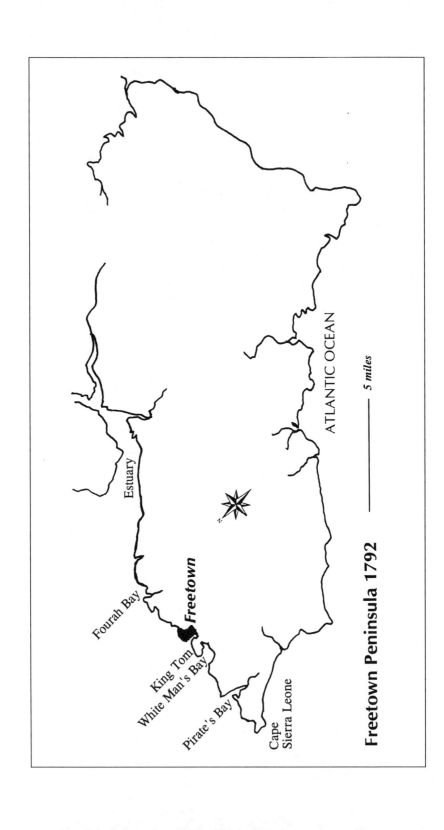

ATLANTIC OCEAN

——— 5 miles

Estuary

Fourah Bay

Freetown

King Tom
White Man's Bay

Pirate's Bay

Cape
Sierra Leone

Freetown Peninsula 1792

Chapter 20

Plans to Govern Freetown

John Clarkson kept the directors informed of his work in Nova Scotia. They had expected he might be able to recruit a hundred families to go to Freetown. When they learned that many more were signing up, the directors began to envision a more secure colony, with trade and revenue much larger than their earlier expectations.

As Clarkson's glowing reports of successful recruitment reached London from Halifax, the Sierra Leone Company directors were able to add to the 500 initial investors and increase the initial capitalization of the company from £42,000 to £235,000. A total of 1,100 people purchased shares in the company, all of whom expected some return on their investment.

The incorporation act, passed on May 30, 1791, did not specify a trading monopoly and limited the life of the company to 31 years. The Sierra Leone Company came into being on July 1, 1791.[1] The stated goals of the company were trade, development of tropical agriculture, and the spread of Christianity—to be brought about by the black settlers.

Granville Sharp was not happy with Parliament's decision. He wrote of his disillusionment with the "very disagreeable circumstance" in a letter to William Thornton:

> ... the community of settlers, though they are now restored to their actual possessions in the settlement, are no longer *proprietors of the whole district* as before, as the land has

been granted ... to the *Sierra Leone Company*, so that they can no longer enjoy the privileges of granting land by a free vote of their own Common Council, as before, nor the benefits of their former Agrarian Law, nor the choice of their own Governor and other officers, nor any other circumstances of *perfect freedom* promised in the *Regulations*; all these privileges are now submitted to the appointment and controul of the Company, and no settler can trade independently of it.

I am very sure that such restraints cannot accord with your ideas of perfect liberty and justice. But I could not prevent this humiliating change: the settlement must have remained desolate, if I had not thus far submitted to the opinions of the associated subscribers.[2]

Sharp lobbied valiantly to write safeguards for the rights of the black colonists into any company charter. Although his suggestions were supported by Prime Minister William Pitt and Member of Parliament William Wilberforce, they were strongly opposed by London, Bristol, and Liverpool slave-trading interests, as well as by West Indian sugar planters whose prosperity would be threatened.[3] The governing charter that Sharp presented was not adopted. Parliament passed only an incorporation act for the company (changing its name from St. George's Bay to the Sierra Leone Company), enabling it to take over the original land grant and buy additional land. The fact that the tract had been assigned in the original agreement to the black settlers in Granville Town and their heirs in perpetuity was ignored. The directors reasoned that the original title had been negotiated by an agent of the Crown, and the settlers had abdicated their rights to it by deserting the Province of Freedom. A clause in the incorporation did prohibit the company from engaging in the slave trade.

The regulations governing the Sierra Leone Company were published in November 1791, but Chairman Thornton did not write John Clarkson until December of the new provisions, sending the letter to Freetown to await his arrival.

We have proposed ... to indemnify ourselves for all our huge expenses at the first, by a rent on the lands, which will be more easy to collect, than by high profits on trade. I trust the Blacks will not consider this as a grievance especially as it will be very light at first & that they will consider themselves as hereby paying the necessary expence of government

& return to the English Subscribers who have stood forth so
liberally to serve them.[4]

The blacks will not consider this as a grievance? Clearly the new
regulations conflicted with the promises Clarkson made in Nova Scotia to the black emigrants. The directors were not motivated, however,
by any malice or ulterior motives. They sincerely believed themselves
embarked on benevolent good works. They had been active in a long
effort to abolish slavery in England and end the slave trade on English
ships. Sharp, then middle-aged, had been associated with the abolition
cause for years. He had raised funds and invested his own money in
assisting impoverished free blacks. After the debacle in Granville Town,
however, his colleagues no longer felt confident that his resettlement
scheme was practical, and they drew together to improvise a more
efficient way of providing a home for the objects of their pity.

The other important Sierra Leone Company directors were young
men, well-to-do, four of them bachelors. Henry Thornton came from a
prosperous family and was at age 32 both a Member of Parliament and
a successful banker; he was elected chairman in the hope that his financial skills would direct the company toward profitable enterprise.
William Wilberforce, also an MP and close friend of Prime Minister
Pitt, was 31 and from an even more prominent and wealthy background;
he was also an enthusiastic leader in the abolition movement. The Clarkson brothers came from a devout clerical family; Thomas Clarkson, also
31, was an inveterate writer of books and pamphlets condemning slavery. His brother, John, was just 27. (Both kept extensive journals, which
provide a window to what was going on in their circles at the time.)
These were men of strong and upright character, who empathized
acutely with the plight of the black poor.[5] Thornton wrote that "every
measure will be taken for laying a foundation of happiness to the natives,
by the promotion of industry, the discouragement of polygamy, the setting up of schools, and the gradual introduction of religious and moral
instruction among them."[6] Thomas Clarkson described the Sierra Leone
project as "the Noblest Institution ever set on foot, an Institution which
embraces no less than an Attempt to civilize and Christianize a great
Continent, to bring it out of Darkness, & to abolish the Trade in Men."[7]

Since the freed blacks would not be allowed to govern themselves, the company directors sought suitable white officials to send out to Sierra Leone. Their first choice to be superintendent, Henry Hew Dalrymple, demanded 150 soldiers to accompany him; when the directors agreed to only 15, he promptly resigned. The logical second choice was Alexander Falconbridge, who had returned to London from the Province of Freedom in Sierra Leone in September, bringing with him King Naimbana's son John Frederick to be educated. When Falconbridge found himself working for a radically changed company—with hundreds of colonists expected from Nova Scotia—he immediately criticized such "a premature, hair-brained, and ill digested scheme, to think of sending such a number of people all at once, to a rude, barbarous and unhealthy country."[8]

Offended by his testy criticism, the directors compromised by offering him the post of chief commercial agent, a position for which he had no experience whatsoever. Needing the salary, he accepted, but he was furious at being passed over in favor of John Clarkson, a much younger man who had never been to Africa. Falconbridge had recently married a very attractive young woman, against her parents' wishes, and may have had high hopes of impressing both his wife, Anna Maria, and his in-laws with his status and acumen.

In addition to the council members, three Swedes who had applied in 1787 to go to Granville Town (intending to plant a Swedenborgian church in the heart of Africa) were also welcomed. Finally, 85 junior company employees (including 16 soldiers) were sent from London ahead of the fleet from Nova Scotia. They idled on their ships in Freetown harbor awaiting the arrival of their new superintendent.[9]

Chapter 21

To the Cotton Tree

John Clarkson left Halifax bone weary and with a nasty cold. After less than a week at sea, he turned his duties over to his deputy, Lieutenant Samuel Wickham, and took to his bunk for four weeks. His flagship's log recorded storms, with strong gales and squalls of snow, hail, or rain. Sixty-five of the settlers (including Adam Abernathy, the Preston farmer whose wife had headed a school) and two of the ships' captains died en route. Clarkson himself was back on his feet when the fleet reached tropical latitudes in February, and he was able to be rowed about among the ships. He arrived in Sierra Leone in very weakened health. Lieutenant Wickham was told to supervise the landing operation.

Clarkson expected to find an English governor awaiting him with the beginnings of an organized colony. He was astonished when a group of councilors dressed in cockaded hats and gold-braided, epauletted waistcoats rowed out to meet him. Although the company directors had reluctantly sanctioned the wearing of these conspicuous uniforms by their officials, the inappropriate garb must have been the first hint to Clarkson of where their priorities lay. They told him, again to his surprise, that the directors had decided that he himself should step into the superintendent's position on his arrival.[1]

Clarkson was appalled to learn that the scores of officers and artisans sent from London had done absolutely nothing to prepare for the needs of the black settlers except to erect a single canvas shelter on shore in which some of them slept. In the daytime they used it for "dining, preaching, praying, working, palavering, & Council Chamber." Clarkson immediately sent men on shore to clear a path to the tall cotton tree that stood like a beacon on a narrow plateau halfway up the mountain slopes. On March 10, Alexander Falconbridge, second in command, conducted his sixth and last council meeting on board the ship, and swore in Clarkson as governor—first among equals in a council of eight.[2]

On the first Sunday after their arrival—March 11, 1792—everyone, black and white, went ashore from their anchored ships, which rocked gently on the broad estuary. Balmy aromatic breezes blew from the Bullom Shore, a low, dark line along the horizon to the north, shimmering across the placid harbor.

Two young men from Moses Wilkinson's congregation carried him between them on their clasped hands. He must have gazed up at the warm tropical sun cresting the mountain rim high above the landing and felt exaltation for the new day that was finally bringing happiness to his people. Scripture may have echoed through his mind: "The people who walked in darkness have seen a great light ... for Thou hast broken the yoke of bondage, the rod of their oppressor."

Thomas Peters gazed at the emerald green slopes and found their luminance dazzling to his eyes. Surely all the lush vegetation surrounding them promised abundant harvests from the gardens and fields they would plant there.

Mary and Caesar Perth walked with their daughter Susan between them, their clasped hands trembling with anticipation. The hymn they were all singing sounded to Boston and Violet King like a choir of angels. David George remembered the trials endured by his mother in Essex County, Virginia, and wished she were there with him to give thanks for the triumphant delivery of all the free blacks around him from the bonds of slavery. Surely all of them walked with the reverence of pilgrims approaching a sacred shrine.

They gathered under the huge cotton tree that thrust its mighty crest almost 100 feet above them like a watch tower guiding them to safety. Anthony Elliott, 15 years old at the time and later a preacher himself, described the service of thanksgiving that followed—the glorious christening of a settlement named Freetown:

Pioneers ... were despatched on shore to clear, or made road-
way for their landing, which being done they all disembarked, and marched towards the thick forest, with the Holy
Bible, and their preachers (all colored men) before them,
singing the hymn ...

> 'Awake! and sing the song
> of Moses and the Lamb,
> Wake! every heart and every tongue
> To praise the Saviour's name! ...
> The day of Jubilee is come;
> Return ye ransomed sinners home.'

They proceeded immediately to worship Almighty God,
thanking him for ... bringing them in safety to the land of
their forefathers.[3]

The Anglican Reverend Nathaniel Gilbert raised his arms over the
hundreds of uplifted faces and expounded on the first verse of Psalm
127: "*Except the Lord build the house, they labor in vain that build it:
except the Lord keep the city, the watchman waketh in vain.*" Voices were
lifted in hymns of praise to the God who had watched over them during the bitter winter passage from Nova Scotia. David George articulated their humble gratitude in the first Baptist sermon preached in
Africa. The town site was dedicated. All heads were bowed in earnest
prayer for safety and prosperity in this, their new home, their promised
land.

Chapter 22

An Erratic Beginning

As he listened to David George's inspiring sermon, John Clarkson probably looked around and grimaced because no streets had been laid out, no surveying done, no wood cut for building, no wharf built for unloading supplies, no storehouse erected to protect them, no houses started—in spite of the many letters he had written to Henry Thornton in England stressing the importance of appointing sympathetic officials who would exert themselves on behalf of the settlers. Clarkson's experiences gathering the blacks together in Nova Scotia had made him very aware of how sensitive they were to the way whites treated them. He empathized completely with their feelings, but wrote to Thornton of his worries about "captains of your vessels, sailors, keepers of the storehouses and inferior people, who would think no harm in calling these people what I cannot mention on paper…. You may probably say that none will be appointed but those who detest slavery … but consider the education of many … and you will have reason to fear."[1]

Clarkson immediately gave surveyor James Cocks a plan for laying out town lots on the slopes above the landing, drawn up at his request by the chief surveyor in Nova Scotia. Twelve streets, each named for a company director, were to be cut—nine running up the slope at right angles to the waterfront, and three broad avenues (80 feet wide) parallel to the river. One of the three, Water Street along the waterfront, was to be double the width of the others. The streets would be paved in Bermuda grass and cropped by cattle, sheep, and goats. Two squares were to be laid out, one with a tower in which to hang the great bell that would be rung at sunrise to start the day's work. Above this grid the hump of the mountain above the cotton tree was named Thornton Hill after chairman Thornton and designated for the governor's future residence. Settlers were to occupy the town lots in whatever random order they were laid out, until such time as a lottery could be held to determine permanent locations.

As quickly as possible—for the rains were expected soon—large tents were erected to shelter the company's business and stores. Smaller tents for the white officials were put together from the sails of the transport ships. Anna Maria Falconbridge and the other European wives stayed aboard the transport ships, gossiping and embroidering the respective status of their husbands in the company pecking order.

There was no time to fell the huge trees in the surrounding bush and saw them into lumber for building frames and siding. The settlers were told to erect any covering they could devise as quickly as possible before the rains began. They looked around and saw what appeared to be deceptively simple African huts in King Tom's village near the watering place, built with only mats and thatch.

Mary and Caesar Perth would have set to work immediately cutting saplings, jamming them into the earth, and tying them together for the frame of a temporary hut. Mats made by the Africans were available to wrap around the framework. The roof was the hardest part. The Africans used thatch, so Mary Perth and Susan, then only ten years old, would have hiked up the river with the other women to cut tall grass. Staggering quantities were needed, for 2,000 settlers would require at least 500 shelters. As Mary and Susan brought their bundles of thatch, Caesar tied them as best he could in tight rows over the saplings. He was an energetic and determined worker, but he had never before attempted to make a thatch roof waterproof. Some of his less nimble neighbors had difficulty even securing the bundles in place because the bone-dry grass bent and crumbled and filled the air with aggravating chaff.

This was the end of the long dry season. The merciless sun and daily temperatures close to 100 degrees made the sweat pour off their bodies as they labored. Barely two weeks after their thanksgiving service, the first violent storm broke over the mountains, bringing gale winds and great streaks of lightning. Thunder reverberating through the hills did indeed sound like lions roaring—the sound that had prompted the Portuguese explorers of the fifteenth century to name the peninsula *Serra Lyoa* ("lion mountain"). The lashing winds tore away the clumsily constructed thatch roofs.

Caesar struggled during the next ten days' respite to shore up his flimsy shelter, but then another storm battered them. Torrents of rain soaked the flimsy huts and drenched the settlers. The interludes between storms shortened until rain poured down every day in July and August— drenching, vicious, deafening, flooding in torrents down the slopes and gullies, turning the red laterite soil where the jungle had been cut into a sea of mud.

They had no furniture, so they were all sleeping on the ground. Only candles were available for light; they must have spent many hours in darkness while the wind and thunder howled around them. Dry wood for cooking fires simply couldn't be found. Mary and Caesar's clothing, blankets, and food were soon sodden. Nothing ever dried out: leather boots molded, knives and axes rusted, cloth rotted. Mary despaired of keeping her New Testament dry. If Caesar grumbled and griped over the foul weather and the dilatory white officials, Mary surely reminded him that they must soldier on; they were free of their owners and poised on the threshold of a new life.

Occasional bursts of bright sunshine made the landscape steam and brought out brilliant birds to preen in the fierce light. Lizards crawled over everything. Mary was particularly distressed when spitting cobras began creeping into their hut to escape the driver ants; green mambas slithered into the thatch. Green mambas, kraits, and night adders were deadly poisonous.

Wild animals also sought the shelter of the tents. Leopards mauled the pet dogs her neighbors had brought along. Thieving monkeys swung through the trees. Rats attacked everything edible. Every rain brought out the deep bass chorus of singing frogs. Crickets made a monotonous sound so piercing that Mary's head ached, but they helped drown out the wild drumming in King Jemmy's town, which lay "a musquet shot distant." What kind of nefarious rites could those pagan Africans be celebrating to indulge in such incessant drumming?[2] The Nova Scotians had scarcely the vaguest idea of what the first rains meant to the

Africans—the promise of abundant harvests to come after long months without rain.

Nights were raw, and clouds of insects bred furiously as soon as the rains began. Clarkson wrote that

> crickets, cockroaches, spiders, etc., are driven out of their crevices and jump about the floor in a distressing situation among their enemies [ants]. The large black ants conquer every living animal and devour it unless it escapes by flight.... As it is impossible to turn these swarms of black ants either to the right or to the left, when the settlers see that their course is directed through their houses, they have recourse to fire or scalding water, with which they attack them as they are pouring along the ground like a rivulet.

Cuffey and Judith Preston burned down their hut and all they owned trying to divert a column of marching ants.

The ants were formidable, the spiders were fearsomely large and furry, and biting chiggers buried their eggs under human skin. The settlers became vigilant in watching for these predators, but the more debilitating enemy was barely visible. Mosquitoes, breeding copiously in every stagnant puddle and discarded calabash, carried the malaria parasite. No one at that time knew that the searing fevers were caused by the bite of a fragile, winged creature no different from those they had slapped on another continent. White men then believed that malaria (derived from two Italian words meaning "*bad air*") was borne on the miasma from the tropical swamps and the mists of the rainy season in Africa. They covered their bodies with woolen underclothing and flannel next to the skin to protect themselves from foul air, only increasing their body temperatures in the tropical heat. Think of Falconbridge's animated young bride, Anna Maria, proudly wearing her satin and taffeta trousseau gowns, with sleeves to her wrists, a high neckline just under her chin, full skirts covering her ankles, sweating in the tropical heat. Her parasol sheltered her from the tropical sun, but mosquitoes and flies zeroed in ferociously on any inch of exposed skin.

Settlers developed dysentery, tuberculosis, and malaria and began collapsing. Strong drink was prescribed to assuage fevers. John Clarkson's first encounter with Dr. John Bell, the chief physician, had been on March 12, when the doctor returned from a visit to Bunce Island, feverish and too drunk to recognize anyone. He died the following night. Clarkson protested that Dr. Bell's drunken behavior set a very bad example to the settlers, but the councilors immediately lowered the flag to half-mast, for he was one of their own. The next morning they donned their fancy gold-braided uniforms to accompany the coffin in a solemn burial at sea. The *Harpy*'s guns were fired at one-minute intervals as Bell's body was removed. During the salute, one of the gunners lost a hand when gunpowder exploded. He died as well on the following day.

The other doctors were of very little use to the settlers, for they knew almost nothing about treating malaria (which they called "ague"), sunstroke, scurvy, dysentery, or rheumatism. They had only chinchona bark (from which quinine would later be derived), opium, and laudanum to work with. Dr. Charles Taylor had ministered to the sick during the winter passage from Nova Scotia, but chills and fevers raging in the soggy equatorial heat were not part of his experience. Knowing how little he could do to aid the stricken, the hapless doctor wandered away almost daily to King Jemmy's town nearby, where (according to his journal) he admired the flora, fauna, and nubile young women (who wore nothing but wraparound skirts and strings of beads). The spectacle of these half-naked women was shockingly enticing in the pious atmosphere ordained by the colony's sponsors. Taylor and another surgeon soon asked to return to England, as did a third man when Clarkson refused to double his salary to compensate for the frustrating conditions.

Those who fell sick had very little effective medical attention, save for the healing skills of a young African woman who sought refuge in the settlement. She had fled Signor Domingo's village upriver because he intended to sell her—or so she claimed. Mary Perth and her friends welcomed her when they learned that she feared for her life.

When this clever refugee saw how many of the settlers were stricken with fever, she immediately began brewing infusions of local barks and herbs, which eased the symptoms for many of the sick. They were so delighted that Mary sent Caesar to Clarkson to ask him to buy her. Caesar and his friends pledged their own labor to pay for her. The governor was very reluctant to get involved in the slave trade, but how could he refuse to redeem slaves who claimed refuge in Freetown—particularly at the urging of leading settlers?

116

In any case, this African woman was allowed to stay in Freetown after promising that she would wear a blouse with her *lappa* (wrap-around skirt). The Nova Scotians were dismayed that the African women who brought fruits and vegetables to the landing were half-naked, their pendulous breasts hanging loose over their ribs and flapping as they unloaded their baskets. Their children, wearing nothing more than leather bracelets around their waists and forearms, stood sucking their fingers behind their mothers, clinging to their legs. Flies crawled unprotested around their eyes and noses. The vivid scars on the African faces were disturbing as well, for how could one condone such ghastly mutilation? Cutting incisions in one's flesh so that benevolent spirits would recognize a person was surely a heathen practice. Disturbing, too, were the teeth filed to sharp points and stained from chewing kola nuts (a stimulant and painkiller, offered to guests as a symbol of goodwill and hospitality).

The only thing to admire about the native women were their bright head scarves, tied in perky crests to protect their heads from the burning sun. The fact that one African woman seeking refuge knew herbal medicine made her more than welcome among the anxious settlers. The unseen Africans in the bush upcountry were clearly inhumane; they were still selling each other into slavery, capturing their neighbors, and sending them down to the port to be picked up by the white slavers.[3] A ship loaded at the English factory on Bunce Island every month.

Chapter 23

Continuing Confusion

Mary Perth would have been very aware that the slave trade went on almost under her nose. Whenever she straightened her tired back from her laundry tub or cooking fire, she glanced out over the wide sheet of water below her. More often than not a sailing ship was either approaching from the sea, anchored in the estuary, or passing below the watering place in one direction or the other. More often than not, they would be Guineamen.[1] She must have watched them with distaste. Clarkson noted in his journal:

> I uniformly send, or go on board, to advise the Captain not to anchor off our settlement, as his seamen will certainly desert from him, and plague me; some take the hint, and thank me for it, others do not, and they are sure to lose their seamen, give me an immensity of trouble, unsettle the minds of the Nova Scotians, and mix their morals. We begin already to feel the bad effects of so many strangers of different characters coming among us.[2]

Moses Wilkinson, unable to move about without help, surely had a stool or rock to sit on and meditate while others were busy around him. A furtive seaman doubtless approached him from time to time, asking for shelter or a hiding place. He would have sympathized, of course, with any harassed black or white, for anyone who was mistreated. Did he murmur quiet instructions that would shield the victim from discovery?

When ship captains complained of losing their crews, Clarkson replied:

> If the seamen are in the Colony, I never see them. I told the [chief mate of the *Fisher*, now at Bunce Island] he was at liberty to go where he pleased in search of his people, and to do what he could to induce them to return with him; that I should not take a part either way, but that if I could be assured that they would be properly treated, it would be more agreeable to me that they should leave the Colony, as it is extremely prejudicial to the peace of the settlement to have a number of dissatisfied seamen lurking about.

Finally, Clarkson posted a notice on the storehouse door "warning all seamen from taking refuge in the Colony, and declaring that I had given orders to the constables to apprehend all such as should be found in any part of our district." Even this did not keep them away, for seamen from passing ships frequently sought out Clarkson to complain of brutal treatment by their captains.

> These frequent applications from seamen place me in a trying situation. I am fully convinced that the complaints made to me are in general too true and that their return to their ships is in many instance returning to their graves, but I am also well acquainted with the untoward conduct of seamen in general; on the other hand the mischief they do to the Nova Scotians cannot be estimated, and I am induced to believe, after much reflection, that in point of genuine humanity it would be better for me to leave the seamen to their fate than have the chance of their becoming inmates of this Colony.[3]

Because they were so far from home, captains of all ships carried mail and passengers for each other as they went back and forth between England, the West Indies, and Africa, and they let each other know when they were sailing. In one letter to the factor at Bunce Island, Clarkson wrote, "If you could spare me a pair of brass hinges and a brass lock I shall be much obliged to you, and if you could send me down your news papers they will be very acceptable."

This rapprochement between Freetown officials and the slave factors and captains made all the black settlers very uneasy, but, as John

Clarkson wrote in his journal, "These little civilities and attentions are necessary in a country where you stand in need of mutual assistance, and I have invariably found great benefit from such a conduct." Sierra Leone Company ships were repaired at Bunce Island, and company doctors treated officials there. Even the black artisans often found paid work at Bunce Island.

Before March ended, Violet King was afflicted with fever, but daily proclaimed her ardent faith in the Lord's benevolence. Boston King surely sought the African woman's remedies for his wife, but to no avail. Violet died surrounded by her friends singing hymns.

Anna Maria Falconbridge noted all this in her diary. By mid-April she estimated that at least 700 settlers were laid low by "burning fevers … two hundred scarce able to crawl about … five, six, and seven are dying daily, and buried with as little ceremony as so many dogs and cats." She herself suffered three weeks of "a violent fever, stoneblind four days, and expecting every moment to be my last."[4] Before long, Clarkson ordered the carpenters to stop making coffins, for their lumber was needed more urgently to build houses.

Later in the season, great banks of soupy fog rolled in and blanketed the landscape between rains. Those who evaded malaria, yellow fever, typhus, typhoid, and dengue fever[5] were weakened by the foul weather, the pervasive dampness, and the meager diet. The settlers caught fish and an occasional deer and wild pig to eat, but African fruit and vegetables were in short supply until the new harvest matured toward the end of the rainy season.

Mary and Caesar Perth were probably not aware that hunger menaced them, for little care was taken of the provisions brought with them. The storekeeper and accountant did not arrive until May. In the meantime, supplies were unloaded from the ships and taken ashore, unpacked, then left where they were scattered. Settlers and Africans alike appropriated what they found lying about—knives, hoes, axes, and other tools. The rains, of course, soon ruined everything left out in the open. The store tent became unfit to work in. Clarkson wrote of the "nauceous putrid stenches produced by stinking provisions, scattered about the town—rotten Cheese, rancid Butter, bad provisions, damaged pickled Tripe. Sacks of flour infested by insects and drenched with Molasses leaking from the Casks."

The Perths struggled with their shelter, confident that there would at least be enough to eat, for the provisions sent on the ships were intended to supply three months of full rations and another three months of half rations. Barely three weeks after their arrival, shortages forced Clarkson to cut rations by half. Everyone was dismayed, then watched the horizon hopefully for a supply ship to ease the shortages. They were elated when the *Trusty* arrived in May, but she had been so badly packed in London that the cargo was worthless—lime and coal in casks so old they fell apart in the sunlight; beef and pork tainted; biscuits, flour, and oatmeal in leaking bags rather than casks; butter rancid ; molasses leaking from barrels into the dry staples.

Clarkson wept over this catastrophe. He was too sick and depressed to deal with this much waste and disorder. So weak that he needed support to walk, he came ashore from the *Amy* every day so that he would be available to deal with the settlers' endless problems, and was assailed by one crisis after another. Susana Smith asked for soap to wash her clothes: "Sir I your hum bel Servent begs the favor of your Excelence to See if you will Pleas to Let me hav Som Sope for I am in great want of Som I hav not had aney Since I hav ben to this plais I hav bin Sick and I want to git Som Sope verry much to wash my family Clos for we ar not fit to be Sean for dirt."[6]

Andrew Moore wanted "Nourishmen Such as Oat meal, molassis or shugger, a Little Wine and Spirits, and Some Nut mig" for his just-delivered wife.[7] One group was unhappy that their town allotments were not adjacent to each other, another group because food distribution seemed unfair. One settler wanted to hire African laborers to clear the lots; another entertained an African visitor who assaulted a sentry while drunk.

The haughty behavior of the company personnel disgusted the settlers. The councilors seemed more eager to attend official receptions and lengthy council meetings than to supervise the work of building a town. They bickered endlessly over every step to be taken, and when agreement was finally reached among the eight, they then jockeyed with each other to control the execution of every decision.

Alexander Falconbridge and James Cocks were drinking too much, deluded that alcohol would protect them from disease. Clarkson noted as well that the captain, mates, councilors, and clerks living on board the *Harpy* consumed 144 dozen bottles of porter and 96 dozen of port wine in less than three months. Occasional fist fights resulted. "Drunkenness—Pilfering the Cargoes—insulting the Natives—and debauching the Nova Scotian women were the most prevailing acts at the Commencement of this intended religious Colony."[8] Clarkson spoke at Anglican services every Sunday, which all the settlers were expected to attend, urging the congregation to behave in an exemplary manner, to set a good example for their brethren and for the heathen Africans.

The surveying was assigned to Cocks and Richard Pepys. Pepys was chief engineer, as well as a councilor, and felt that surveying was beneath his dignity. Unpopular with the other officers, Pepys only increased their jealousy when Clarkson put him in charge while he took a short recuperative cruise. Falconbridge was the logical second in command, but he was regularly too drunk to be reliable. In early August, Clarkson wrote that "Mr. Falconbridge talks of making a trip to purchase stock for the Colony, but from his constant drinking, he has rendered himself incapable of being trusted, and I do all I can to amuse him, in order to keep him quiet; if he had not one of the strongest constitutions, he must have been dead long ago."

Surveyor Cocks was amiable, but inexperienced. He had been given charge of the tiny band of company soldiers, and preferred dressing up in his uniform and marching his battalion up and down to laying out lots and farms. Company plans were to augment the 18 European soldiers with 20 blacks. Cocks offered the Nova Scotian men extra provisions and free rum if they would enlist. Some did, but the white soldiers died one after the other until only four were left. They were sent home at their own request in September, leaving Freetown with only a black militia. Not many years passed before Sierra Leone would be known in England as the "*white man's grave.*"

Both Pepys and Cocks assigned the surveying to junior officials. They quarreled over which laborers should work on their various projects. Work parties ventured out to cut the great trees—African mahogany, cottonwood, ironwood, golden walnut, pearwood—and saw them into building lumber. Soon they were lured away by a different councilor promising higher wages, abandoning one work site for another. Pepys insisted that the survey parties deserved a daily rum ration, a custom of long standing in the British navy. Clarkson very reluctantly agreed, but later regretted the concession because other work parties then demanded the same privilege, and the men gradually acquired a taste for rum. When the workers were defeated by the huge trees entangled in masses of vines and creepers, white officials quickly lost their tempers, shouting angrily at the settlers, calling them "black rascals."

By May, Cocks was ill, and in June he received permission to return to England. Pepys agreed to take charge of the surveying if he could add Cocks's title to his own, but he was soon embroiled in a feud between his wife and the large family of storekeeper White, and later got himself involved with the wife of one of the ship captains. In mid-August Clarkson wrote that "Mr. Pepys has unfortunately made himself so unpopular with his brother officers and particularly of late—respecting his conduct about Mrs. Wilson, that many unpleasant things are said of him which would never have been agitated had he conducted himself otherwise."[9]

The accountant, John Wakerell, was too often sick to tend to the store, "and in consequence of the death of so many clerks in the Storehouse, it will be impossible for him to draw out any account which may in the least be depended on." With a bickering council unable to reach agreement, Clarkson dealt with each crisis as best he could.

Chapter 24

Ill Will Between
John Clarkson
and Thomas Peters

The saddest aspect of those first three months in Freetown was the deterioration in the partnership between John Clarkson and Thomas Peters. Clarkson found himself in a situation much different than he had expected, but as the appointed superintendent of the colony he tried valiantly to keep it functioning in the changed circumstances. Peters regarded the new government by a council of eight Englishmen as an indefensible betrayal of the settlers by the directors in London. He observed the faltering beginning of the Freetown settlement with a fierce, unyielding rectitude, and his anger grew. He had clashed with Clarkson in Halifax, but they had worked out their differences. Now that they were on the ground of their promised land, Peters simply would not accept the compromises that Clarkson found necessary.

He was a proud man, who knew he had played a significant role in setting in motion the exodus from Nova Scotia. He had proved his merit during the American Revolution, when British officers had valued his service in the Black Pioneers. He had braved the stormy Atlantic crossing to England to seek redress for his people. He had recruited over 300 settlers eager to voyage to Sierra Leone and aided Clarkson in facilitating the embarkation. As the white officials in Freetown bickered and stumbled, he met with his fellow Methodists daily, reminding them that the Sierra Leone Company had betrayed them. Perhaps he saw himself in the role of their savior. He must have realized very quickly that many of the white council members were both pretentious and incompetent. The council arrangement put in place, in effect, eight different governors, and Clarkson had no authority to overrule them. Furthermore, both Clarkson and Peters were in poor physical shape. Clarkson was weakened by fever caught en route and exhausted by the confusion and by the dreadful weather, neither of which he could control or abate. Peters must have been infected shortly after their arrival, perhaps with malaria, for he was dead before June ended.

On March 22, Clarkson wrote in his journal that Peters called on him that day with "many complaints; he was extremely violent and indiscreet in his conversation and seemed as if he were desirous of alarming and disheartening the people." Were Peters to describe the same conversation, he might have said that he was feverish, but determined to articulate the very real concerns of his fellow blacks, and spoke forcefully to Clarkson about their needs and interests. In any case, the normally mild-mannered Clarkson lost his temper, told Peters that he could have free passage back to America if he was unhappy in Freetown, and vowed never to quit the new settlement while Peters remained there. The battle was joined.

Needless to say, the various congregations gathered daily for prayer meetings, at which all the settlers' problems were debated vigorously. Some of the preachers—David George and Cato Perkins among them—attempted to act as peacemakers and reassured Clarkson of their continued loyalty. In fact, it was unfair of Clarkson to accuse those who felt betrayed of disloyalty for expressing their strong feelings about the actions taken by the company directors. He, after all, had made sweeping promises to them, and the directors had placed Clarkson in an impossible position. But much of the discussion among the settlers took place with only one side represented. The freed blacks had little experience to prepare them for the hard realities of government and politics. The sentiments that surfaced in each congregation doubtlessly reflected the eloquence and perspective of their leader in articulating their grievances. Peters was a commanding figure, older than most, hardened in the crucible of the recent war. He was very aware of the disorder in

Freetown, and was clearly furious with the waste, the lack of progress, and the bickering and fumbling of the white administration while the rains poured down and people were dying daily.

Cooler heads like David George sensed that matters were getting out of hand and urged patience. Rations were reduced on April 7. On Easter Sunday, April 8, after the weekly Anglican service with the whole settlement in attendance, two members of the Preston Methodist congregation gave Clarkson a note warning him that other factions among the Methodists were pushing to make Peters governor in his place. It is easy to imagine the blacks expressing their preference for Peters's leadership among themselves when no whites were present. Clarkson, in his anxious mental state, unfortunately interpreted the suggestion as a threat of mutiny.

He had not read the note until after dinner, on board his ship. His immediate reaction was to buckle on his sword, go ashore, and tell Pepys to ring the bell. As a golden sunset bathed the harbor in opalescent hues of rose and lavender, the settlers hurried through the lengthening shadows to the cotton tree. Under its great spreading crown, Clarkson confronted Peters and told him that "it is probable that either one or other of us would be hanged upon that Tree before the Palaver was settled." He wrote in his journal that it would be better to "hang three or four who might be the cause of future Misery ... than to suffer the whole to experience wretchedness." This threat must have resulted from his naval training, for he had no authority to hang anyone.[1]

Clarkson told the settlers the colony would face ruin if Peters were made governor, for the Sierra Leone Company would withdraw its support and leave them on their own. He reminded them of what had happened to Granville Town. He pointed out that large sums of money had been spent to bring them to Freetown in the hope that they would spread Christianity throughout Africa. He accused them of ingratitude, of failing to recognize the sacrifice he and many others had made in their behalf.

The settlers were stunned by his outburst. They replied that they had no intention of displacing Clarkson as governor, but merely wanted Peters recognized as their spokesman, who might "relieve the Governor from the fatigue of so many applications." They gave him a petition that 132 of them had signed, requesting that Peters act as their go-between. They assured Clarkson that they were sorry he was so upset, and begged him "not to expose himself any longer to the Evening air, as they observed [he] was much fatigued."

The petition reassured Clarkson, and he dismissed the meeting, "very glad to close the business with this explanation, for had matters appeared stronger against Peters, I should not have known what to have done with him." As the settlers dispersed, however, Peters's close followers turned angrily on the men who had warned Clarkson, and fist fights broke out between the Methodists and the Baptists.

Clarkson's journal indicates that he continued to brood over the matter. He described Peters as a man of "great penetration and cunning," a "rascal who had been working in the dark from the time he landed to get himself at the Head of the People, and if I had not acted by them as I did ... this Wretch would have driven all the Whites out of the Place and ruin'd himself and all his Brethren." Clarkson decided finally to set spies to watching Peters, as well as to demand that the company directors give their superintendent stronger powers to govern.

Three days later, a general muster was called at which all the settlers and white officials were asked to sign an oath promising to obey the company's rules. When Clarkson learned that Peters was attending nightly prayer meetings at black preachers' huts, Clarkson began to attend as well. After the service, Peters would rise and speak about the unfulfilled promises to the settlers. Clarkson then claimed the floor to reply. His diary indicates that he felt his counterarguments were persuasive. In the last resort, he could always threaten to abandon the settlement, which invariably led the settlers to "beg him ardently not to desert them."

Two weeks later the chaplain Nathaniel Gilbert sailed aboard the *Felicity* for London, carrying Clarkson's report of the settlement's problems and his request for more executive power. He wrote Chairman Thornton that "eight gentlemen, all them invested with great power, each of them acting for himself, and none of them accountable to the other, form ... a system of government as pregnant with contradictions and inconsistencies as can be imagined." He refused to sign the council dispatches and threatened to return to England if he was not given more authority.

No sooner had the *Felicity* sailed than Clarkson received a complaint that Peters had seized and disposed of the effects of John Salter, recently deceased. Salter was a slave from Philadelphia who had been in the Black Pioneers with Peters and had traveled with him to Nova Scotia. In the trial that took place May 1 before a jury of black company captains, Peters did not deny that he had gone to Salter's hut, broken open his chest, and took its contents—some hams and about £20 in cash. Peters stood unrepentant before them, explaining that Salter owed him that much for his help ten years earlier in recovering Salter's wife from slavery. The jury, however, judged Peters guilty and reprimanded him sharply. Clarkson, as presiding magistrate, lectured Peters on the "enormity of the Crime and particularly when committed by a Man who ought to have set the Colony a better example." Peters was ordered to return the property and pay the jurymen for losing a day's work. Peters gave up the property, but appealed the verdict, which Clarkson refused to hear.

As word came again and again to Clarkson from his informants of the discontent expressed by the settlers in their chapel meetings, he realized that they truly did feel that promises of land and self-government were not being kept, and he sought to reassure them. In May, Clarkson held two large settler meetings to discuss wages, land grants, and other matters. He also met with several of the company captains individually, including Peters, urging their patience and understanding. On Sundays he followed the chaplain in the pulpit at Anglican church services, speaking to the whole settlement personally.

In the middle of June, Clarkson was handed a proposal from the blacks that they hoped would counter the weak council government. Twelve black men should act as peace officers to hear small disputes and keep order in the colony. Clarkson agreed that all the males over age 21 should vote to choose 12 such names and submit them to him for approval. Henry Beverhout, in behalf of his company, protested against Clarkson having veto power:

> Thear is non of us wold wish for your honer to go way and leave us hear but your [honor] will be pleased to rember what your honer told the piepel [people] in maraca [America] at Shelburn; that is, whoever Came to Sarakeon [Sierra Leone] wold be free and should have a law and when theur war aney trial, thear should be a jurey of both white and black, and all

should be equel; so we … think that we have a wright to Chuse men that we think proper to act for us in a reasenable manner.[2]

Clarkson received a second, similar letter on June 26, along with word that Peters had died in the night. This must have jolted Clarkson and made him feel very awkward in dealing with the Methodists loyal to Peters. Peters's wife wrote, not to Clarkson, but to Alexander Falconbridge, asking for supplies that were needed for an appropriate funeral:

> This is to beg the favor of you to let me have a Gallon of Wine, One Gallon of Porter, & 1/2 Gallon of Rum, 2 lbs. Candles, 5 Yards of White Linen. My husband is dead and I am in great distress. I apply for the above things. my Children is all sick. My distress is not to be equalled. I remain aflicted
>
> Sarah Peters.[3]

Clarkson ordered the storekeeper to meet all her needs, and when a deputation came requesting pine boards for a coffin, he broke his no-coffin rule. He arranged a pension of £20 a year for Mrs. Peters and her six or seven children. He also granted permission to those wishing to attend the funeral to leave work. His journal notation was cryptic: "Thos. Peters funeral went off without disturbance," attended by "a great many." How much more eloquent that description might have been had one of the black preachers recorded the final rites of the most prominent of Freetown's founding fathers. They would remember him as heroic in stature, having braved the wild Atlantic to take their pleas to England, and standing steadfast both in Nova Scotia and Freetown in demanding that the white officials keep the promises Clarkson had made to them.

Chapter 25

Baptists and Methodists Follow Different Paths

After Thomas Peters's death at the end of June, John Clarkson's personal nemesis was gone, but the division between the Methodists (who comprised between half and two-thirds of the settlers), some of whose leaders were convinced that they had been betrayed, and the Baptists, who seem to have appreciated that Clarkson was doing the best he could in difficult circumstances, remained to plague Sierra Leone Company officials through the decade that followed. Neither denomination was solidly united in its attitude, and the congregations were fluid as leaders disagreed and formed new groupings. Both Moses Wilkinson (so revered that he was now known as "Daddy Moses" rather than "Brother Moses") and Boston King were Methodist leaders. Joseph Leonard, originally Anglican, joined the ranks of Methodist preachers. Henry Beverhout held a revival in Granville Town and substantially increased the Methodist ranks. When issues arose that required the settlers to side with the company or against it, the Baptists generally tried to make the best of things, while the Methodist ranks stood fiercely in opposition.

Clarkson realized that the rift was not based on any religious differences between the Methodists and Baptists but rather in the disharmony between blacks and whites. He soon began to attend evening prayer meetings, first George's, then Wilkinson's, so that after the service he could take a few men aside to discuss whatever was troubling them at the moment, calling on their affection for him to convince them to be patient. He repeated the effort at other chapels until he thought he had won over the important leaders. Most of the settlers trusted him because he had been so uniformly kind to them ever since his arrival in Nova Scotia, but when he left Freetown at the end of 1792, even the Baptists felt they had lost the only white man who really understood their concerns.

When the Sierra Leone Company directors met in London in May to consider Clarkson's demand for more authority, they decided to abolish the council government and replace it with a governor and two councilors, the governor having power to act, when necessary, without the concurrence of his councilors. Dispatches containing the new authority reached Freetown in August 1792, and for a time this restored confidence among the settlers. Tensions might have ended permanently if land had been distributed promptly thereafter, for in the settlers' minds the delays in land distribution in Freetown were a repetition of the delays in Nova Scotia.

Clarkson's health was improving, and he was indeed doing his best to deal with the myriad problems that arose every day. In August when he received notice of his new authority to govern the colony, he spoke from the pulpit on two succeeding Sundays, reading from the directors' dispatch: they intended to do

> full justice to the free blacks from Nova Scotia, giving them the enjoying of British rights, and fulfilling every expectation we have raised in them. Having crossed the seas on the faith of our promises to them by Mr. Clarkson, … we are determined to cooperate with him in endeavoring to render their persons and their property safe, their industry productive, their character respectable, their condition in life more and more improvable and their future days happy.[1]

Unfortunately, the hillside between the harbor and the steeper mountain slopes above was simply not large enough to accommodate all the settlers with farms of the size they had been promised. The Sierra Leone peninsula is highest in the north along the harbor, sloping gradually southward to the sea. But any move to the flatter land beyond the peaks of the mountains would put settlers beyond the protection of the armed white officials in Freetown and the few cannons landed from the company ships. The local Africans had made it clear during the Granville Town experiment that they were not entirely trustworthy neighbors. Nor could a large enough area along the harbor be cleared quickly enough to satisfy all the settlers. The jungle on the Sierra Leone peninsula was an almost impenetrable wall of huge intertwined trunks and vines, which took time and strong men to hack away. The savage greenery surged again as soon as the workmen turned their backs. Much of the terrain was rocky or hilly. The daily downpour prevented sustained work for weeks on end. Surveyor Cocks fell ill.

The nearby Africans protested angrily when surveying parties impinged on their villages, rice fields, and sacred shrines.

> We continue to meet with obstacles in running our lines into the country, as in many instances we interfere with the natives' plantations, and it requires great care in settling little differences with them on this head. In fact we purchased the whole of the land as we believed to a certain distance up the river and then straight into the country; but when the chiefs sold us the country, they had not the least idea that we could want to make use of the whole, and therefore they are not prepared to part with their plots of ground hastily.[2]

Now the surveying had to be halted while Clarkson invited King Naimbanna to come down and "settle the business" in a palaver (from the French verb *palabre*, "to consult") with the local chiefs. Clarkson was no anthropologist, but his journal indicates that he tried very hard to understand the local customs:

> The dominions of King Naimbanna extend from this river up to Rokelle and the interior country eastward, about two and-a-half days' journey, reckoned at forty miles per day, and southward toward Sherbro, four or five days' journey. The power of King Naimbanna is absolute, though in matters of consequence he does not appear to like deciding without the concurrence of the inferior chiefs in the country; but if he grows angry with them, they will all submit to his opinion and pay their homage and obeisance before him, kneeling down and laying both hands on the ground before it on his feet, or kneeling, and at the same time touching the ground with their elbows or else one hand on the ground and the other on their head, bending the head profoundly. It is in

the interest of the king not to appear absolute, but rather to procure a majority of votes on his side.

The kings have some profit, but much trouble in settling palavers, both between white people and those of their own colour. I was informed to-day by a[n African] man who spoke good English, that Royalty is not in general sought after with great eagerness; it is looked upon as an arduous and troublesome office, and declined, if possible, and it often happens that a man is made king by main force, the people generally catching and arresting the heir apparent on the death of his predecessor lest he should run away. It is said that Signor Domingo was chosen King of Rokelle, where he lately resided, but not wishing to accept the office, he escaped and settled here; should he ever return, he would be caught and made king. As none but old men are eligible, it rarely happens that the king's own son succeeds his father, more generally it is his brother, or in failure of these a more distant relation. King Naimbanna will not be succeeded by John Frederic now in England [attending school], till after two intermediate kings have reigned.[3]

So Clarkson sent a boat to convey King Naimbanna down to Freetown. Gifts of rum and cheap trade goods—particularly bright cotton cloth, which the women wore as headdresses—won some favor with the local chiefs, but King Jemmy, the nearest neighbor, was still not completely happy with the settlement scheme. He argued that he should have dominion over a holy place above the freshwater spring "to make sacrifices to a large black snake living under one of the trees for the continuance of the spring, which otherwise would dry up and distress the country." Clarkson agreed to skirt King Jemmy's village of 40 or 50 huts and the adjacent fields, as well as fence the holy place. He also paid 100 iron bars (a common medium of exchange on the African coast) for a family spoon and a gold cross taken from King Jemmy's house three years earlier by a marine from the *HMS Pomona*.

Clarkson notes in his journal that he

> took every opportunity to ingratiate myself with them, and to convince the chiefs of our honourable and peaceable disposition towards them. I told them we should be glad to teach their children book, and to do all in our power to make them have *good heads*; that it was a good plan when either party felt injured, to call a palaver that a clear explanation might

take place; by such conduct we should be sure to live happily together and render each other mutual benefits.

Clarkson bemoaned the fact that these meetings had to be repeated frequently, for although King Naimbanna had stated that King Jemmy, Signor Domingo, King Tom, Gamacoupra, Captain Stuart, Robin Dick, Pah Will, and the others had no authority to sell land, they were constantly dreaming up new complaints that might win them more trinkets. Regular palaver among the males of each clan was an integral part of their culture, and any opportunity to palaver with the white men was regarded as upscale entertainment, enhancing chiefly status. Free feasts of European food and wine served on linen and china with glassware and silver utensils were a pleasant change from African gourd drinking cups and banana-leaf plates.

With the slave trade being carried on in the adjacent river, Clarkson made some effort to understand the African attitude toward slavery. He noted that the local chiefs had a number of slaves

> who are employed in making rice plantations, building, etc.; each of these slaves like their other subjects brings them three or four bushels of rice per year, perhaps also a couple or more of fowls, a fathom of cloth, a goat, or sheep or the like. I understand that great difference is made between purchased slaves, and their children born to their master's service; these latter though in effect belonging to their masters are, however, never sold by them any more than their own children, unless for very heavy crimes. They always call their master "Father," and are considered always as his children. All slaves appear at liberty to carry on trade, make plantations, and do whatever they please, only giving their masters in the proportion above mentioned, but they must provide their own subsistence.

What the Nova Scotians thought about all this can be imagined.

Signor Domingo on one occasion became violent and threatened to shoot one of the inhabitants of Granville Town, the remnants of which lay between Freetown and his village. He claimed that a man named Harford had taken "liberties with one of his wives." Clarkson wrote in his journal,

I had a long conversation with him ... and condemned Harford for his conduct and Signor Domingo for his violence, telling him that Christianity condemned it.... I said, if you had made a complaint to me of Harford's conduct to you, I would have enquired into the business and made him give you every satisfaction. but if you had shot him, as you said you would do, you could not have told what might have been the consequence. I said, Signor Domingo, you no like war, but suppose you shoot my man; you make war upon me, and I could not keep my people from making war upon you, and you know that would be *wicked palaver*. He soon after softened and promised never to take the law into his own hands with any of my people. This was all I could expect from him, and we parted good friends.[4]

The restrictions about impinging on African villages and fields decreased the land available to the Nova Scotians. When this problem became clear, the white officials informed the settlers that in the beginning farms would be only one-fifth the promised size—the rest to be claimed at some later date. Neither Clarkson nor the directors in London foresaw how the settlers would react to this readjustment. Had Clarkson's promises at the Easter meeting with the settlers been fulfilled within the following month or two, harmony might have prevailed. But when no town allotments were ready in July and no farm allotments—even lots reduced by four-fifths—in September, Peters's close associates again began to mutter about betrayal.

Clarkson had found it necessary to ignore some of the company directives received on his arrival. In order to ensure profitable trade, the company directors had ordered that the best land along the waterfront should be held for wharves and warehouses. Clarkson had promised in Nova Scotia that all land would be distributed equally by lottery. Now he proposed a compromise—that land along the three capes where public buildings could be accommodated should be reserved for the company. Luke Jordan and his Methodist congregation already working on those lots reacted angrily. At a large public meeting the suggestion was denounced vehemently, and Clarkson withdrew it.

On a more positive note, the constables elected by the settlers[5] were sworn in during mid-August. Clarkson "addressed them on the important duties they had to perform and particularly desired them to keep a good look out in each of their districts towards the evening, as we have so many strangers of loose character residing and occasionally visiting every part of the town." Some of the earlier settlers from Granville Town had turned to slave trading, which upset the Nova Scotians greatly and "caused great fermentation in the Colony." One of them, named Cambridge, was tried for selling a slave to a Dutch captain; he was found guilty and sent to England for punishment. Clarkson used his sentencing as an opportunity to lecture the settlers on what an abomination it was for freed black men to sell other black men into slavery.

Settler dissatisfaction, combined with the pervasive misery of the rainy season and the mounting toll of deadly illness, caused continuing distress. By September only 995 of the 1,131 Nova Scotians who came to Freetown were still alive; 57 of the colony's 119 white officials were dead. As the white officials died or resigned to return to England, the settlers watched official offices being transferred from one white to another, regardless of qualifications or competence.

Few blacks, on the other hand, were given any authority. Abraham Elliott Griffith's literacy won him the post of chief interpreter, entitling him to a salary and a house. His experience in Granville Town and later interpreting for King Naimbanna was useful at first, but after he supported Peters's bid for leadership, he was no longer invited to dine with the officers. Beverhout was made parish clerk. Richard Dixon was appointed council messenger and part-time clerk, at an annual salary of £25.

The blacks became more suspicious and sullen as the relentless weeks ground by, more and more convinced that the white officials were acting in their own interests and ignoring the needs of the settlers. Some claimed that "If there had been no white man here, we could have laid out all the Lots in Two Months."[6] Privately, Clarkson was inclined to agree with them. He confided in a letter to England that among his colleagues, "Pride, Arrogance, self-sufficiency, Meanness, Drunkenness, Atheism and Idleness were dayly practiced."

In the meantime, the settlers had no source of income except working for the company. They labored clearing roads, building a church, a warehouse, a hospital, and other official buildings, using wooden frames sent from England. They constructed a wharf, and cultivated an experimental garden and a company plantation. Company wages were set at two shillings a day. In May, Clarkson had found that some of the men were spending their pay on rum from passing ships rather than on food, so he changed the payment system. Each workman was given credit for his two days' work in the company store register rather than cash wages. A week's rations was set at four shillings, and the pay and rations transactions were simply posted in the store register. This system was also a grievance, for the settlers had no cash to spend elsewhere.

The blacks protested that working for the company was little better than bondage. Both wages and prices were set by the company, giving them no say in the matter. The company directors, on their part, felt it was their right, even their duty as intellectually superior people, to take care of the weak and oppressed. If the settlers were ungrateful, this proved "but too plainly the importance of bestowing on them an intelligent and protecting government."[7] Directors sitting comfortably in England had no problem putting the company's goals ahead of the settlers' needs.

The lottery for town lots was delayed again and again as disputes arose as to who should get what. The settlers expected each chapel to be assigned a contiguous neighborhood. The Preston congregation had asked Clarkson, even before their departure from Nova Scotia, to be settled together and not intermixed with strangers. Other congregations expressed the same desire. Some of the settlers refused to move off their temporary lots, arguing that they had cleared them and started gardens, which were now producing cabbages, pumpkins, beans, sweet potatoes, yams, cassava, peanuts, rice, corn, and herbs. They were unwilling to simply abandon their efforts to someone else.

Actually, general conditions in Freetown improved gradually as the summer waned. The rains diminished in force and frequency, abating the fevers that had stricken so many. Supply ships had arrived with much-needed food and tools. Dozens of Africans came daily with the fresh fruit of the new harvest (mangoes, plums, bananas, plaintains, limes, lemons, oranges, pineapple, guavas, papayas, and palm oil) and vegetables (yams, beans, pumpkins, cassava, groundnuts, rice, and millet). Pigs and poultry were multiplying. The death of a cow was important enough to be noted in Clarkson's journal; by mid-November all the cattle were dead. James Watt, the plantation manager, had been examining the soil inland and across the estuary in hopes of establishing larger plantations, and was pessimistic about sugar cane, but hopeful that cotton and indigo might thrive.

One fisherman was regularly bringing fish, but the settlers complained to Clarkson that his price was too high.

> Having met the people with the fisherman Robert Horton, we came to a resolution about the fish, and made him sign an agreement to serve the Colony with twelve fish of a certain size for a shilling instead of six, before he offered them for sale to other people; but as a check upon him I furnished American Talbot, James Jackson, Anthony David, and John Strong with materials for building boats that they might take the seine, should he not keep to his agreement.[8]

New officials arrived by ship, some of whom were more enterprising than their predecessors. The Sierra Leone Company recruited Isaac DuBois, an American planter from North Carolina, whose organizing abilities quickly won the approval of the settlers. He soon won Clarkson's confidence as well and was set to work building a new storehouse beside Susan's Bay. Unfortunately, its location impinged on the hut belonging to Nathaniel Snowball, a company captain, who protested about all the work he had done and being moved away from his neighbors. Clarkson was sympathetic:

> I impressed upon him the necessity of individuals giving way for the public good, but added, that ... I should consider him entitled to some remuneration.... he should fix upon two or three of his friends to take the matter into consideration ... and fix the amount of damages to be allowed him for his loss.

His friends decided Snowball's hut was worth £10, which Clarkson paid.[9]

Dr. Thomas Winterbottom[10] had come in July, and, although he soon caught malaria, he proved to be a warm and amiable companion. Adam Afzelius came to collect botanical specimens, paying the settlers a half-penny for butterflies and sixpence for large bats. He also planted a garden, which was thriving by August, to supply the company officers. The mineralogist, Augustus Nordenskiold, was eager to collect samples, so Clarkson sent him to King Naimbanna, "requesting him to furnish Mr. Nordenskiold with ... the best advice as to the route and the means to be used to expect success." Nordenskiold soon wrote back that King Naimbanna demanded 45 bars for use of a boat, so could Clarkson furnish him with a decked vessel to carry him upcountry? Also that purchase of food is "enormously dear ... rum and satin stripe [cloth] is the only thing they will take in exchange for fowls, fish, etc." One more problem for poor Clarkson to deal with. He wrote back that he would pay for the hire of a craft from Bunce Island, then wrote the factor there asking him to furnish one. Early in November, Nordenskiold returned in ill health, having been robbed by slave traders in the interior of all his trade goods.

Michael Wallace ("though once in the slave trade," according to Henry Thornton, "and a little fond of liquor") came in August to replace Falconbridge as commercial agent. Clarkson soon shared Thornton's misgivings about Wallace. A new chaplain, Melville Horne ("lively, animated, zealous beyond measure in his profession, has been in Wesley's connexion, and is prepared to live and die in the service") came in September, along with William Dawes, a new councilor; Mr. Lowes, a surgeon; and Mr. Field, a schoolmaster.

Chapter 26

The Calypso
Passengers Interrupt

In August the settlers learned through the arrival of an unexpected ship in the estuary that the situation in Freetown, bad as it had been, could have been much worse. John Clarkson went out in the *Susan*, his small sailing skiff, to investigate the new arrival.

Imagine his surprise to find on board Henry Hew Dalrymple, who had been the first choice of the Sierra Leone Company directors to be governor in Freetown—he who had resigned when refused 150 soldiers to protect his settlement. Dalrymple had briefly been governor of another enterprise across the bay. The *Calypso*, a vessel fitted out by the Bullom Association, was to establish a plantation colony on the Bullom shore across the estuary to the north, perhaps five miles away from Freetown. (The group, mostly white, had obtained no official government sponsorship before they left England; they were motivated largely by dreams of wealth obtained through the cultivation of export crops in the manner of the West Indies plantations.)[1]

The 153 passengers on board the *Calypso* were in want of provisions, and many of them, including Dalrymple, were ill. Even worse, Dalrymple had quarreled with his council members. John Clarkson wrote in his journal that he had

> never beheld a more motley or miserable set: many of them
> were half pay officers, decayed gentlemen, and dissolute

adventurers, and others respectable characters.... I cannot calculate the consequences likely to result from so many people of mixed character, coming to us at the present time, when our people's minds have become a little settled from the agitated state in which they had been kept for so many months past.[2]

The *Calypso* was one of three ships in the expedition and had arrived ahead of the other two. Dalrymple had gone ashore without making any treaty or agreement with the Africans. Tents were erected and supplies landed. Dalrymple and a handful of men had gone exploring, when suddenly those left behind were attacked by the neighboring Africans. Five men and two women were killed and three or four women taken away and treated barbarously. Clarkson wrote that "the neighboring natives are said to be the most sanguinary and treacherous, the father sleeping with a knife, for fear of his son." Even King Jemmy had complained to Clarkson about the loose behavior of his African neighbors across the estuary.

Many of the passengers in the cramped quarters on the *Calypso*, particularly those who were very ill, applied to go ashore and settle in Freetown. After consulting with his own council, Clarkson refused. He wrote Dalrymple, asking him to control the numbers of his people coming ashore and see that they left before dark, for they were disturbing his own settlers from their work, as well as annoying the nearby Africans. When David George came to him with questions, Clarkson realized that some of the *Calypso* passengers were deliberately spreading misinformation among the settlers. Clarkson quickly posted a notice saying that none of the transients were to remain in Freetown overnight.

He did his best to reassure the settlers. Level heads like George recognized that similar threats hung over his own people; they would be at the mercy of hostile Africans without the English treaty with the peninsula Temne and the English guns and cannons that enforced it. He repeatedly reminded his congregation of their perilous situation and urged them to cooperate with the company officials. His point was reinforced when one of the white officers from the *Calypso* was caught robbing a Nova Scotian settler. Clarkson feared a riot and stationed constables in every street to maintain order.

The *Calypso* passengers were desperate for food and medical supplies and were soon offering outrageous prices for everything in the company store. Clarkson put a stop to that by closing the store. This, of course, upset the Nova Scotians. Boston King wrote to him complaining of not being able to purchase supplies.

By August 24 Clarkson had decided that he needed an English naval ship stationed in the harbor "to attend to the complaints from the shipping continually entering the harbor, and other business requiring local authority to settle, which I feel I do not possess."

Adding to Clarkson's apprehensions was an incident on September 2 with a Dutch sloop "which has long laid in this river." The ship had about 80 slaves on board, and "was cut off this morning about 2 o'clock; one person jumped overboard and drowned himself. Some people were wounded who resisted; the sloop ran on shore. Slaves and cargo lost; cannot learn further particulars."[3]

If some of the Nova Scotian settlers had aided the escaping slaves, they kept it to themselves. The traffic in the estuary constantly reminded them that their margin of safety was very narrow. They were greatly relieved when the *Calypso* finally sailed for England on September 11.

Chapter 27

New Company Officials

Chairman Thornton had written Clarkson introducing William Dawes:

> Mr. Dawes has been at Botany Bay and Port Jackson [in Australia] from the first formation of that Colony, being just now returned. He is a lieutenant of marines and also acted as a surveyor in which and other scientific branches he is a man of capacity. We have also heard of him as a religious man; he seems cool, correct and sensible; he is a man of business and I trust will soon fall into your system and second your views so as to ease your mind, and even to render your return to England, if material to your health, much less dangerous than it would otherwise be to the interest of the Colony.[1]

In October, Clarkson decided to take some of his convalescent officers on a short local cruise in an attempt to improve their health. The accountant, Wakerell, was to use this opportunity to confer at length with his clerk, Mr. John Gray, in an attempt to bring some order into the company books. Although Alexander Falconbridge appeared to "be in a dying state," he, too, was invited to go along. Clarkson saw his own absence as both a much-needed rest and an opportunity for William Dawes to try his hand at running the colony. He spent the final evenings visiting the huts of men he trusted—David George, Moses Wilkinson, Cato Perkins, Richard Crankapone, James Reid, Nathaniel Snowball, and Boston King—"to charge them to pay attention to Mr. Dawes, and not to suffer those of an unruly spirit to trouble him."

Although Clarkson intended to be gone only a week, he wrote Dawes a lengthy letter, containing a very long list of instructions in explicit detail. A very detailed paragraph followed about the care that must be taken in allowing credit at the company store:

> Upon no account whatever must hard money be taken at the retail shop, and the retailer must settle his accounts every week either with the store-keeper or accountant. I gave an order similar to this when I first landed, but I have strong suspicions that vast sums of *hard money* have been paid into the store, which the Company has never received.... Every-one of the clerks who may have defrauded the company are now dead, and we must therefore endeavour to prevent such temptation in the future.

Clarkson went on to describe "every trifling affair relating to the Colony" so that Dawes would have complete understanding of the problems he must deal with.

The convalescent officers did not improve on the cruise, a situation that greatly distressed Clarkson. He himself was having memory lapses and realized that he needed to get away from the endless demands of Freetown. He found on his return that "Mr. Dawes had conducted himself with great *prudence* and *forbearance*," reassuring Clarkson that he could let Dawes oversee more of the settlement's business until Clarkson safely left the colony.

He worried, however, that accountant White's continued illness had resulted in expenses in the colony for which there were no accounts. "I tremble for the effect which this great expenditure and the deficiency of regular and satisfactory accounts will have on the minds of the proprietors and public at large and how materially it may injure the future prosperity of the Colony."[2]

Chapter 28

Land Grants at Last

In November, a drawing was finally held for farm lots: 40 black families, Caesar and Mary Perth among them, received land grants of about five acres each. On November 13, 1792, the fortunate new landowners joined Clarkson and the company officials for a picnic on the way up to Directors' Hill overlooking the harbor. Dinner was served under a tent, followed by a toast to the Sierra Leone Company and the inhabitants of Freetown and Granville Town. Immediately thereafter the 60 survey workers fired their muskets in "three distinct vollies" and gave three cheers, to which the cannons in the town below responded, and the Freetown settlers gave three cheers. The company ships anchored in the estuary, their colors flying, responded, "which had a beautiful effect," Clarkson reported, "and I have no doubt made an impression of the whole neighborhood." Clarkson seized this and every opportunity to "show the natives the armed power we possess."[1]

The ceremony must have lifted the hearts of all the settlers scattered across that emerald green landscape, for those salutes marked the end of a long period of extreme physical discomfort, as well as heralding a conviction that better days would follow.

Scarcely two days had passed when Clarkson began hearing complaints about the land grants: some parcels separated intimate friends, others were "all rocky and not fit for cultivation." He promised that exchanges could be made by those separated from their friends, and that he would try to find a piece elsewhere for those who drew unproductive terrain.

Clarkson had announced a month earlier that he would return to England at the end of the year. William Dawes put Clarkson's mind at ease about leaving. "He appears sedate and a man of business." Clarkson took him about to various Nova Scotian homes in an attempt to win the goodwill of the settlers. "They reply to me when I am recommending Mr. Dawes to their notice, that he is so stiff and serious, they do not like to ask him for anything—they say he may be a very good man, but he does not show it."

Because provisions were short, Clarkson halved rations and cut off provisions entirely to the 40 families who had received land grants. Luke Jordan immediately wrote him: "we wont to know wither we is to pay as much for the half rassion as for the full." Several others signed a joint petition requesting either that their wages be raised to cover full food and liquor rations or be paid half in cash so they could buy things elsewhere.[2] Clarkson granted the full credit at the company store for food, but not for liquor. He was optimistic that many others would soon receive grants, and they would no longer need company provisions. Petitions began coming in immediately, asking if the halving of rations also halved the two days each man worked for the company to pay for them.

Wages, rum, and trade occupied Clarkson's final days before his departure. After the *Felicity* arrived carrying a large number of garden watering pots—presumably to be sold to the Africans for trade goods, Clarkson wrote with veiled sarcasm to the directors suggesting that Freetown offered a better market for European foodstuffs such as wheat flour, tea, oatmeal, sugar, barley, butter, cheese, and molasses; and dry goods such as cloth, needles, thread, pins, shoes, boots, and umbrellas. He asked for more company support in promoting official trade.

Probably no more than a dozen settlers were drinking too much, and none of them were important community leaders. But their behavior—as well as that of Alexander Falconbridge, the derelict white official—led to unpleasant incidents and some actual challenges to official authority. Clarkson regretted having agreed to a rum ration for working parties. Carpenters were now earning three shillings a day, and they were still arguing they should be paid for their company work in coin rather than in credit at the company store. They wanted to make purchases elsewhere. Clearly a number of settlers had figured out how to make a profit in trading with the slave ships or with the Africans and wanted money to invest in goods that could be sold. The Africans, too, had an unquenchable taste for rum and schemed to get it from the settlers. Drunkenness led to dangerous altercations in Freetown, in which officials had to intervene, regardless of who was involved.

Clarkson wrote on November 26:

> I have been informed this evening that five or six barrels of meat and flour went from the Colony this morning to be bartered for rum and other articles from the slave ships in the river, and yet the Colony is distressed for provisions and the people complain of being put on short allowance.... Abraham White's wife had this morning brought from Bunce Island six jars of rum.

Clarkson went to David George's prayer meeting to discuss what might happen if all the workers drew wages instead of credit at the company store, arguing that if the men had more money, "it would enable them to purchase more rum and other pernicious articles." Brother George and his cohorts were reluctant to agree to the payment of scrip wages, but finally promised to "endeavor to convince those more immediately connected with them of the propriety of [Clarkson's] decision" to hold out against paying wages in coin. Clarkson then repeated his effort at other chapels until he thought most of the leaders agreed with him.

Clarkson was disturbed, too, that many of the settlers were simply bartering goods whenever the opportunity arose, for he feared they would be drawn into the slave trade. European ships regularly anchored offshore in the hope of doing a little business with the settlers. They in turn were tempted to follow suit, partly because they had so few other activities from which to turn a profit and partly because trading was obviously the dominant activity in that broad estuary. Little official trading was being done by the Sierra Leone Company, thanks to Falconbridge's endless drinking binges, but clearly anyone with a boat and a little drive and cunning could turn a profit.

Clarkson suspected that the fishing boats he had authorized were trading on the side as well, and he tried to discourage other settlers from joining them. This presented a dilemma; on the one hand, the settlers were showing initiative and adaptability to their new situation, but on the other hand, company control was weakened in the process.

Clarkson worried that Dawes might lack the patience to deal calmly with unruly settlers, whom he described as "very illiterate and suspicious." A journal entry in November stated that

> the late desire for liquor seems to be gaining ground daily, for the carpenters in the Colony have agreed to do no work until they are allowed rum. I have desired Mr. Dawes to leave them to themselves as the only way of bringing them to reason.... Although I find a word from *me* has still great influence over the people, yet I cannot help being anxious for the time to come, considering the feeble means we have of enforcing the laws; I only hope Mr. Dawes will continue to use the same forbearance and firm conduct he has already done, and endeavor to win the confidence and affection of the more serious and worthy part of the settlers.

Clarkson was convinced that such a course was "the only means of rearing this infant settlement."

Life in Freetown was, however, much more bearable than it had been in the spring. Several of the congregations had completed their meeting houses and were proud of their sanctuaries. Mary Perth was delighted to have her daughter Susan enrolled in school. By the end of 1793 the colony's 300 school-aged children were all enrolled in classes at eight schools, seven with black teachers (who were often preachers as well), one headed by a European sent from England. Classes were held in private homes, but the teachers were paid by the Sierra Leone Company. The Anglican chaplain was made superintendent of the schools. To ensure some uniformity, all students were examined together once a month. Boys were taught reading, writing, arithmetic, and church music, while the girls worked on reading, singing hymns, and needlework. Evening classes, mostly in Bible reading, were conducted for adults, instructed either by the school teachers or by literate settlers.

Needless to say, the teachers reinforced the lessons and attitudes of the chapels they led, and dissenter politics impinged from time to time. Henry Beverhout and Miles Dixon were company-supported teachers until their anti-establishment politics led to their dismissal. Joseph Leonard had brought with him the schoolbooks he had used at Brindley Town in Nova Scotia. Clarkson noted in his journal that "Old Leonard and his two daughters [Flora and Phoebe] instruct several children, and the school makes a pleasing appearance as they walk to attend divine service."

At least nine Nova Scotian women taught school at one time or another. Mrs. Lucas drew £24 annually, compared with the £40 the men commanded. Mrs. Abernathy held classes in her small house from 9 o'clock until noon, and 2 o'clock to 5 o'clock in the afternoon. The mornings would have been cool, and the shutters of Mrs. Abernathy's house left open to let the soft breeze from the sea slip through and freshen the shadows. The air smelled sweetly green and luxurious. The children could see the little triangular sails of the Bullom boats (lateen-rigged as Portuguese explorers had taught them three centuries earlier) drifting across the estuary. Hawks wheeled lazily over the treetops above King Tom's village. Flycatchers darted among the branches of the trees along the edge of the clearing; weaver birds mended their hanging nests; crickets sang raucously in the fringe of shade. Somewhere up the hill a faint string of ax blows echoed from a work party. Time seemed to hang suspended in the shadow under the overhanging thatched roof during those hours of tutelage, permitting the children to forget the worries and dissatisfactions that haunted their parents.

The students sat on narrow wooden benches, reading the King James Bible and the *Book of Common Prayer*, learning the pious lessons of their preacher instructors. These books were written in standard English; they would have heard the white officers speaking the standard English of the 1790s. The blacks themselves, however, including the preacher/teachers, would have spoken the black English learned on the colonial plantations of America. With no formal training, they had been forced as slaves to learn enough English vocabulary to understand the instructions of their masters, but they fitted that vocabulary into the grammatical construction of the West African languages they had originally spoken. This would have been particularly evident in an idiosyncratic conjugation of English verbs,[3] but actually followed a logical West African pattern—a pattern that survives in black English today.

John Clarkson worried about the muddled theology of the black preachers, who had little education beyond a rudimentary ability to read and write and whose influence resided in prodigious memories for Bible scripture and an emotional eloquence that transported their audiences.

They preached with a passion and vigor that astonished the staid Anglicans, and were answered with shouting, hand-clapping, stomping, and fervid embracing as the congregations acted out their faith in salvation and redemption. Clarkson wrote that the black preachers

> require instruction; they have had their use in keeping the people together, and it has been principally through them that I have had so much influence over the minds of others. I am continually telling Mr. Horne [the Anglican rector] that he would be more profitably employed in giving up a portion of his time to their instruction than by going amongst the natives who do not understand English. I wish I could induce him to think so himself.

In late December, Clarkson boarded ship for England, ostensibly for a short holiday and consultation with the directors. Before he left, he promised the settlers that farm allotments would be made within the following two weeks. Life was easier now, and, reassured, the Nova Scotians looked forward to his return to a prosperous colony. Forty-nine men and women, including David George, Richard Crankapone, Boston King, John Kizell, Ely Ackim, and Hector Peters, signed a petition to the Sierra Leone Company requesting his speedy return:

> we the humble pittioners we the Black pepol that Came from novascotia to this place under our agent John Clarkson … he ever did behave to us as a gentilmon in everey rescpt, he provided every thing for our parshige as wors in his pour to make us comfotable till we arrived at Sierraleon and his behaveour heath benge with such a regard to us … we … wold desier to render thanks … as our govener is a goin to take his leave of us … our ardent desier is that the Same John Clarkson Shold returnen Back to bee our goverener … and we will oBay him as our governer and will hold to the laws of England as far as lys in our pour….[4]

Clarkson himself set out to visit each household to say good-bye personally, and found himself reduced to tears by the "expressions of Gratitude, Affection, and respect." He was charged with all sorts of errands in England: Mary Perth could no longer read her New Testament and needed spectacles; Luke Jordan, trusted assistant to Moses Wilkinson, wanted a seine and fish hooks; Joseph Brown would like a

150

loom. Others asked that watches be repaired, a spinning wheel and tailor's tools be purchased, and so on. On Christmas Day, Joseph Leonard led his schoolchildren through the town, singing hymns before various houses. Clarkson helped serve communion in the Anglican service.

David George accompanied Clarkson in boarding ship; he had applied directly to Chairman Thornton for permission to study in England and increase his understanding of Baptist theology. Chaplain Horne gave him letters of introduction to several clergymen. George would stay six months in England, tell his life story to Baptist leaders there, and return with new clothes and gifts worth £150, enough to build a new chapel in Freetown.

As Clarkson boarded ship on December 28, settler women came bringing food for the six-week voyage: six dozen chickens, 600 eggs, dozens of yams, onions, fruits, and even a pig or two. As the ship weighed anchor the following day, the battery of cannons on shore fired a 15-gun salute, and the settlers and white officials gathered at the landing "waved their hats and handkerchiefs and gave three hearty cheers." This moving farewell from the assemblage on shore must have lingered with Clarkson long after the estuary faded away behind him.

Chapter 29

Angry Settlers Choose Emissaries to the Sierra Leone Company Directors

Anna Maria Falconbridge wrote that John Clarkson's departure "operated more powerfully and generally upon people's feelings than all the deaths we have had in the Colony."[1] Her diary contains some of the crispest and most outspoken descriptions of the year she spent in Freetown. Alcoholism made her marriage to Falconbridge a disaster— all the more difficult because she had married him against her family's wishes. When Clarkson finally dismissed him as the company's commercial agent, he withdrew to an African hut outside Freetown, leaving his young bride on a ship in the harbor. His death in mid-December left her without any reason to remain in Freetown or any male protection in a time when proper women could not live alone. She solved that problem by marrying Isaac Dubois a week after she had buried Falconbridge, and she gave a large New Year's party to celebrate. Needless to say, the tongues of the white officials in Freetown wagged, but Anna Maria and her new husband were both spirited enough to ignore the gossip.

Affection for Clarkson had given the settlers patience with the white administration, but now he was gone, and they were nervous because of recent tensions with the neighboring Africans. Rumor had reached the settlement that King Jemmy was seeking allies among the slave traders for an attack on Freetown. Richard Pepys had been "molested by the natives" for infringing on their land. Clarkson had held another palaver with King Naimbanna, agreeing to greatly restrict the area available for settlement, but the Temne people living on the peninsula still objected when labor parties intruded into the forest near their villages.

Contrary to Clarkson's promise that their land allotments would be delivered within two weeks, Acting Governor Dawes ordered Pepys to halt all surveying work and start work immediately on a fort on Thornton Hill above the cotton tree. Dubois protested that the stone storehouse he was working on was needed much more than a fort; he was immediately relieved of his responsibilities for that project and told to lay out a company cotton plantation. Acting Governor Dawes put Pepys in charge of all public works.[2]

Both Dawes and Pepys were convinced that the drumming and drunken gunfire heard from King Jemmy's town indicated that the Africans intended to attack Freetown, as they had attacked Granville Town in 1789. After a few Nova Scotian traders in the interior were seized and sold into slavery, a permanent night watch was set to guard against outside infiltration into Freetown. Official preparations for attack unsettled the Nova Scotians, even though many Temne people came peacefully enough every day with food to trade, while others worked as day laborers on the plantations. Nervous settlers felt they should be armed to defend themselves, particularly since the slave ships passing so regularly up and down the river seemed a constant threat to them.

Freetown was in many ways an anomaly, located, because of its excellent harbor, in the center of a major slave-trading territory. Clarkson had promised freedom to slaves who sought refuge in Freetown, leading the settlers to encourage slaves to escape, hiding them in their homes.

William Dawes was a rigid, pious man—a much different personality from Clarkson. He had developed a taste for missionary work at Botany Bay, which brought him to the attention of the Sierra Leone Company directors. One of his first acts after Clarkson's departure from Freetown was to ring the great bell every morning and evening to summon the colony to Anglican prayers.[3] This conflicted with the prayer meetings in the chapels and led the settlers to suspect that Dawes intended to draw them away from their chapels and convert them to the Anglican faith. Dawes's experience in a convict colony in Australia had accustomed him to arbitrary government, where orders were given and obeyed without question. He was not of a mind to tolerate initiative among his officials or to consult the settlers before announcing his decisions. Not for him was the patient convincing and cajoling of illiterate blacks that Clarkson had believed necessary. Dawes's immediate termination of the farm surveys roused the settlers' wrath. When he tried to include 20 feet from William Grant's town lot inside his new fortifications, a crowd gathered around the lot and berated him. When Dawes threatened to leave them if they did not behave, Mrs. Falconbridge (now Mrs. Dubois) heard them shouting, "Go! Go! Go! We do not want you here, we cannot get a worse after you." Dawes withdrew.[4]

Rumors spread that the farm surveys would take another year. John Gray, the commercial agent, wrote to Clarkson that the colony would be ruined if farm grants were delayed a year, for the settlers would "go and take Possession of Land where they like…. they are Grumbling now more than ever I remember them to have done before."[5]

In January 1793 King Naimbanna, paramount chief in the area, died. To make matters worse, his son, who had been sent to England in 1791 to be educated by the company, died on board a company ship just as he was returning to Sierra Leone.[6] Other sons of King Naimbanna accused company officials of complicity in the death. Several colonists were murdered by vengeful Temne, and Nova Scotian patrols were armed to prevent further attacks.[7]

More anger was added to the tension when in February the bell was rung to call together a mass meeting, and Pepys announced that the settlers were all to give up their temporary town lots for new ones, which would exclude 500 feet along the waterfront for company use. An uproar followed. Needless to say, all the black congregations met that night in heated discussion. Pepys happened by one of the meetings and was called in to explain the company's policies. When black leaders reminded him of Clarkson's promises that they would be treated equally with white men, Pepys was intemperate enough to reply that Clarkson must have been drunk when he made such promises in Nova Scotia.[8] He stated as well that Clarkson would not be coming back to Freetown, and so the settlers had better forget him and obey their new governor.

154

After Pepys had stalked off haughtily, Moses Wilkinson, Boston King, Cato Perkins and the other black preachers agreed on one thing: Clarkson was the only white official they trusted. They were certain that the directors in London would not want them treated so arbitrarily as Dawes and Pepys were treating them now. They discussed how to make their needs known, finally agreeing that two representatives might be sent to London to ascertain exactly what Clarkson's promises to them meant, just as Peters had been sent to London from Nova Scotia in their behalf. On the spot they chose Cato Perkins (a Huntingdonian pastor and carpenter) and Isaac Anderson (one of the settlers who had led the resistance against Dawes's attempted occupation of the town lots) as their delegates. Anderson, born a free man in Charleston, South Carolina, had no memory of slavery to make him cautious. His name would reverberate through the 1790s as a ringleader in the opposition to company rule in Freetown.

Pepys seems to have had much to do with the latest wave of dissatisfaction. He had schemed from the beginning to widen his influence in the colony. Now he cunningly cultivated Acting Governor Dawes, as well as the new councilor, Zachary Macaulay, a former plantation overseer in Jamaica who had arrived in mid-January. The three of them joined forces to heap odium on Clarkson's character both in dispatches to the directors in London and on the spot in Freetown. Macaulay wrote Thornton that before Dawes took charge, "the colonists were turbulent and disorderly, and the colony exhibited constant scenes of lamentable riot and licentiousness." Clarkson's regime had lacked Dawes's "steadiness, firmness," and now that Dawes was in charge, the settlers were happier and more respectful of their governor than they had ever been of Clarkson.[9] The intention of such reports may have been to camouflage their own decreasing popularity with the black settlers or to wean the settlers away from their loyalty to Clarkson. Of course, such slander actually alienated many of the settlers even further.

The directors in London put more faith in the praises Pepys, Dawes, and Macaulay heaped on each other than in Clarkson's judgments after seven months of experience in governing Freetown. This bias may seem curious, but was based on the fact that the three councilors now in charge in Freetown shared with Chairman Thornton and his closest associates an enthusiasm for the evangelical piety of a growing Anglican sect in

Clapham. Indeed, Dawes and Macaulay won their appointments because they had joined Thornton's circle at Clapham.

Thornton had been born in Clapham; as a successful banker he bought and enlarged a lovely house there. The business of the Sierra Leone Company was largely conducted in offices next door to Thornton's bank, where, surrounded by great comfort, the evangelicals planned the future of the penniless freed blacks in Freetown as one segment of their campaign to reform Protestant religion and end the slave trade.[10]

Clarkson arrived in England in February and wasted no time informing the directors of the heavy toll sickness had taken in Freetown, exacerbated by widespread incompetence among the white staff and a shortage of basic supplies. Chairman Thornton, the largest shareholder in the Sierra Leone Company and now a Member of Parliament, took Clarkson's criticisms personally, believed they reflected badly on him and the other directors, and was deeply offended. He pointed out that war in Europe had affected shipping and justified all actions taken by the board of directors as vital to maintaining a public perception in England that Freetown was thriving.

Mrs. Falconbridge, never one to mince words, assessed in her diary the differences of opinion with a much clearer eye. "Let the Directors shake off a parcel of hypocritical puritans they have about them, who, under the cloak of religion, are sucking out the very vitals of the Company; let them employ men conversant in trade, acquainted with the coast of Africa, and whose *religious tenets have never been noticed.*" Instead, "they employ a pack of canting parasites, who have just cunning enough to deceive them."[11]

Meanwhile, Clarkson was receiving letters from the settlers informing him that the surveying had stopped, that he was being accused of making drunken promises to the settlers, and that Dubois (whom Clarkson knew to be one of the more efficient white officials in the colony) had in frustration asked to leave Freetown. Isaac Anderson and Luke Jordan wrote him that "Our present governor allows the Slave Traders to come here & abuse us."[12]

On the day that Clarkson left London to be married, Thornton offered him a handsome stipend if he would resign as governor. Clarkson refused and was promptly dismissed.[13] With Clarkson disposed of,

Freetown was firmly in the hands of Thornton's pious evangelicals, for Macaulay would, at age 26, follow Dawes as governor.

Clarkson recognized, however, that the Freetown colony was still fragile and would suffer if his views were circulated in England. He restrained his public comments because he knew that Freetown could not survive without British funds and protection. Instead, he wrote his black friends in Freetown that they must "be obedient to the laws or else the Colony will be at an end." He assured them of his firm belief that the Sierra Leone Company would do everything in its power to protect them and further their prosperity.

Chapter 30

Two Governors:
Richard Dawes
and Zachary Macaulay

Richard Dawes's chilly personality, in stark contrast to John Clarkson's warmth and empathy, rankled the settlers and caused distrust. Actually, rigid as he seemed to the settlers, Dawes involved them where they could assist him in governing. He had, even before Clarkson's departure, suggested that every ten settler households should elect a tithingman, and every ten tithingmen should choose one hundredor—a surviving aspect of Granville Sharp's old plan for the government of Granville Town. The duty of these officials would be "to keep the peace and decide causes of less importance." The new system was instituted the day after Clarkson's departure, with both men and women, white and black, privileged to vote. Dawes intended to use these minor officials as the mechanism for enforcing company rules in Freetown. The hundredors would be junior magistrates and serve on juries.[1]

Settlers like Hector Peters soon recognized that the hundredors could be a mechanism for making their wishes known to the governor and his councilors, and set out to make the most of the new arrangement. Others, particularly in the Methodist congregations, maintained their opposition to a governor and council appointed by the Sierra Leone Company without the settlers having any say.

Those who were disgruntled were continually reminded of their fragile situation by the regular passage of the slave traders up and down the estuary. John Kizell, hoeing in his kitchen garden, watched with brooding eyes any ship coming downstream. If others were working near him, he described his memories of the cramped rows of tightly packed bodies shackled in the hold, the hunger, thirst, sickness, and revolting smell that intensified as the agonizing days followed one another.

The settlers also feared an attack by their African neighbors. Their dependence on the Sierra Leone Company for protection and all other amenities frustrated them. The company was the only employer and used its monopoly power to keep the settlers in line. Fractious workers could be, and were dismissed. Furthermore, the company controlled trade and the supply of goods to the colony. It paid the settlers wages in company currency, which was useless anywhere but at the company store. The company added freight, insurance, and commission costs to its 10 percent profit when pricing its goods, which doubled the costs of goods sent from London. Since they could buy nothing elsewhere, many settlers felt they were being exploited. In March 1793 the Huntingdonian paster Cato Perkins, a carpenter himself, led a strike for higher wages. The strikers had no other means of subsistence, and gave up within a week.[2]

Another rainy season soon set in, with its inevitable toll of disease and death. Caesar Perth, surrounded by weeping friends, was among those who succumbed in the spring of 1793. He had managed to complete a two-story, shingled wooden house on his town lot on Water Street, set up from the ground on stone piers, with storage space underneath. He and Mary had paced off their seven-acre farm and planned what they would plant among the rough tree stumps, but nothing would grow until the rains came. Now, when it was time to begin planting, he was dead.

Mary and her daughter Susan sat down together after the funeral to decide how they would manage without Caesar's strength to sustain them. Mary had been a house servant, and knew nothing of farming. She was sure she would do better staying in the town and starting some sort of business there. So she sold the farm allotment and opened her house on Water Street to boarders, particularly company staff who needed a bed until they could find permanent shelter for themselves. Susan could help her with the cleaning and cooking.

At the daily prayer meetings in all the chapels, piety was expressed, but injustices like the abortive carpenters' strike were hashed over as well. Repeated angry discussions finally led to the decision to act. The settlers' charged their two representatives, Isaac Anderson and Cato Perkins, with carrying a petition signed by 31 hundredors, tithingmen, and preachers, to the board of directors in London. Donations were solicited to pay their expenses. Anderson and Perkins boarded ship in June and, reaching London in mid-August of 1793, immediately sought out Chairman Thornton, confident that the directors were not fully informed of the situation in Freetown. In very simple, polite language, their petition indicated that the settlers disliked and mistrusted Dawes and Pepys:

> When the Gentlemen you send here talks one against another and does not agree among themselves we cannot think things are going on right ... we could have laid out all the Lots in Two Months but Mr Pepys ... took off the People that was working on them to build a Fort ... which we do not think will ever be done ... but Mr Dawes says he would rather [lose money] than not do what he wishes...."[3]

They wanted John Clarkson to return to Freetown as governor, and grants of free land, fair prices at the company store, and wages rather than credit paid for their labor so they could trade as they wished.

Meanwhile, letters to Thornton from Dawes and Macaulay in Freetown labeled all the settler complaints "frivolous and ill grounded." Anderson and Perkins soon ran out of money and were told to find jobs or mortgage their farms (not yet received) if they wanted loans. They got in touch with Isaac and Anna Maria Dubois as soon as they reached England in October, and Dubois carried a letter from them to Clarkson. Clarkson wrote Thornton that he would join Anderson and Perkins for a conference with the directors. Thornton ignored the suggestion.

When Anderson and Perkins presented him with a letter from Clarkson, Thornton told them to board the *Amy* and return to Sierra Leone, where they would receive their answer. When they protested, they were told to put any further complaints in writing. In subsequent correspondence (perhaps written with Isaac Dubois's help), they were much more insistent that they would not be governed by the company's present agents in Sierra Leone and wanted to have a voice in the selection of any future governor:

> We did not come upon a childish errand, but to represent the grievances and sufferings of a thousand souls. We expected to have had some attention paid to our complaints, but the manner you have treated us has been just the same as if we were *Slaves*, come to tell our masters of the cruelties and severe behaviour of an *Overseer*.[4]

When the directors realized Anderson and Perkins were in touch with Dubois, he was dismissed from company employ. Thornton stated publicly that the settlers' petition had been "Hasty, and the facts therein ... chiefly founded on mistake and misinformation." Malicious advisors like Dubois were at fault, for any hardship in Freetown had been caused by a temporary shortage of provisions; since that problem had been corrected, Anderson and Perkins should go back to Freetown and stop causing trouble.

The two lingered for a year in England, earnestly seeking redress. Perkins met Lady Ann Huntingdon, who put him "to Collidge" while he waited to meet the company directors. Meanwhile, in Freetown Governor Dawes was working on methods to pacify the neighboring Africans. He established a school for African children, with Mingo Jordan as schoolmaster (at £40 per year—a top salary for a black in Freetown) and invited the African chiefs nearby to send their children to Freetown for education.[5] Soon the Africans living on the Bullom shore across the estuary asked for the same privilege. Boston King, now widowed, volunteered to go and live among them, acting as missionary and schoolmaster. David George conducted missionary work among the Temne as well, baptizing several Africans that fall. All the preachers agreed that Christianizing their pagan neighbors was part of their mission.

In the fall of 1793 two hundredors—Baptist preacher John Cuthbert (an escaped slave from Norfolk, Virginia) in Freetown and James Reid (a royal artillery veteran) in Granville Town—were appointed marshalls, both authorized to summon juries, arrest offenders, execute writs, collect fees and fines, supervise the jail, and direct the tithingmen. Simon Proof was appointed jailor at £10 a year.[6]

Tension between the whites and blacks in Freetown was increasing, however. In November 1793 the storeship *York* caught fire in the harbor and burned for two days, but the settlers refused to help extinguish the blaze. The company lost £15,000 worth of African exports, trade goods, rum, beef, and pork, plus all of Macaulay's careful accounts. Macaulay wrote Thornton that the settlers were

> rejoicing in the calamity as a just judgment of heaven on their oppressors. Some said it was but right that the goods, withheld unjustly from them by the Governor and Council, should be thus destroyed, and their sinister aims should be thus frustrated. They declared the *York* to be the repository where Mr. Dawes' gains and mine were stored.[7]

Dawes returned to England in March 1794, taking with him a Temne chief's son for schooling, along with King and Cuthbert for training as teachers. Council member Macaulay had visited King's mission on the Bullom shore, where he taught 20 African pupils the alphabet, simple spelling, and the Lord's Prayer.[8] Macaulay told Dawes that preaching to the adults was difficult because King had to use an interpreter; therefore, he could never succeed in winning their parents from their pagan ways until he knew their dialect and had a broader understanding of the gospel. (Macaulay probably never considered how little Christianity would appeal to Africans who saw Christians as foreigners who regularly came to cheat and sell them.) This led to Governor Dawes's invitation to King to spend two years at Kingswood School near Bristol, an opportunity that thrilled King. King returned to Freetown in 1796, first teaching at Granville Town and later in a Freetown school.

Macaulay, then 24 years old, became acting governor when Dawes departed. One of 13 children of a Scottish clergyman, Macaulay had been sent to Jamaica at age 16 to work. He became bookkeeper and later overseer on a sugar plantation and so was accustomed to tropical climate and disease. His brother-in-law, a member of the Clapham sect, brought Macaulay to Thornton's attention, and he lived for some months in Clapham. Thus, he won an assignment to Freetown.[9]

Macaulay was the ideal company official, zealous in keeping records and gathering information and intent on carrying out policy, but not adept at initiating it. He displayed little of Clarkson's empathy and none of his humility. In June 1793, shortly after Dawes had left him in charge, a settler named Robert Keeling got into a shouting match with Captain Grierson of the slave ship *Thomas* over racist remarks. Keeling and his friend, Scipio Channel, were joined by a crowd of Nova Scotians, principally Methodists, in arguing with the slave captain. Grierson complained to Governor Macaulay, who sided with Grierson and dismissed Keeling and Channel from company employment "on account of disrespectful conduct." This preferential treatment of a slave captain infuriated the hundredors and tithingmen. They met and demanded Keeling's and Channel's reinstatement, threatening mass resignation otherwise. Joseph Leonard, preacher and leading school teacher, and Myles Dixon delivered the hundredors' protest to Governor Macaulay.[10]

Macaulay responded with equal warmth. "No one within the colony has a right to censure the Governor and Council or to interfere with them, in regard to their employing or discharging the Company's servants." Nor could the hundredors and tithingmen resign without giving "timely notice."

Anderson and Perkins arrived back from London, empty-handed and disheartened that the Sierra Leone Company directors had treated them so cavalierly, to find the Freetown Methodists seething with anger at Macaulay. They saw the directors' dismissal of their grievances now reflected in Macaulay's arbitrary treatment of the settlers. Incited by their preachers, a group gathered to demand that Macaulay justify Keeling's and Channel's discharge. The crowd grew rapidly as Macaulay argued with them. When Richard Crankapone (who succeeded John Cuthbert as town marshall when Cuthbert went to England) tried to disperse the mob, he was attacked by Lewis Kirby and Simon Johnson, who threatened to hang him if he continued. Crankapone and Macaulay hurried to headquarters to prepare a warrant for their arrest, but the mob refused to give them up. When Crankapone appealed to the hundredors and tithingmen for assistance, they ignored his pleas—in effect abrogating their police function. The angry mob then "approached to the Gate of the Governor's yard bidding defiance to all law and authority and threatening instant destruction to whoever should oppose them."[11]

Macaulay and his white councilor, James Watt, announced that all company salaries would be stopped, then armed the white employees under the command of Pepys to protect the governor's house on Thornton Hill and sent word to the English crews of company vessels to be ready to intervene. David George was told to gather any of his Baptists whom he could trust to side with the whites, but the mob attacked the black settlers who tried to disperse them. A cannon was mounted at Macaulay's gate to intimidate the crowd gathered there, and white patrols arrested three settlers during the night.

Angry groups of settlers raged back and forth through Freetown for two days, until finally on Sunday they paused to attend church. Macaulay had a proclamation read at all services warning the worshippers that destruction of the company government would put them all at the mercy of the slave traders. By permitting disorder, they would lose all the advantages they enjoyed in Freetown. Anyone who wished to return to Nova Scotia could have free transportation. All public works were halted, company employment was ended, and the company stores closed.

These measures stunned the congregations and brought them back to their senses. On Monday the hundredors and tithingmen finally agreed to arrest the riotous ringleaders, and the insurrection was over. The brig *Venus* in the harbor was designated to carry disaffected settlers who wished to return to Nova Scotia, but it rode at anchor empty. Instead, eight of the ringleaders—Scipio Channel, Samuel Goodwin, Simon Johnson, Lewis Kirby, Joseph Tybee, James Jackson, and John Manuel—were sent to England for trial on the charge of inciting rebellion, accompanied by seven settlers who agreed to act as company witnesses. The eight defendants were found guilty and banished from Freetown forever. Lesser offenders were dismissed from company employment for life, an equally severe punishment. One man was fined by the local court, and three women were flogged for their part in the rioting.[12]

Peace was restored, but the settlers seethed because Macaulay had used company employment as a weapon to subdue them. Barely a month later, settlers assisted five slaves in escaping from a English ship anchored at Freetown. Captain Horrocks complained to Macaulay, demanding return of his property. Macaulay returned the slaves because they were the property of an Englishman, and severely reprimanded the settlers for violating property rights. The settlers defied him for siding with slave traders against black slaves and continued to shelter any refugees who came to them. The chaplain preached a sermon support-ing Macaulay, reinforcing the settlers' belief that the Anglicans repre-sented arbitrary authority. They saw their outspoken evangelism as far superior to the punitive theology of the white Anglicans.

Macaulay did not share their confidence in their quixotic beliefs. Although the settlers were practicing Christianity, Macaulay knew that most of them were illiterate; he considered them befuddled in their understanding of true Christian principles. Their preachers had only a vague understanding of complex theology and were lax in instructing their congregations to accept the strict obedience to God's word expected by the Clapham sect. Macaulay felt that the untutored Africans were much purer targets for conversion, for they had no preconceived ideas of personal discipline or redemption. He gradually gathered together under his wing a large group of African children whom he intended to educate and Christianize as the first step in converting the indigenous tribes.

Chapter 31

A Chosen People

Because they were Christians, dressed as civilized people dressed in England, and some of them could read and write, the Nova Scotians felt far superior to the half-naked, animist Africans who lived in the jungle around Freetown. Dismayed by the incomprehensible African dialects, the drumming and pagan rituals of the Poro society, the charms and amulets worn on arms and necks, the facial scarring, the spirit worship and superstition in the African villages, the settlers developed a sense of themselves as an elite—the select of God—destined to civilize and Christianize a dark continent. Even if they were not completely in control of their political lives, the settlers felt exalted in God's sight, with a significant religious mission to fulfill.

Though they professed to follow different denominations, their essential beliefs were much the same. They were certainly echoing the pious Christian objectives expressed by the white officials running the Sierra Leone Company, but the psychological impact of finally finding themselves elevated above a whole race of ignorant heathens to whom they could provide enlightenment gave the Nova Scotians a lasting sense of cohesion and destiny. This was expressed in meticulous attendance at divine services. Daily prayer meetings were held in the chapels, which provided the ties for each individual's social bonds and his assurance of mutual assistance in time of need. As many as 11 chapels existed at any one time, with 22 preachers. Weekly classes and family prayer circles were held in private homes, where elements of English culture, copied from the white officials, were adjusted to the lessons learned from slavery and the heady assumption of status derived from feeling so much more civilized than the tribal Africans who surrounded them. The distinct culture that developed around the Freetown chapels was legitimized by their preachers. The hundredors, often preachers themselves, always submitted their proposals to the "Junto of preachers" (Macaulay's phrase) for approval before taking action. Macaulay complained that in Freetown "a religious society is erected into a kind of Jacobin Club for controlling Government."[1] These pious men were not paid for their services, nor had they been educated for their calling. Some of them were illiterate. The chapels might be numerous and fluid, and a new group organized by a man whose strong personality won a following, but the doctrines remained consistent. The preachers cherished an image of themselves in the mold of Moses, who had led his people out of slavery in Egypt. Like Moses, they had successfully survived ten years of plagues (in Nova Scotia), had crossed the sea, and reached the shores of the promised land. Would they allow their vision of Zion to be tarnished by the authoritarian doctrines of the Anglican clergy and the mercantile preoccupations of the Sierra Leone Company, permitting its officials to divert them from their mission, making them wander in the wilderness for the biblical 40 years? No, indeed.

The *Missionary Magazine for 1796*[2] printed a sermon, possibly by David George, that reflected their credo, written down by an Englishman who attempted to capture the preaching style:

> We was in slavery not many years ago! Some maybe worse oppressed dan oders, but we was all under de yoke; and what den? God saw our afflictions, and heard our cry, and showed his salvation, in delivering us, and bringing us over de mighty waters to dis place. Now, stand still and see de salvation of God. God make his salvation go from dis city, tro' dis heat[h]en land; and as Moses and de children of Israel sung a song when dey were delivered, and had seen de salvation of God, so I hope to see de heat[h]ens about us going tro' de streets of dis city, singing hallelujahs and doxologies to God. I hope to see it. Now, it is said, dey soon forgot his works, dey murmur 'gainst God, and his servant Moses. Take care, my friends, and do not like dem' stand still, & see what God is still doing for our nation, putting into de hearts of his

people, to come from far distant nation, to come over de mighty waters, and great deep, to bring de salvation of God to dis nation, to Africans.

Politics as well as religion were debated in the chapels and were colored by denominational overtones. Congregations expressed unified political attitudes, first demonstrated in the rift in June 1793 between Thomas Peters's Methodists and David George's Baptists. Settler conviction of their spiritual superiority was strengthened by the Anglican church's association with the unpopular company government and the slave traders. All the settlers were expected to attend Anglican services on Sunday, conducted by either the Anglican chaplain or the governor. When the Anglican chaplain went so far as to support company policy from his pulpit, the preachers began to view the Anglican establishment as one more threat to their independence.

They were pained that Chaplain Melville Horne insisted on his right to preach in each chapel once a fortnight. When in a Sunday sermon the chaplain condemned "dreams, visions and the most ridiculous bodily sensations as incontestable proof of their acceptance with God," Henry Beverhout accused him of emulating Pharaoh. Beverhout urged those in attendance to bear their sufferings like the Israelites until God delivered them, then led his Methodist congregation in walking out of the service in protest.[3]

After Horne returned to England, schoolmaster Jones was appointed acting chaplain and managed to make even George aware of his contempt for what he viewed as the befuddlement of the black preachers. In his sermons Jones stressed his own views on universal atonement, which denied that the black preachers were an elect of God. After the June 1795 insurrection, Jones was heard to call the Methodists "a rotten society," a remark immediately circulated on the jungle telegraph. Insulted, the Methodists declared him no longer welcome at their meetings and boycotted Anglican services, which they had attended from the day they landed in Sierra Leone. Finally they began holding their own Sunday services at the same hour to make sure their people did not attend the Anglican service.

One of the most poignant incidents related in Macaulay's diary dealt with an invitation he extended in 1798 to George to walk with him to his mountain farm. Macaulay had berated George earlier for allowing his son to bring home the girl he intended to marry when their marriage banns had been published only once. Macaulay chose this long walk up the mountain as an opportunity, Bible in hand, to prove to George that he had broken three commandments. He criticized the Baptists for their drinking, for neglecting to instruct their children, for unchastity. He chided George for assuring his parishioners that they would always remain secure in Christ in spite of their sins. He overwhelmed George's arguments with scripture until the "poor old Man burst into tears!" The harangue lasted from noon till midnight, with Macaulay proud that he had indeed enlightened his grateful listener. "Rivers of water ran down David's eyes because men kept not God's law." What an example of hubris—this arrogant young man in his 20s humbling a middle-aged black man who had survived far more trial and tribulation than Macaulay would ever encounter.

Chapter 32

The Outside World Intrudes

No one knows what further tensions might have arisen in Freetown had not eight ships sailed into the estuary flying the English flag.[1] The entire population of Freetown rushed to the waterfront that morning of September 28, 1794, to welcome the new arrivals. How stunned they must have been when suddenly the fleet began bombarding the town with cannonballs. Zachary Macaulay's first thought was to defend his settlement, but he realized immediately that the 24 rusty cannons at his command were no equal to the broadsides from eight ships.

His next thought was that the captains must be confused as to where they were, not realizing this was an English settlement. He immediately ran up a white flag. The bombardment continued, injuring several on shore. Finally, he shouted to his white officials and settlers to seek safety in the bush.

Although some of the ships were English, the seamen who landed from the ships were French—the disguised fringe of the Napoleonic wars that followed the French Revolution in faraway Europe. Macaulay surrendered and was taken aboard one of the ships. The sailors proceeded to loot Freetown, destroying whatever English property they could not carry to their ships, burning every company building—the governor's house, a large courthouse with a veranda all around, a simple church large enough to seat 1,000 people on benches, offices and houses for white officials, and two hospitals.

Dr. Winterbottom's dispensary was wrecked and his medicines

destroyed. The company's new printing press was smashed, records destroyed, telescopes and weather instruments thrown into the harbor, the apothecary's shop and the library sacked. In the church, Bibles and prayer books were torn up and the clock smashed. Fruit trees were uprooted, donkeys killed, botanical specimens destroyed. Twelve hundred hogs were killed and carted off, and most of the poultry. The French privateers ate well in Freetown.

Richard Pepys was the principal casualty of the French attack. He apparently feared for his personal safety outside of Freetown and fled into the woods with his wife and son. Although the settlers offered him shelter, he refused any help except transportation to the Bullom shore across the estuary. He died there of exposure on October 6, and was commended in the Sierra Leone Company's 1795 report for "extraordinary exertions" in surveying the land.

As the days passed, the blacks gradually realized that the white English officials were the French target—they had no quarrel with former slaves. Settlers living on the periphery hid white officials in their homes and fed them. Others slipped quietly back to their houses in the town. When the French ignored them, they set about saving whatever property they could—lumber, iron ware, boats, barrels of molasses and rum—which they hid in the forest or in their homes. They even persuaded the French invaders to share some of the loot and to let the settlers dismantle public buildings and save the frames before they were burned.

After a two-week occupation, the French fleet weighed anchor and sailed away, carrying off two Nova Scotian boys and leaving behind a hundred English prisoners captured elsewhere. English officials came out of hiding and surveyed the destruction of their houses and official buildings. Governor Macaulay was both fearful and appalled. He decided to move his residence from the waterfront, where he was exposed, up to Thornton Hill above the cotton tree.[2] He rented the best of the settlers' houses for himself and other officers until new government buildings could be erected. White artisans rented rooms in settler houses until they could rebuild. When Macaulay totaled up company's losses, he was aghast to realize that the destruction mounted to some £40,000, not counting buildings.

In his dismay, Macaulay resorted to the only measure immediately available for restoring property, however meager. He called the hundredors and tithingmen together and demanded that all company property saved by the settlers be turned over to him immediately. He argued that this was owed the company in return for all it had done in support of the settlers. Knowing that his demand might not sit well, he threatened those who failed to make immediate restitution with loss of all company employment, support, or services (including school and medical facilities). Each settler was to sign a declaration, agreeing to return salvaged goods or to pay a penalty twice their value before any further company services would be available.

This single act drastically widened the rift between the settlers and the Sierra Leone Company. The settlers had reason to be proud of their conduct during the siege, and were furious at now being called thieves. A few nails and tools and some lumber were handed over. David George and the other Baptist preachers urged their flocks to act responsibly, but only 120 (about a third of the household heads) settlers stepped forward to sign. The rest, led by Moses Wilkinson and the other Methodist preachers, insisted that the company's title had been forfeited when Macaulay surrendered to the French. Several Methodists pointed out that the goods they had saved—worth perhaps £1,000 all told—had either been given to them by the French, or been saved from destruction at great personal risk. Fearing reprisals for their intransigence, some of the settlers armed themselves and prepared to resist Macaulay by force.

Wilkinson wrote John Clarkson:

> We wance did call it Free Town but since your Absence We have A Reason to call it A Town of Slavery. We take it our duty to write unto You letting you know that the French have Attacked us and Destroy all the Compy Property and likewise our little Affects.... if any man see A Place is to be Destroyed by fire and Run the Risk of his life to care of that Ruin afore it is Destroyed, so you not think the Protector of the Articles have a just Right to these property?[3]

The settlers sent two lengthy petitions to the governor and council; Clarkson received letters from several other settlers as well, communicating their anger with the English officials.

Although Governor Macaulay had bragged earlier that "our schools are a cheering sight, three hundred children fill them, and most of the grown persons who cannot read crowd to the evening schools," he immediately dismissed most of the settlers from company jobs and cut off all free services. Four schools were closed and the number of children in classes was reduced by half—to 150.[4] Those in dire need of medical care had a fee five times the usual cost deducted from their store credit. Banned from the company school, a group of settlers soon formed a private school and hired an Englishman named Nicholson, put ashore by a whaler because of illness, to be their teacher. In the next five years private schools were set up to serve the separate interests of the bulk of Freetown's black children, further widening the gulf between them and the colony's white officials.

Many of the residents had lost their land grants when the French sacked their homes, so Macaulay decided to issue new ones. He included in them the proviso that the owners must pay an annual quitrent[5] to the company of a shilling an acre. The settlers regarded this move as a trap, and fewer than half of the 300 grants prepared were picked up by their owners. Those most dissatisfied with white control began to move beyond the company's jurisdiction. Robert Keeling went to live in an African village, where the chief gave him land to till. Nathaniel Snowball and Luke Jordan, both leading Methodists, sought out neighboring chiefs and negotiated a new land grant from Prince George and Jemmy Queen, then moved their entire company to set up a new settlement on Pirate's Bay, halfway between Freetown and Cape Sierra Leone. Snowball was elected governor of the breakaway group, with America Talbot their preacher.

Those who remained in Freetown but refused to sign the oath were deprived of their right to vote. In the 1795 election 70 families remained unrepresented. To forestall further French attacks, however, the settlers remaining in Freetown worked with the white officials on defenses and in the reorganized militia. Six howitzers were placed before the governor's house on Thornton Hill above the cotton tree; a dozen cannons stood in the central square near the bell; nine cannons were lined up at the landing place. All male residents of Freetown, black and white, were organized into companies of 35 men, with elected captains, lieutenants, and sergeants. They all received firing practice and mounted guard duty. Those blacks who had served in the American Revolution had an advantage over white settlers with no military experience; they commanded companies containing white troops.

Although whites and blacks drew together in fear of French ships cruising the coast, the settlers' sense that they were completely at the mercy of the Sierra Leone Company was much diminished. During the French occupation they had survived largely untouched, while the company officials hid under their protection, and many of them were increasingly confident that they could survive on their own in the future. Those who had received land grants tended to move out of the town onto their farms, where they felt more secure. Rather than objecting to this migration, the council realized that this relieved them of some of their responsibility. They encouraged the movement by giving a small monetary premium to help any settler wanting to build a house more than a mile distant from the town. A few ventured even further in the hope of benefiting from the flatter land beyond the mountain crest, but the open hostility of the surrounding Temne villagers made such ventures dangerous.

The French war interrupted shipping. Ships sailed uninsured because wartime insurance costs were so high. Those captured by the French were a complete loss to the company, so the directors reduced the supplies sent to Freetown. The Sierra Leone Company had spent more than a quarter of its capital supplying the settlement through its first two years. When the losses from the *York* fire and the French occupation were added, the directors began cutting expenses. The numbers of white officials were reduced; those remaining were preoccupied with rebuilding government buildings destroyed by the French and with promoting trade to recoup company losses. As official posts were abolished and salaries reduced, jobs formerly held by whites opened up for the Nova Scotians. Universal company employment for the blacks was ended and replaced by contracts for specific tasks such as unloading ships, transporting goods, building, carpentry work, and the like. John Cuthbert and Richard Crankapone, for example, were hired to unload salt and crockery from a chartered ship at a rate of two shillings a ton.

Because David George, ever loyal to the company, rallied the Baptists, they won far more contracts, licenses, commercial privileges, and company positions than their numbers warranted when compared with the more numerous Methodists. They were encouraged to apprentice themselves to artisans and supervisors so that they could learn the required skills and eventually fill those positions. Jess George and Eli Ackim became apothecaries; James Edmonds assisted the company

174

surgeon; William Pitcher shadowed the master of works, Scipio Lucas the master shipwright; Joshua Cuthbert was employed in the dispensary; Nathaniel Snowball, Jr., was given command of the company ship *Dawes* trading upstream; while Thomas Cooper became superintendent of the company's factory in the Rio Pongas region. Some of these individuals became patriarchs of Freetown families that would be prominent for decades to follow.

Loans were made available for boat construction and the purchase of trade goods, which could be sold at a stipulated mark-up. Mary Perth, John Cuthbert, Martha Hazeley, Robert Keeling, James Reid, and Sophia Small were licensed to purchase wholesale provisions from the company warehouse and open retail shops. Sophia Small also kept a tavern and invested her profits in Freetown real estate until she became wealthy. She and a white man had a daughter named Jane, who on her marriage to an English carpenter, George Nicol, commanded a dowry sufficient to establish him as a leading businessman.[6]

One can imagine Mary Perth displaying and selling goods in the front room of her house, while her boarders lived in the upstairs bedrooms. An African cook, working in a small detached shed in the back yard (separate from the house to avoid fires as on southern plantations in the colonies), would prepare meals for her boarders to eat in a back dining room. Fruit trees and coconut palms surrounded the house, with a kitchen garden in back and poultry scratching underneath.

Six months after retail stores were licensed, taverns and the retail of spiritous liquors were licensed—even more profitable than the provisions trade. The settlers were fond of liquor. No stigma was attached to drinking, only to drunkenness. Even Baptist preacher George, who had a salaried job as a messenger in the company secretary's office, opened an ale house to help support his large family. (When Macaulay rebuked him for the example he was setting, George gave up the license.)

Settlers tied thus to the company through private enterprises had a vested interest in the company's success, and they worked to ensure that success. When fire broke out on the company brig *Beginning* in October 1795, a group of Nova Scotians immediately went to save it. Eighteen of them were given rewards for their loyalty.

Chapter 33

Mary Perth
as Housekeeper

Zachary Macaulay admired Mary Perth for her fortitude. Widowed, she had shown considerable enterprise in looking after herself and her daughter. He was also impressed by her quick action when the French attacked Freetown. As Mary fled the French bombardment, she paused at the governor's house to gather together the African children he had brought into his household. She led them to safety in Pa Demba's town, inland against the base of the steep hills above the town.

As the siege wore on, Macaulay was released from the French flagship and found shelter in a settler's house in Granville Town. Mary sent a message to him there, inviting him to come to tea and see that his charges were safe. He came, and was much impressed by the piety with which Mary offered prayers for their safety and salvation before the food was handed around.

After the French departed, Macaulay had a new residence built above the cotton tree on Thornton Hill—a single-story wooden building surrounded by an airy veranda. (Within the next two years, the other official buildings were reconstructed as well.) Macaulay asked Mary to bring the children back to his house, then suggested that she take charge of their care and keep them safe from the contaminating influences of the town. Thus, Mary became Governor Macaulay's housekeeper.

Mary's daughter Susan had been ill for some months. When her mother was told that the Freetown climate was disastrous for the child, Mary sent £150 to Chairman Thornton to invest for her in the hope that Susan could be taken to a northern climate, as the doctors recommended.

Governor Macaulay, troubled by what he viewed as muddled doctrines extolled by the chapel preachers, was convinced that the innocent Africans could be introduced to a purer Christianity than the freed slaves who had already adopted Christianity, but got it wrong. The black children gathered into his household would make better missionaries than the Nova Scotians because they spoke the local dialects and could reach their people as the freed slaves could not.

Macaulay's dream of turning these children into missionaries seemed daunting until a generous donor in England, Robert Haldane, provided more than £6,000 to send them to England for training. Macaulay was overjoyed. Mary's services were so valued that when Macaulay left Sierra Leone in April 1799, he took 25 black pupils with him to be trained as missionaries, along with Mary and Susan. The governor's invitation to accompany him to England, where Susan could receive medical care, must have seemed to Mary like a gift from God.

The Clapham sect quickly organized its own Society for the Education of Africans, raised funds, and took charge of Macaulay's children, providing a resident schoolmaster and his wife under the watchful eye of the Clapham rector, John Venn.

Records indicate that the children were not all indigenous Africans, but included offspring of several Nova Scotians, including Abraham Hazeley, David Edmonds, Sophia Small, and John Kizell. Unfortunately, by 1805 all but six of the African children had died.

Mary Perth stayed with the African children at the school in Clapham until 1801, but Susan apparently did not survive.

Chapter 34

Quarrels Over Religion

While Zachary Macaulay was on leave in England in 1795–96, he made a special effort to learn how to run Sunday schools. On his return to Freetown, he devoted himself to the religious instruction of the colony. A Sunday school was organized for about 200 settler children and met at 5 p.m. each Sunday afternoon. The new chaplain who came from England with him, John Clarke, taught Bible study and the catechism. The children's teachers were to attend with their classes. (One of the white Methodist teachers, John Garvin, resigned in protest and began preaching instead. He would be a ringleader in opposing Macaulay's effort to reform religious practice in Freetown and bring the chapels more into line with conservative Anglican doctrine.)

After the settler Sunday school, a separate session was held for the African children and houseboys in Macaulay's household. In June the children who had behaved well received prizes—hats for the boys and handkerchiefs for the girls. On New Year's Day, three outstanding pupils were given complete outfits, with lesser rewards to 50 others. Then they all marched from the church to the governor's house on Thornton Hill, where a dinner of stewed beef with yams and rice pudding was served under a tent. A sermon by chaplain Clarke was followed by hymn singing under the stars. Macaulay's journal indicates the great satisfaction he found in such uplifting rituals.

While on leave, Macaulay's zeal had been enhanced by meeting Reverend John Clarke, a Scots Presbyterian. Though Clarke was nonconformist enough to refuse to take Anglican orders, he was sufficiently evangelistic to win the appointment as company chaplain in January 1796. In Freetown, his initial open admiration for Nova Scotian piety soon won him settler acceptance and approval of his Saturday evening catechism classes. But as he began to visit the settlers in their homes and listen carefully to the fervent sermons of his black colleagues, Clarke recognized their limitations and proposed that the preachers alter their hours of worship so that more settlers could attend his services. The Methodists were very much opposed to what they viewed as proselytizing. In one chapel Clarke was shown two books by John Wesley that the Methodists said "we abide by." When Clarke asked if they could read them, they responded, "We can't read it is true, but *our souls* can read them."

Soon Clarke began to intimate his disapproval of the homegrown theology of the uneducated black preachers, who had always been fearful that the company would force Anglican doctrine on them. When Macaulay named Clarke the superintendent of all the schools, his position was elevated above that of the black preacher/teachers. When the black Methodist preacher in Granville Town began boycotting Clarke's catechism class, Macaulay abruptly closed the settler school where he taught. To the settlers affected, this seemed an attempt by the Anglicans to take control of religious affairs in Freetown; they were outraged. In barely three months Clarke had destroyed his initial popularity.

Most of the white employees sent to Freetown by the Sierra Leone Company had enough schooling to be literate, but few of them were men of extensive education or sophisticated background. They obviously had to make a living and had not found suitable niches in England. Their employment in Freetown was motivated primarily by self-interest, and any altruistic sentiments they cherished were likely to be very narrowly focused by the prevailing Anglican doctrines. Although several of the single men kept black mistress-housekeepers, few of them could empathize with or tolerate the naiveté and artlessness of the freed blacks from America as John Clarkson had.

James Wilson, who had come out on the same ship as Clarke to manage a sugar mill, wrote back to England of the importance the settlers attached to their status as free blacks in a land where the whites were intruders:

> They are open and free, and their regard and love for white
> people is almost childish. If I look any of them in the face,
> I am almost sure of a curtsy or bow, if not a shake by the
> hand, which they reckon a great compliment. They talk pretty
> good English and are very dressy after the English style.[1]

The aspect of Nova Scotian character most troublesome to rigidly pious company personnel like Zachary Macaulay was the casual sexual mores born in the restrictive conditions of colonial slavery. Mild David George could not have articulated the adaptations in their culture, but he knew that the white colonial masters had either forbidden or ignored any formal marriage bond for their black slaves. As a result, the marriage ceremony was no more sacrosanct to the settlers in Freetown than the more familiar common-law arrangements they had adopted in the slave quarters on southern plantations.[2] Community leaders—Baptist preacher Hector Peters and Methodist preacher Henry Beverhout—lived openly with their women without the sacrament of a formal marriage contract. Illegitimate children were honestly declared and listed in the census returns; they inherited their father's property without question. Chaplain Horne expressed the negative English reaction to what he regarded as loose morals in a letter to a friend:

> The conjugal union is little understood or regarded and a
> woman who has preserved a character for chastity ... is
> barely to be found. The young people are licentious, but this
> is easily accounted for by those who understand the manner
> of life common among slaves in America and our Islands.[3]

The white officials, accustomed to passive and dependent European women, were particularly uncomfortable with the feisty women in black society, and seldom regarded them as ladies. Almost every Nova Scotian woman had an occupation—preacher, teacher, shopkeeper, trader—with an income independent of her husband's. To the settlers this was a normal result of their slave experience, where women often had complete responsibility for their children, but the eighteenth-century Europeans regarded independent black women as bold, impertinent, and probably immoral.

When Macaulay tried to uphold British standards by refusing to baptize bastard children and fining those living in sin, the settlers saw his actions as one more example of white interference in long-standing black customs. After Macaulay discovered two cases of bigamy in 1796 and instances of marriages dissolved by mutual consent of the couples, he ruled that only an ordained Anglican chaplain or the governor could perform a legitimate marriage ceremony. The hundredors engaged in heated debate over the decree, and the settlers were furious. Even David George thought the governor had gone too far and warned Macaulay that the settlers would never submit to such a law. A protest meeting of the settler preachers was called. When a Sunday demonstration under Moses Wilkinson's leadership was planned, however, Brother George became alarmed at the prospect of insurrection and withdrew.

Beverhout demanded that those who remained in the gathering should indicate whether they stood with the company or with the chapels. Isaac Anderson, Luke Jordan, Stephen Peters, and Nathaniel Snowball were eloquent in their condemnation of the company, and consensus was reached immediately. The Methodists gathered as a body to plan their opposition. Beverhout instructed Elliott Griffith (the interpreter from Granville Town) to write a letter to the governor indicating that the settlers would defy the law.

> We consider this new Law as an encroachment on our religious rights, and as such we not only Mean to be inattentive to it, but influence the minds of all ... against it.... we consider ourselves a perfect Church, having no need of the assistance of any worldly power to appoint or perform religious Cerimonies for us, our ministers we consider as much in Holy orders as if they had been sent out by the Presbytery in the Kirk of Scotland.... Our meeting House sanctified by the presence of the Almighty we count as fit for any religious purpose as the House you call the Church. We cannot persuade ourselves that Politics and religion have any connection and therefore think it not right for a Governor of the One to be Middling with the other.[4]

Ten preachers and 117 settlers signed the letter in the name of the Independent Methodist Church of Freetown.

Macaulay responded by ringing the bell to assemble the settlers under the cotton tree, where he read the marriage section from Blackstone, ignoring the fact that an 1781 act of Parliament gave non–Anglican preachers the right to perform marriages for members of their churches. He stated that marriage was a civil ordinance under English law, required by the legal constitution of a British colony. Anyone not complying with his directive would be charged with sedition and rebellion, the penalty for which for hanging.[5] The settlers backed down before this threat, but they seethed over what they saw as an insult to their religious liberties.

Chapter 35

Growing Prosperity

The discovery by settler Andrew Moore in 1796 of wild coffee growing on Directors' Hill was a new spur to agricultural production. The council immediately offered prizes for finding more and cultivating it for export. That prospect lured more settlers out of Freetown, inspired by the hope that they could succeed on their own as plantation farmers, growing export crops. For a time coffee was the main export from Freetown.

Unfortunately, the soil was poor on the peninsula, for the heavy annual rains eroded away topsoil and leached nutrients faster than they were replaced. Settlers who had labored on fertile southern plantations soon shared with their African neighbors a bewildered sense that dark forces somehow held the land in thrall, for nothing really thrived around them except the jungle that bound the soil in place and formed a huge but permeable umbrella to break the force of the rains and winds. Cut the great trees, kill their roots, and soon nothing remained but a sticky, red clay composed of iron, aluminum, manganese, and other insolubles that would barely support decent grass.

Furthermore, many of the settlers were reluctant to invest their earnings in farms that could be repossessed if the quitrent was not paid. They soon realized that they would do better investing in trade goods, and the farms they had sought so assiduously were often abandoned.

Governor Macaulay never acknowledged that the quitrent partially accounted for the reluctance to farm. He decried the laziness of the settlers, bemoaning "their fickle, unsteady & naturally indolent tempers." To set an example to them, Macaulay bought a farm three miles from town and hired Africans to work it. It yielded some fine cabbages and 20 pounds of "pretty good" cane sugar, produced by paid labor— hardly an enterprise to inspire penniless settlers when quicker returns were available in building and trade.

Even the company plantations yielded insufficient returns to make their expansion worthwhile. The plantation John Clarkson started on the Bullom shore dwindled to four acres planted in coffee, plantains, cinnamon, and mangoes. The cotton plantation started by Isaac Dubois on Thompson's Bay lapsed until an overseer (paid £60 a year) and 12 African laborers were hired to grow plantain, yams, corn, and coffee. Few of the settlers could amass the necessary capital to copy these examples.

Nathaniel Wansey was one settler who did make a valiant effort to farm on the slope above Directors' Hill. John Kizell was also determined to eke a living from the land. Born in the Sherbro country, son and nephew of chiefs, he was about 12 years old when he was captured, sold into slavery, and transported to America. He remembered his childhood very well and still spoke the Sherbro dialect. He had been to England as a witness in the 1793 treason trial and had sent a son to Clapham for education. He received a nine-acre farm allotment in Freetown and tried to cultivate sugar cane, cotton, pepper, and ginger for sale to the company store. Unfortunately, commercial agent Gray, attempting to boost export income, would buy crops only from those who were trading with Africans outside the colony. Nor would James Wilson, who ran the company sugar mill, pay a high enough price for sugar cane to encourage settlers to grow it. Kizell quoted Wilson as saying that sugar manufactured in Sierra Leone would spoil the West Indian trade.[1] Later Kizell and Job Allen grew and cured tobacco, but they received no encouragement to sell it commercially.

Kizell never gave up. He had learned to read and write in Nova Scotia. He ran a liquor store, and served as a tithingman. In 1796 he returned from England with a supply of trade goods to find Freetown devastated. He used his profits to aid his suffering fellow Baptists. Then he, Richard Crankapone, and Abraham Smith borrowed £5 from the council and built a craft large enough to carry 12 tons of cargo. They sailed to the

Sherbro country and bought rice and bullocks for sale in Freetown. They set up a Friendly Society—a marketing cooperative to break the white stranglehold on trade. Other settlers followed their example.

Commerce was an uncertain business, however. Traders mortgaged their Freetown homes to procure needed credit, and if things went wrong, they had no other resources to fall back on. Kizell was among those who were forced to give up their Freetown property, worth hundreds of pounds, when prices fell at the wrong moment.[2]

Because of his facility in the Sherbro dialect, Kizell was sent in 1805 by Governor Ludlum to negotiate with the Sherbro chiefs to carry on trade from York Island. In 1810 Governor Columbine sent him upcountry to explain that Britain had abolished the slave trade. Kizell sent back letters filled with sharp observations. Finally he obtained land from the local chief on the south shore of Sherbro Island and established a trading post and a church there, preaching in the Sherbro language.[3] Possibly he felt more at home there, in a homogeneous environment, than among the diverse and quarreling settlers and English officials in Freetown.

A few settlers tried to make a living herding cattle, pigs, and goats. African rustlers stole so many beasts that in 1799 settlers took guns in hand and marched into King Tom's territory to seize their lost animals. King Tom quickly captured three settlers and demanded a palaver. An agreement was reached to settle that particular incident, but it hardly guaranteed an end to African abduction of straying animals.

Company policy had changed after the French attack, when the settlement badly needed provisions—yams, rice, sheep, cattle, goats, fowl, fresh fish—that could be obtained through settler trade with the native Africans. Camwood and ivory were soon added to the inflow of African produce. By 1797 white officials of the Sierra Leone Company as well would be permitted to enter local trade as long as they did not compete with the company or trade in slaves. Several received large credits from the council to start their businesses. Before long they were bartering goods with the slave traders, and eventually several, including commercial agent John Gray, were involved directly in selling slaves.

As food supplies became more abundant, prices declined. Wages rose in the free labor market, as did living standards. Life in Freetown was easier now. True, the rainy season was always a trial, but the weather was never bitterly cold, as it had been in Nova Scotia, and no one died of exposure or starvation. Settlers doing well as artisans or traders built sturdy clapboard houses with wooden shingles and shuttered windows, and they could afford to hire African servants and field hands. Settlers who established their economic independence were less inclined to be frustrated by white political domination of the colony.

Actually, the degree of emancipation the settlers enjoyed in Freetown was impressive had they compared their situation there with their slave status in the American colonies. While Macaulay was governor, he encouraged settler participation in government. All council resolutions were submitted to the hundredors and tithingmen for their approval, and their initiatives in introducing measures to encourage order were welcomed. Gradually the white council came to recognize these elected officials as a sort of legislative body, and they consulted the hundredors and tithingmen for their opinions on important matters. In fact, in 1796 Macaulay actually used the word *legislature* in speaking of the elected constables and ruled that in their quarterly deliberations a majority vote was binding. Each family was to pay a shilling a year for a clerk to keep the record of their deliberations. The hundredors were expected to meet monthly with their tithingmen, and the two groups gradually became the accepted spokesmen of the settlers.

These representatives were granted the power to impose taxes, disperse public funds, and organize work parties. Macaulay offered them a £50 loan to start a public treasury. They were responsible for organizing the militia, whose members supplied their own arms but were issued ammunition paid for by the treasury.

The hundredors and tithingmen proposed and won approval for a law to prevent hogs, sheep, and goats from roaming loose in the town. They set price ceilings on fresh meat and bread; levied fines for disorderly conduct, selling liquor without a license, and using bad language; and laid down penalties for adultery. They chose black surveyors of streets and roads. They granted Peter Francis a divorce from his wife, who had left him in Nova Scotia. As the years went by they would impose a road tax of six days' work annually, forbid strangers from obtaining land in Freetown without the council's permission, and set a residence requirement of a year and a day for new citizens to vote or serve on juries. Most of the settlers were very law-abiding and paid their road tax without protest. Warrants were generally served when needed, court sentences carried out without protest, and militia duty cheerfully performed.

Macaulay actually took the trouble to draft a constitution that would have established a formal legislature, elected by the settlers, to pass and submit bills to the governor and council for approval. Unfortunately, at the same time the governor was directed to impose a quitrent on land as a way of recouping some of the huge losses resulting from the French raid on Freetown. The directors in London based their projections on the total land grant in Sierra Leone—250,000 acres of farmland yielding a shilling an acre. Exports were not bringing in any substantial revenue, but a quitrent should be a painless way to channel dividends to the Sierra Leone Company stockholders. In Sierra Leone, however, little of the area ceded by the African chiefs was suitable for farming. Only 2,560 acres of land had been allotted to 500 men and women, which would have brought in very little revenue.

Macaulay and his council also decided in 1796, as a way of diluting the black vote, that white residents should own land and vote in elections and extended the franchise to every resident earning £40 a year. Some of the settlers were adamant against including whites among their hundredors. The other settlers were determined not to pay quitrent, both because John Clarkson had promised them in Nova Scotia that land would be free and because the tax would make them seem mere tenants of their land. The quitrent was violently denounced at meetings and demonstrations. Thinking that the hundredors could abolish the quitrent, Ishmael York and Stephen Peters led a campaign in the 1796 election against the white candidates running for office and defeated all of them. York and Peters both retained their seats as hundredors; Nathaniel Snowball and Isaac Anderson won seats—all four of them long-standing opponents of company government.

Macaulay was aghast when faced with a legislative body with no white faces; he ridiculed the newly elected blacks because not one of them could read the oath of office distinctly. He saw Peters's influence as "considerable among the Methodists, he being one of their great thundering Orators." York was regarded by Macaulay as "a noisy factious fellow, exceedingly griping & selfish, which makes him of little weight. An elder of Lady Huntingdon's Sect, and a great talker about religion, but sadly unprincipled." Macaulay charged York with bribing voters with free drinks and withdrew his liquor license.[4]

Some of the settlers were so incensed at the controversy that they withdrew completely from Freetown. The Baptist preacher Hector Peters, for example, went upriver to Rokelle and began to trade in slaves. He did not return to Freetown until a general amnesty was declared after the slave trade became illegal in 1807.

Macaulay regarded the new hundredors as extremists—"in general the most ignorant, hard headed & perverse of our colonists"—and shelved the constitution.[5] He reported his dismay to Chairman Thornton in Clapham. To decrease the weight of the settler vote, the two agreed that women should no longer vote in future elections. Intemperate politics in Freetown had ended a privilege that women in America would not enjoy until the twentieth century.

The Freetown settlers were hardly powerless, as some of them saw themselves, but they had had their expectations of self-government raised by Clarkson beyond the level the Sierra Leone Company directors could accommodate. Deprived of a strong legislative voice, many settlers turned to the courts to express their grievances. In fact, they filed so many petty law suits that a 15-shilling fine was imposed on any petitioner who lost a civil suit—in a fruitless attempt to discourage frivolous litigation over tiny debts and minor insults.

Trial by jury was authorized (a privilege not granted to blacks in the United States until after the Civil War), with at least half of the jurors the same race as the defendant. White company officials sat as justices of the peace and judges, but the black settlers took their jury duties very seriously in deciding guilt and setting penalties—imposing fines, confinement in stocks, or whipping.

Chapter 36

Insurrection and Defeat

The first payment of the quitrent was set for July 1, 1797; James Wilson was appointed collector. The Baptists, after long and heated discussions led by David George, agreed they would pay it. The members of the Countess of Huntingdon's connection left it up to their members to decide, although the leaders of her group announced they would not pay. The Methodist leaders were adamantly against the quitrent and warned that anyone paying it would be expelled from the congregation.

In the face of such opposition, Macaulay scheduled a meeting and delivered a lengthy address to the 150 heads of household who came to hear his explanation of the legitimacy of the quitrent. In addition to the usual statements of how much the settlers owed the Sierra Leone Company, the governor asserted that none of them had received land in Nova Scotia as they had here, and that they knew before they left Nova Scotia that the quitrent would be levied—neither of which was true. The huge gap between his perceptions and those of his audience was evident when he denounced them for failing to trust him and the company and for listening "to every prating, malicious, designing tale-bearer; to every selfish and base deceiver, who ... would abuse or revile your Governors and misrepresent their conduct. You have often been made to see the folly of acting thus, and yet you return like the sow, to flounder in the same dirty puddle."[1] Macaulay's sarcasm hardly endeared him to his listeners.

Macaulay left the meeting without responding to any of the settlers' questions, but Isaac Anderson immediately rose and reminded the group that he and Cato Perkins had gotten no satisfaction from the company on their abortive mission to England in 1793. Stephen Peters delivered a tirade against the governor, but when Thomas Cooper, a black man born in England, rose to defend Macaulay, the crowd refused to listen and the meeting ended in tumult.

Macaulay sent gloomy reports of the "mutinous spirit" in the colony to London at the end of 1797. The election in December of that year passed quietly, with women excluded from voting for the first time. Two whites were among the 24 tithingmen chosen; the antiwhite faction protested briefly at the swearing-in ceremony. In a final gesture of defiance over the quitrent, three settlers—Isaac Anderson,[2] Stephen Peters, and Ishmael York—carried a petition to the senior naval officer on the coast, Captain Ball of the frigate *Daedalus*, asking him to arbitrate over the quitrent. Rather than act in their behalf, Ball took their petition immediately to Governor Macaulay.

Rumors of another impending French attack led to a temporary truce as the settlers helped strengthen the defenses, shared militia duty, and transported valuables inland to safety. The enemy fleet had no sooner left the West African coast than King Tom demanded palaver over disputed land on the eastern boundary. Negotiations led to a cessation of the dancing and drumming in King Tom's town on Sundays, which had disturbed chapel services. When another rumor circulated that the Africans were plotting to kill Macaulay and seize Fort Thornton, the settlers who had no guns were allowed to buy them.[3]

Early in 1799 the hundredors and tithingmen accused the white judges of racial discrimination in company courts, in company stores, and at public auctions. They announced that the solution to this problem would be the election of judges from among their own numbers, and so informed Governor Macaulay. The choosing of judges became a central issue in achieving their sovereignty. Macaulay responded that the idea was impractical because none of them was versed in English law. At an impasse, the governor agreed to transmit to the company directors a settler petition asking permission to appoint black judges.

Macaulay's replacement arrived in April. Thomas Ludlam was 23 years old, slight of build, with "mild and conciliatory manners," in contrast to Macaulay's "cultural arrogance."[4] Ludlam had no African or colonial experience. With him came John Gray, veteran commercial agent, returning from home leave. They brought renewed demands from the directors that the quitrent be paid, but with a teaser that it would be spent locally for colonial needs, rather than paid to stockholders in London. Again, new land grants incorporating the terms were offered, and again, only a handful of settlers responded. Macaulay was unable to collect any rents before his departure on home leave in April. His fear of settler attack led him to keep loaded guns in his bedroom and a light burning through the night during his last weeks in Freetown. Gray then acted as governor for seven months; Ludlam took over that post in November.

Without waiting for the reply to their petition for black judges, the hundredors chose schoolmaster Mingo Jordan to be a judge and John Cuthbert and Isaac Anderson to be justices of the peace, sending their names to Governor Gray. Needless to say, the directors in London rejected their demand and so informed Ludlam in November. When Ludlam refused to recognize their appointments, the dissident settlers proclaimed that they were Africans, not Englishmen.

In the meantime, one of Ludlam's first actions on assuming the governor's post was to drop the conditions imposed on school enrollment after the French invasion. Macaulay had excluded from company schools all children whose parents refused to take the loyalty oath or return confiscated property and who later refused to pay the quitrent. In 1797 the council had permitted those children excluded to re-enroll if their parents paid $1 a quarter in advance. Ludlam sensed how important education was to the settlers and immediately abolished all fees and conditions for school enrollment and reopened three company schools.

Ludlam also let the quitrent die, since no payments were forthcoming. He computed that the levy of a shilling an acre would force a settler to pay the full value of his land to the British government every 20 years. He understood the settlers' resistance to the idea, and their fear that the land improved by their hard labor could be lost in a lean year. He hoped that these concessions would undercut the radical leaders. But the rejection of the settlers' plan to appoint judges refueled the acrimony.

Macaulay reached London in July 1799 and was appointed permanent secretary of the Sierra Leone Company. Two major steps were taken that summer in London. To replace the company incorporation act (which had not, in fact, granted the Sierra Leone Company the judicial power its officials had been exercising in Freetown), the company applied for a royal charter, "which should convey to them a clear, formal, well-grounded authority, to maintain the peace of the settlement, and to execute the laws within the territory."[5] Clearly the directors were weary of supervising a contentious colony that required enormous resources, but brought scanty return. The directors asked also that a navy ship be posted in Freetown harbor to uphold the company government, that government funds be appropriated to run the colony, and that British troops be stationed there to put down any rebellion.

At the same time the company was negotiating to move more than 500 exiled Jamaican Maroons (descendants of runaway slaves who had revolted against British rule and been banished to Nova Scotia) to some other location in Sierra Leone at British government expense.[6] In return for the royal charter, annual subsidies, and British military support, the directors agreed that the Maroons should receive four-acre land grants similar to those of the Nova Scotians, but with a quitrent attached.

In December the last election of hundredors and tithingmen proceeded in Freetown. Those candidates demanding a black judiciary were all returned, including three (Anderson, Nathaniel Wansey, and James Robinson) who spoke openly in favor of the settlers exercising their God-given rights regardless of the council's actions. Ludlam reported that "almost every friend of the Government among the Hundredors & Tithingmen was thrown out at the ensuing election; and the boldness, turbulence and power of the factious leaders continued thro' the whole of the year 1799 rapidly increasing."[7]

In February, Wansey drew up a list of grievances against the council government, and requested an appeals court to hear them. In April, an armed brig, the *Nancy*, arrived in the harbor, sent by the company to defend its officials against external and internal aggression.

In May, Ludlam informed the settlers that no justices could be named from among the settlers because the impending crown charter would give all governing power to the Sierra Leone Company. (The crown charter would be approved in July 1800.) He also warned them of the imminent arrival of an armed force to uphold the company's authority. He did not tell them that 500 Maroons, fighters legendary for their courage and cruelty, were expected as well.

Clearly, if action was to be taken before the company received enlarged powers, the time had come. All the hundredors, led by Anderson, and half the tithingmen, led by Robinson and Wansey, were in favor of some action. Those moderates who spoke in favor of conciliation were ejected from the discussions and replaced by company opponents. Someone suggested that they put all the whites in an open boat without sails, oars, or compass, and set them adrift. Others sought out King Tom to gain his support in a bid for independence. Several worked out a plan for black juries to exonerate defendants of any political charges brought by the governor until black judges were appointed.[8]

The names that rocked Freetown in 1800 are not the familiar ones of the previous two decades. Twenty-five years had passed since Lord Dunmore's proclamation in Virginia, and many of the black loyalists from the American colonies were at or beyond the average lifespan of their time. Some of them had already died. Most of the younger men haranguing the meetings now had been children when they left the colonies or were born in Nova Scotia. They had grown up listening to intense debates about company government and diatribes against the quitrent. They were vigorous men, willing to undertake the hard labor of digging and hoeing a farm out of the jungle. But they were determined not to pay rent, for they knew that they would be obliged to pay for their land over and over again, and that they could lose everything in one poor growing season if their labor yielded too little to pay the tax.

On September 10, 1800, as many as 150 heads of families gathered in Perkins's Huntingdonian chapel to discuss alternatives. In a town of 1,200 residents, this represented probably half of all the households. Perkins, who was married with children when he left Charleston, South Carolina, must have been getting on in years. He may have offered prayers for their safety, but left the heated arguments to younger men.[9] Anderson emerged as the consensus leader, with Cuthbert named judicial officer and Zimri Armstrong secretary. These names were seldom mentioned in the governors' diaries or reports to the directors of the Sierra Leone Company. True, Anderson had been sent to London as a settler representative, but his humiliating reception there had turned him into a fiery opponent of the company government. Cuthbert had served as a company marshall and kept a retail shop, but had little experience in negotiating compromise. Armstrong had suffered in New Brunswick from agreeing to a two-year indenture in exchange for a promise of freedom, which was never kept, but played no leading role in Freetown before this time. These three were apparently the most hot-blooded in the group that strongly opposed company rule and the most vocal in giving vent to their frustrations.

The group drew up a code of laws that said, among other things: "The Governor and Council shall not have anything to do with the Colony no farther than the Company's affairs, and if any man shall side with the Governor, etc. against this law shall pay £20."[10] Only the hundredors and tithingmen could issue summons or warrants. No company debt could be collected without their concurrence. Trade would remain in company hands, but the company was required to take the settlers' produce in exchange for company goods, which were to be duty-free. Price ceilings were set for basic commodities. Fines were set for minor crimes like trespassing, stealing, scandalizing, adultery, and the like.

These laws were announced on September 10, to come into effect on September 25, when Anderson, Robinson, and Ansel Zizer would take charge of affairs in Freetown. On that night the new settler constitution was posted on Adam Smith's window shutter, signed by Robinson, Zizer, Anderson (all three hundredors), and Wansey (elected chairman of the tithingmen).

The next morning, as other settlers gathered to learn the import of the announcement, two white officials, Gray and James Wilson, copied it down and read it aloud to those who had not joined the conspiracy. Those who listened must have felt a dismaying sense of foreboding as they carried the news to David George and the other loyal Baptists.

When Ludlam was informed, he called his supporters to Thornton Hill and armed them. That evening, when he learned that the rebels were meeting at Ezekiel Campbell's house, he sent Marshal Crankapone and an armed party to arrest them. The confrontation disintegrated into a brawl, and shots were fired. Robinson and Zizer were taken into custody. The official report states that six of the marshal's party were wounded by rebellious settlers. John Kizell and Eli Ackim testified that the conspirators were unarmed, and had resorted to defending themselves with sticks only after the governor's party opened fire.

The following day, both sides prepared for battle, but held back.

The rebels feared that loyal settlers like David George and Hector Peters would continue to support the company. Freetown was unnaturally quiet. The streets were deserted, for settlers stayed in their houses, fearful that the neighboring Temne would join the rebels and destroy their tenuous foothold on the African coast. Certainly, George understood how perilous the impasse was.

Governor Ludlam issued warrants and promised rewards for the arrest of Anderson, Wansey, Daniel Carey, Charles Elliot, and Frank (Francis) Patrick on charges of treason. He also proposed that the first naval captain to arrive in the harbor should arbitrate the dispute.

On Sunday, September 28, Anderson threatened to attack Thornton Hill if the prisoners were not released. Some of his supporters stole powder, shot, money, liquor, tea, and the like in Freetown. Ludlam announced that all looters would be treated as traitors. Cuthbert and Perkins went up to Thornton Hill to mediate with the governor. King Tom warned that, as landlord, he would step in and settle the dispute if the colonists could not.

Then, like the dramatic climax of a comic opera, a naval transport sailed over the horizon and anchored that evening in the estuary. On board the *Asia* were 47 British troops escorting 550 Maroons from Halifax. When informed by Ludlam of "the rebellion raging in the heart of the Colony," the 150 Maroon men responded gleefully to a suggestion that they "stretch their legs a little" and help the British troops restore order.[11]

The faint-hearted among the dissidents had slipped away to their homes to await the outcome of the impasse. The intransigent rebels, believing that half the population of Freetown was in silent support of their demands, must have expected mild-mannered Ludlam to give way, as he had given way on the quitrent and the opening up the company schools. Isaac Anderson went so far as to send an anonymous and threatening letter to the governor. The radicals raided outlying farms of those loyal to the company for food and finally took up a position just outside Freetown on the road to Granville Town. Henry Washington (former slave of George Washington), who farmed east of Freetown, joined the rebels. On October 1, a last invitation to surrender was sent through intermediaries to the fifty armed rebels gathered at Buckle's Bridge. When they temporized in replying, British officers led several detachments ashore the next morning in a surprise attack. A heavy thunderstorm interrupted the plan to encircle the rebels. Two were killed, but the rest fled into the bush. Some of those who escaped were hunted down or turned over by King Firama for a promised reward.[12]

No prison adequate to hold the captives existed, nor could the company afford to send them to England for trial. A military tribunal headed by the three British officers from the *Asia* was hastily convened to try the rebels. Of the 55 active participants in the rebellion, Anderson and Frank (Francis) Patrick were singled out and hanged as a warning to others. Thirty-three others were banished, and their property was distributed to the Maroons. Nine Freetown settlers were rewarded for assisting the company officials. The voices demanding self-rule were silenced, and the freed blacks from Nova Scotia finally relinquished their dream of governing themselves.

Governor Ludlam, unwell and deeply troubled by the uprising, resigned even before the trials were completed. He remained on the council in Freetown, but the directors persuaded William Dawes to return and replace him as governor. Dawes arrived to a warm welcome on January 6, 1801, his previous unpopularity apparently forgotten. He immediately saw to the building of a blockhouse and barracks for the English troops and the improvement of the gun emplacements around the town.

Chapter 37

Transition

The new charter granted to the Sierra Leone Company in 1801 gave the company full authority over the colony and the land ceded to it, augmented by armed strength to enforce the law. Judicial powers were invested in the company council. Black participation in the legislative process was ended. The hundredors, tithingmen, and town marshal, who had all been Nova Scotian before 1800, were replaced by a white mayor (Thomas Cox, the company's storekeeper), three white aldermen, and a white sheriff. (Richard Crankapone continued as undersheriff.) The council was to appoint commissioners to a Court of Requests from among Freetown's "principal Inhabitants." That and jury duty were the only small roles left for the loyal blacks to play.[1] Fifty European soldiers of the Royal African Corps, formed in 1800 for service at Gorée (an island off Dakar), were sent to garrison and rebuild the Freetown fort.

One of the first acts of the council under its new charter was to declare that all settlers must receive new farm grants and must agree to pay the quitrent or their land would revert to company ownership. The most industrious farmers—young, active men—who had rebelled to fight the quitrent, now forfeited their farms after the revolt was put down. Soon, both escaped rebels and Temne neighbors were harassing the outlying farms, causing their owners to abandon them and seek safety within the town. Even those settlers who accepted the new grants refused to pay the rents.

Mary Perth returned from England to Freetown in 1801, having buried her daughter Susan in Clapham. She must have felt a deep sense of homecoming after seven years in England. One can imagine David and Phillis George enfolding her in their arms, inviting her to dinner, and relating the traumatic events of the preceding year. Brother George would now be close to 60 years old; he had been married to Phillis for 30 years. They probably had grandchildren.

Resilient to the end, Mary had brought Elizabeth Gould from England to live with her and help in her shop and boarding house, where she would provide meals for Church Missionary Society clergy sent out from England. She returned to a colony even more troubled than the one she had left.

The arrival of reinforcements in 1800 and the strengthening of the town's defenses—clear indications that Freetown was no transient undertaking—unsettled the local Africans. In October 1801 the Temne chiefs ordered several hundred traders and grumettas working in Freetown to leave the settlement. Governor Dawes thought they had been ordered home for the rice harvest. An African attack on Thornton Hill a month later indicated otherwise. It was led by two escaped Nova Scotian rebels, Nathaniel Wansey and Daniel Carey. The timely arrival of the *HMS Wasp* brought guns and crew to the colony's aid. Mayor Cox was shot dead. Dawes, although badly wounded, led a charge, sword in hand, that drove out the invaders. Eighteen settlers (including women and children) were killed. Most grievous was the loss of ever-faithful Richard Crankapone, who had rushed to the governor's house to warn him of the attack.[2]

After the attackers had been driven off, it seemed wise to fortify less-defensible Granville Town. The company had intended to settle the Maroons elsewhere, but their usefulness during the rebellion and the reluctance of the indigenous Africans to grant more land led the council to locate them in Granville Town. Although they were allotted farms there in 1801, most of the Maroons preferred to work as laborers in Freetown. Their timely arrival and their willingness to work hard endeared them to the council, which held them up as an example of loyalty that the Nova Scotians should emulate. When the council declared September 30 an annual day of thanksgiving for God's "providential deliverance of this colony from the late unnatural rebellion,"[3] the Nova

Scotians realized that company officials regarded the Maroons as the counterbalance that would keep the Nova Scotians in their place. If God had intervened to save the colony for the Sierra Leone Company, how could the black settlers go on believing that this was their promised land?

After the second Temne attack, the Maroons who had settled in Granville Town crowded into Freetown, along with outlying Old Settlers (as they came to be known) who feared for their safety, and were settled on the west side of the town. Detachments were sent out to burn the Temne villages nearby until a truce was arranged. In negotiations with King Tom in December 1801, the company requested the whole Sierra Leone peninsula in the hope of making more land available to distribute to the Maroons.

The few months of quiet were broken again in April 1802, when King Tom and Wansey led 400 Africans and 11 rebel Nova Scotians in another attack on Freetown. The defenders were better prepared this time and quickly drove away the Africans, leaving 100 dead on Freetown streets. Three settlers lost their lives; all European women in the colony were evacuated. Local trade came to a halt, and more farms were abandoned for the safety of the town. No land was cultivated in 1802, leading to a serious food shortage.

Elliott Griffith (the talented interpreter first encountered in the Province of Freedom) was arrested for debt to the company in 1802 and died in prison at Fort Thornton, where James Reid was jailer.[4] Boston King passed away that year in Sherbro country. Whether he was seeking food or other trade goods there or still trying to carry God's message to the animist Africans is unknown. William Ash, prominent Huntingdonian preacher, had drowned in 1801 (his widow left his town lot to the congregation); Cato Perkins, also leader of a Huntingdon chapel and a vocal opponent to company government, would find his rest in 1805.[5] Perkins was succeeded as Hungtingdonian preacher by John Ellis.

The native rice crop failed in 1803, and the company again resorted to shipping food from England. Granville Town was abandoned to the jungle. No revenue was flowing to the company, so the office of commercial agent was abolished in 1803. The costs to administer and defend Freetown soared. By the end of 1803 the Sierra Leone Company's total assets had fallen to £31,643; by 1807 to £11,111.[6] Only an annual government subsidy of £10,000 kept the company going.[7]

Numerous discussions during prayer meetings and chapel services must have focused on the changing status of the original settlers. The Maroons gave the company new strength and became another element in an ethnic rivalry that gradually honed the Nova Scotian culture. Unfriendly Africans always lurked in the lush, green jungle. The taste of economic disaster that followed turbulence in Freetown was fresh in everyone's mind. Most of the dissidents against company rule had been banished or had left Freetown voluntarily. Cooperation with company government now seemed the only way to survive.

Councilor Ludlam gave serious thought to settler concerns; he argued convincingly against enforcing the quitrent. He pointed out that any sensible settler would do better to work for wages, save money to buy land, and then be free of the quitrent. Finally, in 1803, the council agreed with him and abolished the obligation.

Palavers with the local chiefs gradually improved relations with the neighboring Africans. A party of white officials talked the Temne into giving up rebels Wansey, Carey, and Sampson Heywood. Some farming was resumed, but most of the Nova Scotian owners preferred to engage Maroons in share-cropping arrangements, so they could be free to trade or work as artisans.

The quitrent had been abandoned before a new governor, Captain William Day, arrived in February 1803. Economic activity was almost at a standstill. Thomas Ludlam, who had understood Old Settler opposition to the quitrent, remained on the council to champion their needs. The new governor devoted his immediate attention to strengthening Freetown's defenses and the formation of a paid Volunteer Corps to patrol and defend the town. Eventually some 270 men—almost the entire male population of the colony (more than half Maroon)—were enrolled and given a small monthly wage.

The local Temne soon saw that Freetown was no longer vulnerable and retreated to their villages on the mainland. The Maroons were resettled on the small peninsula that had once been King Tom's headquarters.[8] Settlers who had lost their means of livelihood were resilient and found jobs constructing and supervising fortifications, clerking in stores, teaching, and other community enterprises. Indeed, Freetown again had more jobs than laborers, thanks to generous government subsidies (£28,000 in 1804) for defense and administration. Salaries were never as high as those paid to whites, but salaried employees saw their interests interwoven with their employers' and their safety dependent on the British. Optimism and goodwill increased as the settlers became more prosperous. Their improved morale in turn made them seem more reliable and meritorious in the eyes of company officials.

The contrast between the Old Settlers and the Maroons, however, was heightened by the vigor and self-confidence of the Jamaicans. Their rough and loud manners contrasted with the steady piety of the Nova Scotians. They preferred to live in their own districts and have separate schools for their children. Few Maroons attended church or had any interest in becoming literate. Women were kept subordinate; polygamy was widely practiced. The council feared outright violence if they tried to suppress these common Maroon practices. Nova Scotian preachers valiantly sought to wean the newcomers from their pagan ways and convert them to Christianity.[9]

The rough-and-tumble aspect of the Maroons' lifestyle in Freetown reinforced the Old Settler sense that theirs was a culture superior to that of other blacks. They kept the English names brought from America, and wore a distinctive style of western dress—the women in bright petticoats and shawls over cotton print gowns, with a colored head scarf, often topped with a beaver hat; the men in jackets, waistcoats, and trousers (wool, duck, or cotton) and straw or beaver hats.

The Old Settlers were all active in their chapels. David George, Moses Wilkinson, and Cato Perkins had passed their productive years, but were still preaching. They urged their children and grandchildren to value education; some of them were prosperous enough to send their children to school in England. Many of them could afford to hire Africans as servants, apprentices, or grumettas to work in their fields. Apprentices were bought and sold, considered the property of their masters during their indenture. If this smacked of slavery, the Nova Scotians rationalized that the local blacks were an inferior people, deserving of a subservient status, whereas the immigrants identified themselves with the ruling elite.

Nothing was to be gained, now that the peninsula belonged to them, from appeasing neighboring chiefs. Rather, the Old Settlers supported company officials in defending the peninsula from incursions by indigenous Africans. They clung for over a century and a half to the culture that distinguished them from the Maroons, from Africans put ashore in Freetown from slave ships, and from their less civilized, "upcountry" African neighbors.

Curiously enough, the early missionaries sent out from England reinforced these distinctions. The Church Missionary Society was founded in 1799 by several of the men also involved in the Sierra Leone Company—Granville Sharp, Henry Thornton, William Wilberforce, and Zachary Macaulay—to encourage Anglican mission work in Africa.[10] They could offer Sierra Leone as the ideal untainted ground on which to work, but found few ordained Anglican clergymen willing to undertake the task. They turned then to the Lutheran Berlin Seminary for candidates, brought two—Melchior Renner and Peter Hartwig—to England for training, and sent them to Freetown in 1804. Mary Perth probably welcomed them into her boarding house and provided their meals until they were sent out to proselytize among the African tribes.

When the local Africans showed no interest whatsoever in their preaching, the two returned to Freetown to act as colonial chaplains. The Old Settlers were perfectly willing to listen to their sermons and let them participate in chapel services, but their own persuasions were too strong to tempt them to convert to the Anglican faith or baptize their children as Anglicans. The German accents and general indolence of the missionaries were a source of mirth among the settlers. Hartwig's eventual abandonment of preaching to become an active slave trader only reinforced their poor opinion of white missionaries.

Three more Germans were sent in 1806—Leopold Butsher, Gustavus Nylander, and Johann Prasse. Again Mary would have welcomed them to her boarding house and fed them well. Nylander won settler approval by marrying the 21-year-old schoolteacher, Phillis Hazeley, daughter of settlers Abraham and Martha Hazeley. Governor Dawes had taken her to England in 1793 to be trained; she opened a school when she returned. She died eight months after her marriage, to her husband's great grief. Nylander than married Ann Beverhout, daughter of Methodist preacher Henry Beverhout, who also taught school. Many of the Nova Scotian dissenters, particularly Methodists, attended Nylander's Anglican communion services and asked him to perform marriages, but adamantly refused to join the Anglican Church.[11]

Nylander and his three companion missionaries were assigned outside Freetown in 1808, where their objective was to turn the indigenous Africans into copies of the Nova Scotians, thus reinforcing the Old Settler belief in their own superiority.

The Reverend Charles Wenzel, after the death of his English wife, married Ann Beverhout's sister Fanny. In 1812 when the Reverend Renner was assigned to the Rio Pongo mission, he, too, took a black wife, Elizabeth Richards, who was much admired by his colleagues. She taught 60 girls at his mission, and served Renner as his advisor and interpreter with the Susu people. He wrote glowingly to the CMS secretary: "The Lord has joined black and white together in love, peace & harmony."[12]

Chapter 38

The Crown Replaces the Sierra Leone Company

The Sierra Leone Company continued to run the colony using an annual subsidy from the British government until 1807. Negotiations to dissolve the company began as early as 1803, for continuous deficits and the 1800 rebellion had convinced the company directors that their African enterprise would never fulfill the expectations of its founders. They feared that eventual insolvency might cause the colony to disintegrate.

The 1807 purchase of all land on the peninsula in effect removed the Temne to the mainland, where they were no longer a menace to Freetown. For a brief time, peace and harmony prevailed in Freetown. The dissidents were gone. As security increased and wages rose, Nova Scotian traders, artisans, businessmen and women (Mary Perth among them), and gentlemen farmers prospered. For the first time, social mixing among whites and blacks became common. The Old Settlers could feel that they were finally being treated with respect by the white company officials in Freetown, who attended wedding feasts and sponsored Nova Scotian frolics, to which the Maroons and indigenous Africans were not invited. White officials took Old Settler mistresses and produced families of mulatto children, consolidating an assimilated community, aware and protective of its privileged position.

As the company was about to end its days, Thomas Ludlam (who became governor again when William Day died in 1806) was instructed to tell the settlers on the directors' behalf of "the satisfaction we have felt in contemplating their increasing good order, under trying circumstances, for several years past; and to assure them, that although we cease to govern them, we shall not cease to do whatever may be in our power to promote their happiness."[1]

In 1808 the Sierra Leone Company was dissolved by an act of Parliament, without compensation for the property in Freetown transferred to the Crown. All authority in Sierra Leone was then invested in the British Crown—Britain's first permanent colony in Africa. The Sierra Leone Company directors regrouped themselves as the Africa Institution to promote commerce and civilization in Africa and to provide continuing advice on British colonial policy there.

In 1807 Parliament also legislated the abolition of the British slave trade.[2] British captains could no longer trade in slaves, but Americans, Spanish, and Portuguese stepped in quickly to replace them. In 1807 the United States prohibited any further trade in slaves, as well, although renegade American and English ship captains continued clandestine voyages across the Atlantic.[3] Britain worked actively thereafter to end the trade, stationing a squadron of warships along the West African coast to seize slave ships en route to plantations in the West Indies and the United States and paying bounties to the owners and the expenses to resettle the slaves. Captured slave cargoes were often put ashore at Freetown, where a Vice-Admiralty Court was set up to forfeit captured slaves to the Crown and decide their fate.

Still secretary of the Sierra Leone Company in London, Zachary Macaulay suggested that they be apprenticed to the Old Settlers in order to teach them useful skills for earning their living. Thus, they were settled on the edges of the town, often grouped together according to their tribal origin—a Congo Town and villages for the numerous Ibos and Yorubas. The Maroons welcomed tribesmen from the Gold Coast (now Ghana), claiming to have come from the same region. Macaulay won the profitable appointment as agent for those Royal Navy captains claiming prize money, established a commercial firm in Freetown, and grew rich on the commissions charged for negotiating the bounties.[4]

The brief period of harmony in Freetown ended abruptly when the first Crown governor arrived. Thomas Petronet Thompson, friend of

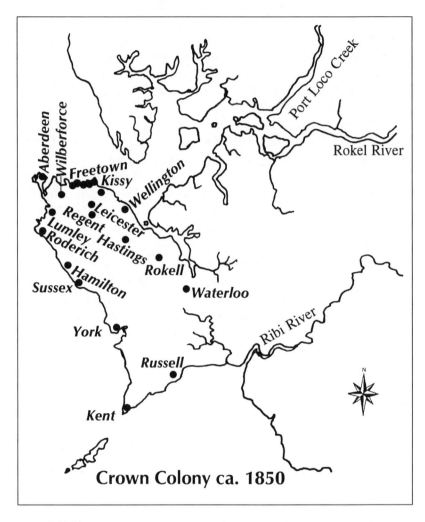

Crown Colony ca. 1850

William Wilberforce, the son of a rich banker in Hull, 25 years old, a blunt military man, had little empathy for easygoing Old Settler society.[5] When he found over 150 indigenous Africans chained in Fort Thornton for trying to escape after Governor Ludlam had apprenticed them to Nova Scotian masters, Thompson decided on the spot that the Old Settlers and former company officials were deliberately taking advantage of the system to gain cheap, unskilled, bonded labor for their farms and businesses.

Thompson released the Africans immediately, and declared all apprenticeships null and void and any kind of slave dealing a capital offense. He further punished the Nova Scotians by cutting wages for skilled artisans in half, by canceling licenses and trading monopolies, and by giving the Liberated Africans part-time employment and land on which to start farms so that they could compete with the settlers. As their numbers increased, he preferred to apprentice them to Maroons, whom he trusted would train, rather than exploit them. John Kizell complained that the government "took the Captive and the Kruman and set [them] before our children and us ourselves, this is hurtful."[6]

Governor Thompson immediately disbanded the Volunteer Corps in its smart blue and gold uniforms because its members were paid. He replaced it with an obligatory, unpaid militia of all males between the ages of 15 and 60.[7] The Old Settlers met and decided to reject his plan, and they sent ten delegates to inform the governor. Thompson immediately called the settlers to a mass meeting, where he disqualified the ten delegates from holding any public office in the colony and charged them with treason. Then he publicly reduced the Old Settler officers of the Volunteer Corps to the ranks and appointed new white officers over them.

Thompson soon reported to the British secretary of state that he found the Nova Scotian "vain, loquacious, full of the idea of his own importance, insidious, fawning, and suspicious, with all the vices of civilization and none of the greatness of the savage."[8] It never occurred to him that the example the Old Settlers had copied was set by the white officials of the Sierra Leone Company, many of whom were very haughty and status-conscious, disdained hard manual labor, dressed extravagantly, quarreled frequently among themselves, and were overly fond of alcohol and illicit sex.

When the Old Settlers defied Thompson by pointing out that this was Freetown, he changed the name to Georgetown, gave some of the streets the names of British military leaders, and abolished the money called dollars and cents. When the settlers continued to denounce his Militia Act in their chapel meetings, Thompson formed a special constabulary of all the whites in Freetown and mobilized the Liberated Africans for action against any violence, thus reintroducing racial division into the colony. He went so far as to leave a Maroon headman in charge when he left the colony briefly in 1809 with a detachment of troops to restore order after a riot on Bunce Island. Another Maroon was appointed to supervise all grumettas and Liberated Africans hired by the government.

The Old Settlers must have felt betrayed once again as Thompson wielded his coalition of whites, Maroons, and Liberated Africans against them. The very people whom they considered inferior were now being raised above them. When the senior leaders—Moses Wilkinson, David and Phillis George, Mary Perth and her new husband (name unknown)—met in the lanes of Freetown as they went about their daily business, surely they stopped to commiserate that another tyrant ruled them.

Thompson was particularly incensed by liaisons between young settler women and white officials; he blamed the company governors still in Freetown for encouraging such laxity and immorality. William Dawes and Thomas Ludlam in turn demanded an enquiry into these charges; they were ultimately exonerated. When Thompson's accusations of mismanagement, corruption, and the reintroduction of slavery reached the former company directors in London; they felt personally insulted and began pressuring the secretary of state for his recall. Barely eight months after his arrival, Thompson was ordered to return to England.[9]

Too late. Those few halcyon months of harmony between the settlers and their white officials were over. Up to 1,000 Liberated Africans were being put ashore in Freetown every year from captured slave ships. They soon ringed Freetown with a dozen new villages, outnumbering the original settlers.[10] Myriad customs, traditions, and racial stocks were thrown together. White European missionaries sent out by the Church Missionary Society labored among the Liberated Africans to make Christianity and education the cement that would transform them into copies of their teachers. They in turn would be the shining example for all the African hinterland pagans to follow. (Fourah Bay College would be founded by the CMS in 1827 to train Africans for the priesthood.)

A huge government effort was needed to feed, house, and clothe the slaves liberated from slave ships, then train them and find jobs for them. This meant more contracts, more work for artisans, and more profit for tradesmen. The apprentice system was reinstituted by Thompson's successor, Captain Edward Columbine, so that the Liberated

Africans again provided cheap labor for both the Nova Scotians and the Maroons, augmenting their prosperity.

Gradually the numbers of Liberated Africans grew beyond the possibility of apprenticing them to trades, so that the Old Settlers and Maroons could secure their indentured services for three to fourteen years, depending on their age, and use them for whatever menial tasks they preferred not to do themselves. Eventually, as the slopes above the watering place were crowded full, the Crown government began establishing rural villages with quaint English names like Regent, Bath, and York elsewhere on the peninsula. Because Whitehall refused to finance these villages beyond a small rice subsidy for those unfit for military service or apprenticeships, they were not included in any central administration. Instead, CMS missionaries were put in charge and would act not only as ministers of the faith but as schoolteachers, administrators, and magistrates.[11]

Illness forced Governor Columbine to resign after only 14 months in Freetown. Ludlam died and Dawes resigned—the last two friends the Nova Scotians had in positions of authority. Columbine was replaced by Lieutenant Colonel Charles Maxwell, who transferred as commander from Senegal, bringing his own council members with him. His primary concern was fighting the slave trade and defending Freetown against neighboring Africans. In November 1811 he proclaimed a new Militia Act, which required universal service and strict military discipline. The Old Settler and Maroon leaders again felt that an English governor was dividing the colony by pitting the Liberated Africans against them.

Maxwell could rely on his force of loyal captured Africans to keep order. He dismissed the dissidents and deprived them of their Liberated African apprentices, then proclaimed that all males who did not enroll in the militia were outlaws and must forfeit their property. Almost 100 Maroons and 14 Nova Scotians gave up considerable property and their farms and moved to a new settlement outside the colonial boundary. A delegation of Maroons went to England to complain and won the support of Granville Sharp and other members of the African Institution.

Governor Maxwell was distracted from his military preoccupations when the British government ordered that all land claims in Sierra Leone, including the full 20-acre allotment promised to the Nova Scotians by John Clarkson in 1793, must be settled once and for all. Annoyed with the bother that would involve, Maxwell added onerous conditions to the grants: No militia evader could obtain a grant. All grants had to be cleared and fenced and a habitable dwelling built on them. Each grantee must pay quitrent and surveyor's and recording fees.

Most Nova Scotians came forward to register their town plots in Freetown, but few bothered to seek title to their farm grants since no surveyor was available to define the boundaries. At that time barely three dozen Nova Scotians were actually farming the poor soil of the peninsula on an average of 4.5 acres each, and they had no intention of paying the quitrent. The others found greater prosperity pursuing businesses in town or trading with the neighboring Africans.

Chapter 39

Farewell, Cotton Tree

In 1804, when she was in her 60s, Mary Perth married a settler whose name is not recorded. His companionship was surely a solace to her. She must have mourned as old friends from New York and Birchtown passed from the scene. David George, also in his 60s, died in 1810 and was succeeded as the leading Baptist pastor by Hector Peters,[1] whom he had converted in Nova Scotia.

Moses Wilkinson was still alive and preaching, but no longer in charge of Methodist affairs. His infirmities left him with only enough energy to deliver an occasional fiery sermon. His Rawdon Street congregation had been so factionalized by the many controversies over the quitrent that half the congregation had drifted away. In 1807 the three Methodist preachers split their followers into three separate groups — the Great Meeting, the Interceding Meeting, and Christ's Chapel.

Mary doubtless dropped in regularly on frail Daddy Moses to share comfort and gossip. His disabilities made it even harder for him to move around now, but his congregation must have paid an African servant who fixed tea while he and Mary remembered the old days. Surely they reprised together their escape from slavery and their determined pursuit of those fleeting opportunities that brought them finally to this sunswept, green haven on the African coast. Where had they found the courage three decades earlier — to flee their masters and find their way to New York, to cross the ocean to an unknown destination, to struggle to fulfill their dreams?

Neither of them had descendants to found a prominent family in Freetown, but they surely admired and talked about those who did. Sophia Small, Eric Ackim, and David Edmonds had wisely invested their profits in real estate. Abraham and Martha Hazeley had sent a daughter to be educated in England; she married a white missionary. James Wise and Anthony Elliott had become chapel preachers.

They surely were proud that their Nova Scotian community had all their children attending school, and dismissed the rough-and-ready Maroons who did not understand that literacy was always the key to escaping manual labor and winning minor employment in the colony government. Nova Scotian children became teachers, clerks, jurors, policemen. Freetown had six schools in 1810, half of them private institutions charging fees. All but one of the teachers was Nova Scotian. The curriculum was weighted heavily with scripture, proverbs, and hymns, emphasizing righteousness and extolling the unique character of the Old Settlers. Pupils were predominantly Nova Scotian, with interested Maroons and Liberated Africans receiving instruction separately.

The Old Settlers, with little say in governing the colony, had turned again to their chapels for solace. No longer a focus of political activity, the chapels served as the major social grounding and reinforcement of Nova Scotian culture. The preachers who had led their congregations across the wide Atlantic had crossed over Jordan one by one. Now younger men were in charge: Domingo Jordan and Warwick Francis each led small, Baptist-leaning chapels. Mrs. Amelia Buxton held services in her home under the suggestive title "the Speaking Congregation."[2] Mary Perth and Daddy Moses would have discussed the arrival of white missionary George Warren in 1811 to superintend the Methodist Society in Freetown, and the three English schoolmasters who came with him. Did they express secret delight that the pious Methodist curriculum had drawn 90 boys away from the government school run by the Anglican Church Missionary Society?

Mary doubtless congratulated Daddy Moses for his acumen in having Governor Maxwell's new deed for the Methodist chapel on Rawdon Street registered in the names of the church trustees and elders, making the settler members permanent proprietors of their property and independent of any English Methodist Missionary Society. They would have discussed the growing number of Maroons attending Methodist

services and debated whether they should be welcomed into the Nova
Scotian congregations or encouraged to build a chapel of their own at
the other end of town, where they lived.

Old antagonisms died hard. Daddy Moses would have wrestled
repeatedly with the memory of how the Maroons had put down the Old
Settler rebellion in 1800. The two groups still did not mix much anywhere, except in church, and the young men in each community occasionally provoked denominational street fights to vent their antagonism
and dissipate their energy.

In spite of the many trials and disappointments, Mary and Daddy
Moses could console themselves with the fact that their community was
now prosperous and their people well settled in their African home.
They had never been allowed to run their own government, true, but
they were free, as they had longed to be, and many had the means to
leave Freetown and go elsewhere if they wished—even to England if
they desired. The slave trade was now outlawed, and English authority
was forcibly ending the commerce in human lives. It may not have been
all that they had dreamed of, but it was enough that they were content.

Blind Daddy Moses never tired of listening to Mary unfold the
contrasting landscapes in her memory—lush marshes and ranked
tobacco fields along the James River in America, the cruel, pristine
snows in Nova Scotia, England's orderly green orchards and rainswept
fens, crumpled jungle blanketing the misted hills above Freetown. She
doubtless painted word pictures for him of the sailing ships coming and
going in the estuary and of the mighty cotton tree still standing below
Fort Thornton, maintaining its vigil over the roofs of the growing community,[3] but after 1813 Mary's name no longer appeared in the records
of Freetown. Did they bury her beloved New Testament with her? Daddy
Moses surely honored her with a spirited eulogy in his chapel and then
laid her to eternal rest in the grassy churchyard, a world away from their
Virginia birthplace.

In spite of his handicaps, Moses Wilkinson outlived all his contemporaries. Physically unable to work for a living, he had always been
cared for by his grateful congregation, and so it continued until his long
life finally ended.

Epilogue

From 1808 until 1824, the main preoccupation of Governor Charles McCarthy was the civilizing and Christianizing of the thousands of Liberated Africans put ashore in Freetown. In that cause he enlisted the invaluable assistance of the Anglican Church Missionary Society to run schools and administer the nine new village parishes established around the Freetown peninsula. (Not surprisingly, the mortality rate among missionaries sent to Sierra Leone was very high; the numbers sent out to West Africa were never adequate.) The colony government built a church, school, and superintendent's quarters in each of the new parishes and supplied clothing and provisions.

After McCarthy's death fighting the Ashante in the Gold Coast, the CMS asked to be relieved of its administrative responsibilities. Religion thereafter had a lower priority in Sierra Leone than the production of export crops. Government expenditures were much reduced, and the Liberated Africans were left to manage their own affairs. They governed their villages with headmen chosen by consensus, the traditional African style, and moved into trade with the interior tribes. In 1853 they were recognized as British subjects, and admitted to the newly constituted Legislative Council in 1863.[1]

Freetown remained the capital of Sierra Leone, but a very different Sierra Leone from that of 1813. The British were occupied during the second half of the nineteenth century with little wars up the rivers that interfered with trade, attempting to stamp out internal squabbles and domestic slavery among the interior tribes. Finally, in 1898 Britain established a protectorate over the much larger area in the hinterland that very nearly corresponds to Sierra Leone's borders today.

The protectorate, slightly smaller than the state of South Carolina, was opened up to penetration and development when a narrow-gauge railroad was constructed from Freetown to Bo in 1900, then extended to Pendembu in 1906. Railways bring civilization and commerce to inaccessible areas. They not only conquer natural obstacles in their way but also introduce the ideas and practices of the outside world. Rather than benefiting the Freetown settlers, the railway permitted the intrusion of energetic Syrian traders, who hustled far more industriously than the status-conscious Krios and awakened the indigenous Africans of the interior to the possibility of eventually controlling the affairs of their homeland.

Bo became the administrative center of the Protectorate Assembly, made up of the indigenous chiefs and tribal headmen whose native administrations the British would groom to rule the country one day. When independence was granted in 1961, the first prime minister was a Bo resident and leader of the Sierra Leone People's Party rather than a Krio descendant of Freetown.

Appendix:
Roster of Prominent
Emigrants to Freetown

Here follows a list of prominent freed blacks who were evacuated from the colonies in 1783 (with place of origin, if known) and emigrated to Freetown, Sierra Leone, in 1792.

Catherine Abernathy (husband Adam died en route to Africa)   school teacher for Associates of Dr. Bray in Nova Scotia; school teacher in Freetown.

Eli Ackim   apprenticed to the apothecary; bought real estate in Freetown, sired a prominent family.

Job Allen   appointed a peace officer by Governor Ludlam.

Isaac Anderson (Charleston, SC)   born free, a carpenter; served in British Army during American Revolution; led protest against the Sierra Leone Company's taking the waterfront; named a delegate by the settlers to carry a petition to Sierra Leone Company directors; appointed justice of the peace; carried a petition to the senior naval officer on the coast, asking him to arbitrate over the quitrent; elected a hundredor; chosen to be justice of the peace (but never installed); leader in the 1800 revolt, hanged for treason.

Zimrie Armstrong   named secretary in the 1800 revolt.

William Ash (Charleston, SC)   mason; Methodist preacher in the Countess of Huntingdon's connection.

Richard Ball (Camden, SC)   Methodist preacher in Halifax, Nova Scotia.

Henry Beverhout (born free in St. Croix)   moved to St. John in Nova Scotia with Thomas Peters; company captain; Methodist preacher; in Freetown appointed Anglican church parish clerk; company schoolteacher.

John Bull   assisted John Clarkson in organizing the exodus from Nova Scotia.

Ezekiel Campbell   permitted conspirators to meet in his house during the 1800 revolt.

Scipio Channel   dismissed from company employment because of controversy with a slave trader; arrested for inciting rebellion in 1793, sent to England for trial, found guilty and banished from Freetown.

George Clark   appointed a peace officer by Governor Ludlam.

Thomas Cooper (born in England)   ran a company retail shop; then appointed as a schoolmaster; appointed trade superintendent in Rio Pongas; first black named alderman.

Richard Crankapone   elected town marshal in Freetown, then undersheriff; partner of John Kizell in shipping cattle and rice from upcountry; killed in 1801 defending Freetown against King Tom.

John Cuthbert   company captain in Nova Scotia; Baptist elder; elected marshal in Freetown; granted a license to open a retail shop; later chosen to be justice of the peace (but never installed); named judicial officer in the 1800 revolt, banished for his participation.

Miles (Myles) Dixon   Methodist preacher; company school teacher; sent to London as a witness in the 1793 treason trial; elected tithingman and hundredor by the settlers; elected surveyor of streets and roads in Freetown.

Richard Dixon   member of Cato Perkins's company; council messenger; part-time clerk in Freetown.

David Edmonds   captain of a company emigrating from Nova Scotia;

elected a tithingman in 1795, hundredor in 1798; badly wounded in 1800 revolt trying to arrest Nathaniel Wansey.

James Edmonds   apprenticed to company surgeon.

Warwick Francis   appointed a peace officer by Governor Ludlam.

David George (Essex County, VA)   company captain; leading Baptist preacher in both Nova Scotia and Freetown; received missionary training in England; did mission work among the Temne of Sierra Leone.

Jess George   apprenticed to the apothecary.

Samuel Goodwin   arrested for inciting rebellion in 1793, sent to London for trial, found guilty, and banished from Freetown.

John Gordon (born in Africa; slave in Dorset County, MD)   farmer.

Abraham Elliott Griffith (emigrant from London to Granville Town) interpreter to King Naimbana; chief interpreter in Freetown.

Martha Hazeley (Abraham Hazeley's wife from Charleston, SC) granted a license to open a retail shop in Freetown; her daughter was sent to England for education; her family became prominent in Freetown.

Robert Horton   private fisherman in Freetown.

James Jackson   given material to build a fishing boat; arrested for inciting rebellion in 1793, sent to London for trial, found guilty, and banished from Freetown.

Simon Johnson   arrested for inciting rebellion in 1793, sent to London for trial, found guilty, and banished from Freetown.

Luke Jordan (Nansemond County, VA)   sailor; company captain; trusted assistant to Methodist preacher Moses Wilkinson; strong opponent of company government; elected tithingman in 1796, 1797, 1798; led his company to a new settlement on Pirate's Bay.

Mingo Jordan (Isle of Wight County, VA)   emigrated from Digby, Nova Scotia, with Thomas Peters; appointed company school master to African children in Freetown; chosen by hundredors to be a judge (never installed).

Robert Keeling   chief porter on the wharf; dismissed from company employment because of a controversy with a slave trader; later granted a license to open a retail shop.

Boston King (Charleston, SC) Methodist preacher; appointed missionary schoolmaster for African children; volunteered to go as a missionary to the Bullom Shore; spent two years in England receiving mission training.

Lewis Kirby arrested for inciting rebellion in 1793, sent to London for trial, found guilty, and banished from Freetown.

John Kizell (son and nephew of African chiefs in Sherbro country of Sierra Leone; sold into slavery at age 12) farmer in Nova Scotia; sent to London as a witness in the 1793 treason trial; elected a tithingman; ran a liquor store; plantation farmer on his nine-acre allotment; joined with Richard Crankapone and Abraham Smith to borrow £5 from the council and build a merchant craft, bought rice and bullocks in the Sherbro country for sale in Freetown; sent by the governor to negotiate with the Sherbro chiefs; established a trading post and a church on Sherbro Island, where he preached in the Sherbro language.

Henry Lawrence appointed a peace officer by Governor Ludlam.

Joseph Leonard Anglican preacher, school teacher in Brindley Town, Nova Scotia; Methodist preacher and school teacher in Freetown; elected a hundredor.

Isaac Limerick Anglican school teacher in Birchtown, Nova Scotia.

Mrs. Lucas school teacher in Freetown.

Scipio Lucas apprenticed to master shipwright.

John Manuel arrested for inciting rebellion in 1793, sent to London for trial, found guilty and banished from Freetown.

Andrew Moore (Augusta, GA) born in Africa; settled on hill above Freetown; discovered wild coffee in Sierra Leone.

Frank (Francis) Patrick hanged for stealing a gun during the 1800 revolt.

Cato Perkins (Charleston, SC) Methodist preacher of the Countess of Huntingdon's connection; led an unsuccessful strike of the carpenters against the Sierra Leone Company for higher wages; delegate of settlers to carry a petition to Sierra Leone Company directors.

Caesar Perth (Norfolk, VA) military wagoner for a British artillery company during the American Revolution; company captain in Nova Scotia; Mary Perth's husband.

Mary Perth (Norfolk, VA) shopkeeper; ran a boarding house; Governor Macaulay's housekeeper.

Hector Peters (Charleston, SC) played the French horn in a military band during the American Revolution; Baptist preacher who succeeded David George.

Stephen Peters known as a "thundering orator"; elected a hundredor; led the 1796 campaign against the white candidates, defeating all of them; carried a petition to the senior naval officer on the coast, asking him to arbitrate over the quitrent.

Thomas Peters (Wilmington, NC) sergeant in Black Guides and Pioneers during the American Revolution; company captain; Methodist preacher; traveled from Nova Scotia to London to seek redress from British government; strong opponent of company government in Freetown.

William Pitcher apprenticed to the master of works.

Simon Proof appointed jailer in Freetown.

James Reid (Norfolk, VA) served with royal artillery during the American Revolution; captain in Nova Scotia; elected town marshal for Granville Town; surveyor of streets and roads in Freetown; granted a license to open a retail shop.

James Robinson (father and son from Virginia) company captain; sent to London as a witness in the 1793 treason trial; became a spirit dealer on his return to Freetown; elected tithingman; leader in 1800 rebellion; banished for his role.

John Salter (Philadelphia, PA) member of Black Pioneers during the American Revolution; follower of Thomas Peters.

Matthew Sinclair sent to London as a witness in the 1793 treason trial: banished for role in 1800 revolt.

Sophia Small granted license to open a retail shop; tavern keeper; bought real estate in Freetown.

Abraham Smith sent to London as a witness in the 1793 treason trial; banished for his role in 1800 revolt.

Nathaniel Snowball (Virginia)   company captain in Nova Scotia; led his company to form a new settlement on Pirate's Bay; elected a hundredor.

Nathaniel Snowball Jr.   appointed captain of a company trading ship with an African crew.

Murphey Still   sergeant in the Black Guides and Pioneers during the American Revolution.

America Talbot (went to Freetown from St. John in Nova Scotia) given company boat building materials for fishing in Freetown; preacher with Nathaniel Snowball's secessionist colony on Pirate's Bay.

Joseph Tybee   arrested for inciting rebellion in 1793, sent to London for trial, found guilty, and banished from Freetown.

Nathaniel Wansey   farmed the hill above Thornton Hill; elected tithingman; leader in 1800 revolt.

Henry Washington (Virginia; ex-slave of George Washington)   banished for role in 1800 revolt.

Anthony Wilkins   appointed a peace officer by Governor Ludlam.

Moses Wilkinson (Nansemond County, VA)   blind and lame; leading Methodist preacher in both Nova Scotia and Freetown (known there as Daddy Moses); strong opponent of company government.

Thomas Wilson   appointed a peace officer by Governor Ludlam.

Ishmael York   elder in Huntingdon's connection; held a liquor license; elected a hundredor; led the 1796 campaign against the white candidates; carried a petition to the senior naval officer on the coast, asking him to arbitrate over the quitrent; banished after the 1800 revolt.

Notes

Introduction

1. For example, *borku*, meaning "much," is derived from the French word *beaucoup*.

2. According to Roy Lewis in *Sierra Leone* (London: Her Majesty's Stationery Office, 1934), babies are still called *pikins* in Freetown, from *pequeno nino*, Portuguese for "darling child."

Chapter 1. Mary Perth of Norfolk, Virginia

For a more complete documentation of the entire saga of the black loyalists, see Ellen Gibson Wilson, *The Loyal Blacks* (New York: Putnam's, 1976), and James W. St. G. Walker, *The Black Loyalists* (New York: Dalhousie University Press, 1976).

1. Mary Perth's name appears in the diaries of Thomas Clarkson and Zachary Macaulay, governors of Sierra Leone in the 1790s. Much of what is known about the exodus to Freetown comes from memoirs of other blacks, published in various church magazines. See *The Missionary Magazine for 1796*, vol. 1, pp. 177–78; Boston King, "Memoirs of the Life of Boston King, a Black Preacher, written by Himself, During his Residence at Kingswood-School," *American Magazine* vol. 2 (1798); and "An Account of the Life of Mr. David GEORGE, from Sierra Leone in Africa," *The Baptist Annual Register for ... 1793.*

2. First formed in several of the colonies in 1765 to protest the Stamp Act.

3. See Virginius Dabney, *Virginia, The New Dominion* (Garden City, NY: Doubleday, 1971), especially chapter 13.

4. The terminology used by the combatants during the American Revolution may sound strange these days. The British called the American patriots opposing the rule of the British Crown "rebels." They thought of themselves as "loyalists," while the Americans called those white colonists loyal to the Crown "Tories." These terms will be used in this sense throughout.

5. Benjamin Quarles, *The Negro in the American Revolution* (Chapel Hill: University of North Carolina Press, 1961), 21–31.

6. Seven years later, when Mary Perth left New York, her name was recorded along with Patience Freeman, Zilpah Cevils, and Hannah Cevils.

7. John Thornton Posey, *General Thomas Posey: Son of the American Revolution* (East Lansing: Michigan State University Press, 1992).

8. A fashionable custom of the time was to give slaves pompous classical names such as Caesar, Pompey, Socrates, Scipio, and Aristotle.

Chapter 2. Moses Wilkinson of Nansemond County, Virginia

1. Wilkinson's name is listed in the *Book of Negroes*, the record made as the black loyalists were evacuated from New York in 1782.

2. George Whitefield, *George Whitefield's Journals* (London, 1905), 6, 11, 18.

3. Winthrop D. Jordan, *White over Black: American Attitudes Toward the Negro 1550–1812* (Baltimore: Penguin, 1969), 214.

4. Frederick Douglass wrote that when his mistress began teaching him to read, her husband found out what was going on and put an end to it: "Learning will spoil the best nigger in the world. If he learns to read the Bible it would forever unfit him to be a slave. He should know nothing but the will of his master, and learn to obey it. As to himself, learning will do him no good but a great deal of harm, making him disconsolate and unhappy." Frederick Douglass, *Narrative of the Life of Frederick Douglass* (New York: Macmillan, 1962) 79.

5. Granville Sharp, *A Declaration of the People's Natural right to a Share in the Legislature; Which Is the Fundamental Principle of the British Constitution of State* (London: B. White, 1774), 28.

6. Thomas Paine, *The Writings of Thomas Paine*, ed. Moncure Daniel Conway, vol. 1 (New York: AMS Press, 1967), vol. 1, 7.

Chapter 3. David George of Essex County, Virginia

1. "An Account of the Life of Mr. David GEORGE, from Sierra Leone in Africa" (as told to Brother John Rippon), *Baptist Annual Register* 1 (1790–1793): 473–84.

2. George Washington had suggested freeing the slaves to help fight the British, but the southern states vetoed the idea.

3. "An Account of the Life."

4. Wesley M. Gewehr, *The Great Awakening in Virginia, 1740–1790* (Durham, NC: Duke University Press, 1930), 236.

5. After the war's end, Liele was sent to Jamaica as an indentured servant. He worked out his time and established the black Baptist church there. See Carter G. Woodson, *The History of the Negro Church* (Washington, DC: Associated Publishers, 1921), 43–47.

6. Edward McCrady, *The History of South Carolina in the Revolution 1780–1783* (New York: Macmillan, 1902), 661.

Chapter 4. Four Men from Charleston: Boston King, Isaac Anderson, Cato Perkins, and John Kizell

1. King, "Memoirs," 105–110.
2. *Ibid.*

Chapter 5. Thomas Peters of Wilmington, North Carolina

1. The Continental Congress was first organized in 1774 to formulate a uniform response to the imposition of a British tax on imported tea.

Chapter 6. Refuge in British New York

For a detailed history, see Oscar Theodore Barck Jr., *New York During the War for Independence* (New York: Columbia University Press, 1931), and Wilbur C. Abbott, *New York in the American Revolution* (New York: Scribner's, 1929).
1. See Abbott, *New York in the American Revolution.*
2. Barck, *New York During the War for Independence*, 74ff.
3. *Ibid.*

Chapter 7. Peace Treaty Terms

1. David Duncan Wallace, *The Life of Henry Laurens with a Sketch of the Life of Lieutenant Colonel John Laurens* (New York: Putnam's, 1915).
2. The final peace treaty, with Article VII intact, was not signed until September 3, 1783.
3. King, "Memoirs," 157–161.
4. Henry Laurens wrote a letter to his son indicating that he abhorred slavery, but blamed the English for making the southern colonies dependent on slave labor. See Wallace, *The Life of Henry Laurens*, 446.
5. Henry Steele Commager, ed., *Documents of American History* (New York: F. S. Crofts, 1938), 119, and Samuel Flagg Bemis, *The Diplomacy of the American Revolution* (Edinburgh: Oliver & Boyd, 1957), 194–95.

Chapter 8. Evacuation from New York

1. Wilson, *The Loyal Blacks*, 41ff.
2. In 1790 President Washington's administration stopped asking for the return of the slaves. Some compensation was paid in 1798. Ill feeling over the treaty provisions persisted through the War of 1812, when Britain again offered freedom to slaves who deserted their American masters. In 1826 Britain paid $1 million to compensate for 3,601 slaves—half the value claimed by the Americans. See Wilson, *The Loyal Blacks*, 56–57.
3. Washington himself had lost a number of his slaves, among them Deborah (wife of Harvey Squash), Daniel Payne, and Henry Washington—all of whom were evacuated to Nova Scotia. See Wilson, *The Loyal Blacks*, 52.

4. "Book of Negroes," Carleton papers, New York Historical Society, 70.

5. *Ibid.*

6. Some loyalists were sent to England, some to the West Indies, and the bulk to Nova Scotia. Among the latter were some 67 blacks identified as Black Pioneers (21 men, 28 women, 18 children). One-third of them had run away from masters in Virginia, some citing Dunmore's proclamation as their motivation. Black Brigade evacuees numbered 82, apparently the remnant of black units raised at Savannah or Charleston. See Wilson, *The Loyal Blacks*, 34–35.

7. Wilson, *The Loyal Blacks*, 75.

Chapter 9. The Founding of Birchtown

1. Nova Scotia's first settlers had come from Scotland in 1629 and gave their home the Latin name for New Scotland. Three-quarters of Nova Scotia's early settlers came from New England. The major Native American tribe, the Micmac, was neither numerous nor hostile. They fished along the coast in summer and hunted moose and caribou in the forests in winter.

2. Slaves had been brought to Nova Scotia before the American Revolution. The first record of a slave sale there was in 1767, when a slave girl named Louise fetched £15. A census that year listed 104 slaves in a total population of 3,022. Public Archives of Nova Scotia, vol. 443, Poll tax and census rolls, 1767–1794.

3. Parr to Carleton, October 9, 1982, Public Record Office, London, item 30/55/51.

4. Necessaries and Provisions given to Loyalists, June 14, 1783, Foreign Office, London, 4/1.

5. The muster book for the Port Roseway Associates in 1784 listed 4,700 white loyalist settlers, 1,191 disbanded white soldiers, 1,485 free Negroes, and 1,269 servants (largely Negro slaves). Robin W. Winks, *The Blacks in Canada, a History* (New Haven: Yale University Press, 1971), 38.

6. W. O. Raymond, "The Founding of Shelburne: Benjamin Marston at Halifax, Shelburne and Miramachi," *New Brunswick Historical Society Collections* 3; (1909).

7. These names will later be connected with the founding of Freetown.

8. Colonial Office Records, London, item 217/59.

9. Public Archives of Nova Scotia, vol. 213.

10. William Dyott, *William Dyott's Diary, 1781–1845* (London: Archibald Constable, 1907), 57.

11. Colonial Office, item 217/63.

12. Wilson, *The Loyal Blacks*, 88ff.

13. Robin W. Winks, *The Blacks in Canada* (New Haven: Yale University Press, 1971), especially chapter 2.

Chapter 10. Education Mattered

1. Wilson, *The Loyal Blacks*, 94ff.; Public Archives of Nova Scotia; Shelburne Records, University of Michigan.

2. Thomas Clarkson papers, Huntington Library, San Marino, CA.

3. Public Archives of Nova Scotia, Land Papers, vol. 396.
4. Wilson, *The Loyal Blacks*, chapter 5.

Chapter 11. Black Preachers Offer Hope

1. "An Account of the Life," 473–484.
2. Thomas Jackson, ed., *The Lives of Early Methodist Preachers Chiefly Written by Themselves*, 3 vols. (London: John Mason, 1837).
3. Public Archives of Nova Scotia; Shelburne Papers.
4. Winks, *The Blacks in Canada*, 39.
5. "An Account of the Life," 473–484.
6. King, "Memoirs," 209–213.
7. Wilson, *The Loyal Blacks*, 89–90.

Chapter 12. Farms for White Loyalists

1. Wilson, *The Loyal Blacks*, chapter 6.
2. Public Archives of Nova Scotia, vols. 346, 369; Margaret Ells, *Settling the Loyalists in Nova Scotia* (Canadian Historical Association Report, 1934), 105–9.
3. Public Archives of Nova Scotia, vols. 47, 223.
4. *Ibid.*, vol. 213.
5. *Ibid.*, vols. 371 and 394A.

Chapter 13. Thomas Peters in Annapolis County

1. Wilson, *The Loyal Blacks*, 75ff.
2. *Ibid.*, 108ff.; Winks, *The Blacks in Canada*, 36–42.
3. Public Archives of Nova Scotia, vols. 380, 368, 47, 367; Isaiah W. Wilson, *A Geography and History of the County of Digby, Nova Scotia* (Halifax, 1900), 50–51.
4. Wilson, *The Loyal Blacks*, 110–11.
5. Public Archives of Nova Scotia, vol. 395; Winks, *The Blacks in Canada*, 42.
6. Colonial Office, item 217/63, "The Humble Memorial and Petition of Thomas Peters a free Negro."
7. Wilson, *The Loyal Blacks*, chapter 6.
8. Wilson, *The Loyal Blacks*; Winks, *The Blacks in Canada*.
9. T. Carleton to Dundas, Colonial office, item 188/4.

Chapter 14. Refugees in London

1. James Walvin, *Black and White: The Negro and English Society, 1555–1945* (London: Alvin Lane, The Penguin Press, 1973), 46ff. In the fifteenth century Portuguese captains established a monopoly on maritime trade in Africa south of the Sahara. Later they would act as middlemen in the slave trade as other European nations began to compete with them. By the middle of the sixteenth century, English merchants began voyaging to West Africa to bring Negroes back to England.

Queen Elizabeth I gave royal approval to John Hawkins's first piratical engagement in 1563 in the slave trade. (Hawkins made three visits to Sierra Leone, raiding for slaves without paying for them.) Later, a famine in England led the queen to order in 1601 the expulsion of the heathen blacks then employed as domestic servants and entertainers. Her attempt to protect the purity of the English race was unsuccessful. See also Walvin, *The Black Presence: A Documentary History of the Negro in England, 1555–1860* (New York: Schocken, 1972).

2. See Norma Myers, *Reconstructing the Black Past: Blacks in Britain 1780–1830* (London, Frank Cass, 1996), chapter 4.

3. Mary Beth Norton. "The Fate of Some Black Loyalists of the American Revolution," *Journal of Negro History* 58 (1973): 402–26.

4. Wilson, *The Loyal Blacks*, 138.

5. *Ibid.*

6. E. A. Wrigley, "A Simple Model of London's Importance in Changing English Society and Economy," *Past and Present* 5 (1967): 44–70. Estimates of London's population at the time ranged from 10,000 to 40,000. Without a census, such figures are hard to validate. See also Norma Myers. *Reconstructing the Black Past*, 7–8 and chapter 2.

7. Myers, *Reconstructing the Black Past*, 7–8 and chapter 2.

8. In the second half of the eighteenth century, English planters, merchants, and ship captains had a strong interest in maintaining their slave assets, often supported by politicians who had wealth tied up in slaves. A substantial number of members of Parliament owned West Indian plantations. See Stephen J. Braidwood, *Black Poor and White Philanthropists* (Liverpool: Liverpool University Press, 1994), 66; F. O. Shyllon, *Black Slaves in Britain* (London: Oxford University Pres, 1974), chapter 6.

9. Audit Office Records, London, item 12/101.

10. Granville Sharp papers, New York Historical Society.

11. O. A. Sherrard, *Freedom from Fear* (New York: St. Martin's Press, 1959), 109–12; John Peterson, *Province of Freedom: A History of Sierra Leone 1787–1870* (Evanston, IL: Northwestern University Press, 1969), 19.

12. See Folarin Shyllon, *Black People in Britain 1555–1833* (London, Oxford University Press, 1977); Walker, *The Black Loyalists* 96ff.; Braidwood, *Black Poor and White Philanthropists*, 12–19.

13. Sherrard, *Freedom from Fear*, 102.

14. Samuel Hopkins, *The Works of Samuel Hopkins* (Boston: Doctrinal Tract and Book Society, 1852), 2:607; W. E. Burghardt DuBois, *The Suppression of the African Slave-Trade to the United States of America* (New York: Schocken Books, 1969), 34; Prince Hoare, *Memoirs of Granville Sharp, Esq.*, 2nd ed. (London: Henry Colburn, 1837), 2:125–28.

15. The name Sierra Leone then applied only to the small peninsula on the south shore of the Rokel River estuary. Europeans had not yet explored the interior, save by boat up the Rokel. The excellence of the harbor in the estuary prompted the establishment of slave factories on islands behind the peninsula in the Rokel River.

16. Christopher Fyfe, *A History of Sierra Leone* (London: Oxford University Press, 1962), 14.

17. Granville Sharp wrote scholarly and popular tracts condemning slavery;

he drew together powerful friends to form an influential pressure group that worked against the planter lobby; he confronted slaveholders, personally and in court; he cared for 400 "pensioners" out of his own resources. All this was more than most individuals could afford, and it severely taxed Sharp's limited income. See Walvin, *Black and White; and The Black Presence*.

18. Henry Smeathman, *Plan of a Settlement to be Made near Sierra Leone, on the Grain Coast of Africa* (London: T. Stockdale, 1786), 23–24.

19. *Ibid.*

20. Braidwood, *Black Poor and White Philanthropists*, 94, chapter 3; Wilson, *The Loyal Blacks*, 145.

21. Wilson, *The Loyal Blacks*, 143ff.

22. Fyfe, *A History of Sierra Leone*, 14–19.

23. Treasury Records, item 1/621; Treasury, 1/636; Admiralty Records, item 106/2347; Treasury, item 1/638; Treasury, item 1/636; Treasury, item 27/38.

24. Fyfe, *A History of Sierra Leone*, 14; Wilson, *The Loyal Blacks*, 144.

25. Between 1781 and 1785 at least 212 convicts were actually banished to Cape Coast (present-day Ghana) and a few to Gorée (in present-day Senegal).

26. Braidwood, *Black Poor and White Philanthropists*, chapter 3.

Chapter 15. The Founding of Granville Town

1. Wilson, *The Loyal Blacks*, chapter 8.

2. The number was obviously too small to have any great impact on the thousands of black poor in London.

3. Born in Africa, Vassa spent his childhood on a plantation in the American colonies, then was bought by an English naval officer and was educated aboard ship, then sold back into American slavery. He worked assiduously for his new master, saved his wages until he could purchase his own freedom, then served on many merchant ships and became skilled in navigation and the other arts of shipping. Inspired by the preaching of evangelist George Whitefield, he resolved to devote his efforts to helping black slaves return to their country of origin. Ending up in London, he became a leading black abolitionist and friend of the black poor, meeting Granville Sharp in the process. He had unusual natural talents that might have helped establish the new colony in Sierra Leone. Vassa would later become famous as the author of a very eloquent memoir, *The Interesting Narrative of the Life of Olaudah Equiano or Gustavus Vassa the African, written by himself*, published in London in 1789 and a bestseller in his day. The memoir gives a moving first-person account of the Middle Passage (it is reproduced in Paul Edwards and David Dabydeen, *Black Writers in Britain 1760–1890* (Edinburgh: Edinburgh University Press, 1991); see also Walvin, *Black and White*.

4. Admiralty, 1/2594; Admiralty, item 51/627.

5. Parliamentary Papers (1789), vol. 82.

6. Braidwood, *Black Poor and White Philanthropists*, chapter 4.

7. A rail connection did not cross Oguru Gorge to the mainland until 1906. See Roy Lewis, *Sierra Leone* (London: Her Majesty's Stationery Officer, 1954), for a history of modern Sierra Leone.

8. The city of Freetown today has two- and three-foot ditches along the streets to drain heavy rainfall into the sea. The torrents cascading down them are so vigorous that children who fall into them are swept away and drowned.

9. The only really sheltered anchorage for ships on the surf-bound West African coast, the peninsula had been used by ships of all European maritime nations ever since the Portuguese first reached it in 1462.

10. Now immortalized as Pademba Road—a main artery leading south out of modern Freetown.

11. Today, Fourah Bay College stands on the crest of the cliffs above.

12. Colonial Office, item 270/14.

13. Sierra Leone Company Report, 1791.

14. Captain Thompson's log, Admiralty, item 51/627.

15. Fyfe, *A History of Sierra Leone*, 22.

16. Parliamentary Papers, 1789, 1790.

17. Wilson, *The Loyal Blacks*, 164.

18. Parliamentary Papers (1789).

19. Sharp papers.

20. Wilson, *The Loyal Blacks*, 170ff.

21. Hoare, *Memoirs of Greenville Sharp*, 2:150; Anna Maria Falconbridge, *Narrative of Two Voyages to the River Sierra Leone During the Years 1791–1793* (1802; London: Frank Cass, 1967), 67.

Chapter 16. Thomas Peters Travels to London

1. Thomas Clarkson, "Some Account of the New Colony at Sierra Leone," *Universal Magazine*, 3 (1792):229–31.

2. Colonial Office, 217/63, "The Humble Memorial and Petitions of Thomas Peters a free Negro on behalf of himself and others the Black Pioneers and loyal Black Refugees." The text may have been polished by some of the abolitionists Peters met in London.

3. Wilson, *The Loyal Blacks*, chapter 10.

4. Thomas Clarkson papers.

5. Wilson, *The Loyal Blacks*, chapter 9.

6. Braidwood, *Black Poor and White Philanthropists*, 229–31.

Chapter 17. An Emissary from the Sierra Leone Company

1. Thomas Clarkson papers.

2. Colonial Office, item 217/63; Public Archives of Nova Scotia, item 419/1.

3. John Clarkson papers.

4. *Ibid.*

5. *Ibid.*

6. Winks, *The Blacks in Canada*, 68.

7. *A History of Sierra Leone*, 34.

8. *Guinea* was a Portuguese term adopted in the fifteenth century, possibly the Berber word for *black*, used by the Sahara people who carried gold, slaves, and ivory by caravan from West Africa across the desert to North Africa. The designation *Guinea* at that time included all of West Africa. See E. W. Bovill, *The Golden Trade of the Moors* (London: Oxford University Press, 1958).

Chapter 18. Bonds Forged in Nova Scotia Congregations

1. Wilson, *The Loyal Blacks*, chapter 6.
2. The Methodist church was founded in the 1730s by an evangelical clergyman, John Wesley, who sought to reform the Church of England by stressing individual salvation through personal faith and strict discipline.
3. Public Archives of Nova Scotia, Memoir of Bishop Inglis; Colonial Office, 217/68; David George memoir.
4. Winks, *Blacks in Canada*, 39. Shelburne had depended on the uneven rum trade with the West Indies, which was cut off in 1790 by Britain's renewed war with France.
5. Colonial Office, item 217/63; Colonial Office, item 217/72; Wilson, *The Loyal Blacks*, 208ff.
6. Jackson, *The Lives of Early Methodist Preachers*, vol. 3, 157.
7. King, "Memoirs."
8. Marrant was born in New York, spent his childhood in Georgia, and was converted by the evangelist George Whitefield. He sought refuge with the Cherokee tribe, was residing in Charleston at the beginning of the American Revolution, and served the British as a musician on a sloop throughout the war, ending up in England. In 1785 he was ordained in England as a minister in the Countess of Huntingdon's connection.
9. John Marrant, "A Narrative of the Lord's Wonderful Dealings with John Marrant," *The Monthly Review* 73 (1785): 399.
10. The Countess of Huntingdon's followers were Calvinist Methodists, who, upon the break between the Wesleyans and George Whitefield, followed the latter. The Huntingdonians initially intended to supplement regular Anglican worship with daily prayer meetings, revivalistic services, and classes for Christian instruction.
11. Walker, *The Black Loyalists*, 72.
12. The Roman Catholics had few black converts in Nova Scotia because the white communicants would not accept them in regular services. The few black Catholics preferred their own services, led without church approval by one of their own, and they gradually drifted away from the established church. See Winks, *The Blacks in Canada*.
13. Wilson, *The Loyal Blacks*, chapter 5; see also Walter H. Brooks, "The Evolution of the Negro Baptist Church," *Journal of Negro History* 1 (1922):11–12.
14. Dr. Bray's Associates Canadian papers, United Society for the Propagation of the Gospel, London.
15. Wilson, *The Loyal Blacks*, 199ff.

Chapter 19. Still Searching for Freedom and Security

1. Public Archives of Nova Scotia, vol. 48.
2. John Clarkson papers, vol. 1, "Mission to America," New York Historical Society.
3. Colonial Office, item 217/63.
4. Wilson, *The Loyal Blacks*, 219ff.
5. Colonial Office, item 217/63; John Clarkson papers.
6. John Clarkson papers.

7. Christopher Fyfe, ed. *Our Children Free and Happy* (Edinburgh: Edinburgh University Press, 1991), 2.

8. John Clarkson papers.

Chapter 20. *Plans to Govern Freetown*

1. Wilson, *The Loyal Blacks*, 183.

2. Granville Sharp papers, New York Historical Society.

3. James Bandinel, *The Trade in Slaves from Africa* (1842; London: Frank Cass and Company, 1968), 82ff.

4. John Clarkson papers; *Diary of Lieutenant Clarkson, R.N.*, Sierra Leone Studies, no. 8 (March 1927).

5. Bandinel, *Trade in Slaves from Africa*, part 2, chapter 1.

6. Sierra Leone Company Report (1791).

7. Thomas Clarkson papers, Henry E. Huntington Library, San Marino, California.

8. Sierra Leone Company Report (1791).

9. Wilson, *The Loyal Blacks*, chapter 12.

Chapter 21. *To the Cotton Tree*

1. Diary of John Clarkson, *Sierra Leone Studies*, 1927, vols. 7–8. Chapters 21 through 28 of this book are based on Clarkson's diary. These chapters focus heavily on the role of English officials because Clarkson's diary provides an almost daily account of Freetown's first year; his primary concern in this trying period was with organizing the settlement and maintaining order.

2. Falconbridge, *Narrative of Two Voyages*, 139.

3. Christopher Fyfe, *Sierra Leone Inheritance* (London: Oxford University Press, 1964), p. 120, quoting Elliott, *Lady Huntingdon's Connection in Sierra Leone*.

Chapter 22. *An Erratic Beginning*

1. John Clarkson diary.

2. The English knew nothing of the Poro secret society, which was responsible for rites of passage into manhood and acted as a law enforcement mechanism among the local Africans.

3. The slave trade was so successful in Sierra Leone because of the pressure of interior tribes—Mende, Mani, Fulani, and Mandingo (the latter two practicing the Muslim religion)—who were pushing coastward to escape their own internal wars. They sold their captives down the rivers to slave factories on the coast.

Chapter 23. *Continuing Confusion*

1. In the 1780s an estimated 75,000 slaves were transported annually from Africa, half of them carried by British merchants. See Philip D. Curtin, *The Image of Africa* (Madison: University of Wisconsin Press, 1964), 6.

2. John Clarkson diary.

3. *Ibid.*

4. Falconbridge, *Narrative of Two Voyages*, 148, 154–55.
5. Europeans were much more afflicted than the Africans by these fevers, for the Africans had either died of these diseases in childhood or had developed an immunity before they reached adulthood. See Curtin, *The Image of Africa*, chapter 3.
6. Fyfe, *Our Children Free and Happy*.
7. *Ibid.*, 27.
8. John Clarkson diary.
9. *Ibid.*

Chapter 24. Ill Will Between John Clarkson and Thomas Peters

1. The act of Parliament that incorporated the Sierra Leone Company had given the company no judicial authority. See Curtin, *The Image of Africa*, 118.
2. Fyfe, *Our Children Free and Happy*, 26.
3. John Clarkson diary.

Chapter 25. Baptists and Methodists Follow Different Paths

1. John Clarkson diary.
2. *Ibid.*
3. *Ibid.*
4. *Ibid.*
5. Both male and female heads of households voted, a privilege not granted to black males in the United States until after the Civil War.
6. Sierra Leone Company papers.
7. Sierra Leone Company Director's report (1794).
8. John Clarkson diary.
9. *Ibid.*
10. Winterbottom would write the first detailed account of the tribes surrounding Freetown, with small vocabularies included. His second volume was the first systematic account of African medicine. See Thomas Winterbottom, *An Account of the Native Africans in the Neighborhood of Sierra Leone,* 2nd ed. (London: Frank Cass, 1969).

Chapter 26. The Calypso Passengers Interrupt

1. Curtin, *The Image of Africa*, 110.
2. John Clarkson diary.
3. *Ibid.*

Chapter 27. New Company Officials

1. Thomas Clarkson papers.
2. John Clarkson diary.

Chapter 28. Land Grants at Last

1. John Clarkson diary.
2. Fyfe, *Our Children Free and Happy*, 28.
3. In the West African languages, verb forms are constant in every tense. For example, if the third person present tense of the verb *to be* is *he is*, then the conjugation will be *I is, you is, he/she/it is, we is, you is, they is*.
4. Thomas Clarkson papers.

Chapter 29. Angry Settlers Choose Emissaries to the Sierra Leone Company Directors

1. Falconbridge, *Narrative of Two Voyages*, 188.
2. *Ibid.*, 190.
3. Among the white officials, only Isaac Dubois, the commercial agent, John Gray, and Adam Afzelius failed to attend, and their absence was a black mark against them.
4. Falconbridge, *Narrative of Two Voyages*, 203–4.
5. Gray to Clarkson, February 15, 1793, John Clarkson papers.
6. An account of a speech by Prince John Henry Naimbanna after visiting the House of Commons to hear a debate on the slave trade is found in *The African Prince*, published by Zachary Macaulay in 1796. It is reproduced in full in Paul Edwards and James Walvin, *Black Personalities in the Era of the Slave Trade* (London: Macmillan, 1983).
7. Thomas Clarkson papers.
8. Isaac Dubois journal.
9. Wilson, *The Loyal Blacks*, 287–88.
10. *Ibid.*, chapter 15.
11. Falconbridge, *Narrative of Two Voyages*, 186.
12. John Clarkson letters.
13. Clarkson settled down with his bride in East Anglia as a banker and had no more contact with Africa.

Chapter 30. Two Governors: Richard Dawes and Zachary Macaulay

1. Wilson, *The Loyal Blacks*, 299. This and following chapters covering Macaulay's governorship are based on chapters 15 through 19 in Wilson, which are in turn based on Zachary Macaulay's journal.
2. Wilson, *The Loyal Blacks*, chapter 15.
3. Fyfe, *Our Children Free and Happy*, 36–40.
4. Wilson, *The Loyal Blacks*, 297.
5. *Ibid.*, 341ff.
6. Governing Council minutes.
7. Zachary Macaulay journal.
8. Wilson, *The Loyal Blacks*, 337ff.
9. *Ibid.*, 292.

10. *Ibid.*, 313ff.
11. Zachary Macaulay journal.
12. *Ibid.*

Chapter 31. A Chosen People

1. Zachary Macaulay journal.
2. Anonymous, Sermon in *Missionary Magazine for 1746* 1 (1796): 77.
3. Zachary Macaulay journal.

Chapter 32. The Outside World Intrudes

1. Wilson, *The Loyal Blacks*, chapter 16.
2. Fyfe, *A History of Sierra Leone*, 61.
3. Fyfe, *Our Children Free and Happy*, 43–45.
4. Zachary Macaulay journal.
5. Quitrent: A rent paid by a freeman in lieu of services required of him by feudal custom (*American Heritage Dictionary*). Though no longer levied in England, the principle of the Crown's ownership of colonial land led to the demand for quitrents in early British colonies.
6. Fyfe, *A History of Sierra Leone*, 103

Chapter 34. Quarrels Over Religion

1. *Missionary Magazine for 1796* 1 (1796).
2. Colonial Williamsburg reenacts a ceremony called "jumping the broom" to replicate the ties black slave men and women made to each other in the slave quarters, knowing that families could be broken up by auctions or punished with banishment for misdemeanors.
3. Wilson, *The Loyal Blacks*, 348.
4. Zachary Macaulay journal.
5. Macaulay was unaware that the incorporation act creating the Sierra Leone Company gave the company no judicial power whatsoever.

Chapter 35. Growing Prosperity

1. Wilson, *The Loyal Blacks*, 367ff.
2. Walker, *The Black Loyalists*, 349.
3. Colonial Office, item 268/5. The American Colonization Society would later try unsuccessfully to settle there before they moved further east and founded Monrovia in Liberia.
4. Zachary Macaulay journal.
5. *Ibid.*

Chapter 36. Insurrection and Defeat

More detail related to this chapter can be found in chapter 19 in Wilson, *The Loyal Blacks*.

1. Zachary Macaulay journal.
2. In 1798 Isaac Anderson sent to John Clarkson in England a barrel of his first rice harvest to indicate his farming success and his continuing affection.
3. Colonial Office, item 270/4.
4. *Ibid.*
5. Sierra Leone Company Directors' report (1800).
6. Wilson, *The Loyal Blacks*, 388.
7. Colonial Office, item 270/6.
8. Sierra Leone Company report (1801).
9. Perkins was not among those punished after the revolt ended.
10. Fyfe, *Our Children Free and Happy*, 64.
11. Wilson, *The Loyal Blacks*, 393ff.
12. Fyfe, *A History of Sierra Leone*, 85.

Chapter 37. Transition

1. Colonial Office, item 270/5.
2. Fyfe, *A History of Sierra Leone*, 89.
3. Sierra Leone Company Directors' report (1801).
4. Fyfe, *A History of Sierra Leone*, 98.
5. Peterson, *Province of Freedom*, 39.
6. Sierra Leone Company Director's report (1804).
7. By 1823, this annual subsidy to the crown colony government would reach £95,000 (Peterson, *Province of Freedom*, 83).
8. Fyfe, *A History of Sierra Leone*, 99. That residential area is still known today as King Tom.
9. Fyfe, *A History of Sierra Leone*, 88.
10. C. P. Grove, *The Planting of Christianity in Africa* (London: Lutterworth Press, 1948–58), 1: 198–99.
11. Wilson, *The Loyal Blacks*, 373ff.
12. Church Missionary Society, item CA 1/E–2.

Chapter 38. The Crown Replaces the Sierra Leone Company

1. Sierra Leone Company report (1808).
2. Slavery itself in Britain would not be abolished until 1834, after slave insurrections in Barbados in 1816; in Demerara, Guyana, in 1823; and in Jamaica in 1832–33.
3. Bandinel, *The Trade in Slaves*, 124, 176.
4. Richard West, *Back to Africa: A History of Sierra Leone and Liberia* (New York: Holt, Rinehart and Winston, 1970), 79.
5. Peterson, *Province of Freedom*, 50–54.

6. Colonial Office, item 276/92.

7. Peterson, *Province of Freedom*, 50.

8. Colonial Office, item 267/24.

9. Wilberforce personally wrote him suggesting that he be "prudent and judicious" in expressing his opinions upon his return to England.

10. The last slave ship would not be captured until 1862.

11. Peterson, *Province of Freedom*, 60–71.

Chapter 39. Farewell, Cotton Tree

1. Peters became pastor in spite of the fact that he had spent much of the 1790s trading in slaves up the Rokel River. See Fyfe, *A History of Sierra Leone*, 100–101.

2. Thomas Clarkson papers.

3. It still stands today in a major intersection of Pademba Road.

Epilogue

1. The most detailed history of the country can be found in Fyfe, *A History of Sierra Leone.*

Bibliography

Abbott, Wilbur C. *New York in the American Revolution.* New York: Scribner's, 1929.

Adams, John. *The Works of John Adams, Second President of the United States, with a Life of the Author,* ed. Charles Francis Adams. Boston: Little Brown, 1850–1856.

American Magazine 21 (1798).

"An Account of the Life of Mr. David GEORGE, from Sierra Leone in Africa," *The Baptist Annual Register for ... 1793.*

Bandinel, James. *The Trade in Slaves from Africa.* 1842; London: Frank Cass and Company, 1968.

Baptist Annual Register 1790–1793.

Bovill, E. W. *The Golden Trade of the Moors.* London: Oxford University Press, 1958.

Braidwood, Stephen J. *Black Poor and White Philanthropists.* Liverpool: Liverpool University Press, 1994.

Brooks, Walter H. "The Evolution of the Negro Baptist Church," *Journal of Negro History* 1 (1922):11–12.

Carleton, Sir Guy. Papers, New York Public Library, "Book of Negroes."

Clarkson, John. Papers, New York Historical Society.

Clarkson, Thomas. Papers (1787–1846), Henry E. Huntington Library, San Marino, California.

Commager, Henry Steele, ed. *Documents of American History.* New York: F.S. Crofts, 1938.

Cromwell, John Wesley. *The Negro in American History.* 1914; New York: Johnson Reprint Corporation, 1961.

Crary, Catherine S., ed. *The Price of Loyalty: Tory Writings from the Revolutionary Era.* New York: McGraw Hill, 1973.

Curtin, Philip D. *The Image of Africa.* Madison: University of Wisconsin Press, 1964.

Dabney, Virginius. *Virginia: The New Dominion.* Garden City, NY: Doubleday, 1971.

DeHart, J., ed. "Diary of Lieutenant J. Clarkson, R.N. (Governor, 1792)," *Sierra Leone Studies* 8 (March 1927).

Douglass, Frederick. *Narrative of the Life of Frederick Douglass.* New York: Macmillan, 1962.

DuBois, W. E. Burghardt. *The Suppression of the African Slave-Trade to the United States of America 1638–1870.* New York: Schocken Books, 1969.

Edwards, J. Plimsoll, "The Shelburne that Was and Is Now," *Dalhousie Review* 2 (1922).

Edwards, Paul, and David Dabydeen. *Black Writers in Britain 1760–1890.* Edinburgh: Edinburgh University Press, 1991.

Ells, Margaret. "Settling the Loyalists in Nova Scotia," *Canadian Historical Association Report* (1934).

Falconbridge, Alexander. *An Account of the Slave Trade on the Coast of Africa.* London: J. Phillips, 1788.

Falconbridge, Anna Maria. *Narrative of Two Voyages to the River Sierra Leone during the Years 1791–1793.* 1802; London: Frank Cass, 1967.

Fyfe, Christopher. *A History of Sierra Leone.* London: Oxford University Press, 1962.

_____. *Sierra Leone Inheritance.* London: Oxford University Press, 1964.

_____, ed. *Our Children Free and Happy.* Edinburgh: Edinburgh University Press, 1991.

Gewehr, Wesley M. *The Great Awakening in Virginia, 1740–1790.* Durham, NC: Duke University Press, 1930.

Grove, C. P. *The Planting of Christianity in Africa,* 4 vols. London: Lutterworth Press, 1948–1958.

Gundara, Jagdish S., and Ian Duffield. *Essays on the History of Blacks in Britain.* Aldershot, England: Avebury Publishing, 1992.

Hoare, Prince. *Memoirs of Granville Sharp, Esq., Composed from His Own Manuscripts, and Other Authentic Documents in the Possession of His Family and of the African Institution,* 2d ed. London: Henry Colburn, 1828.

Hopkins, Samuel. *The Works of Samuel Hopkins.* Boston: Doctrinal Tract and Book Society, 1852.

Jackson, Thomas, ed. *The Lives of Early Methodist Preachers Chiefly Written by Themselves,* 3 vols. London: John Mason, 1837.

Johnson, L. G. *General T. Perronet Thompson, 1783–1869.* New York: Allen and Unwin, 1957.

Jordan, Winthrop. *White Over Black: American Attitudes Toward the Negro. 1550–1812.* Baltimore: Penguin, 1969.

Kaplan, Sidney. *The Black Presence in the Era of the American Revolution, 1779–1800.* New York: Graphic Society Ltd. in cooperation with the Smithsonian Institution Press, 1973.

King, Boston. "Memoirs of the Life of Boston King, a Black Preacher, Written by Himself, During his Residence at Kingswood-School," *The Methodist Magazine for the Year 1789* 21 (1789).

Kup, Peter. *A History of Sierra Leone 1400–1787.* Cambridge: Cambridge University Press, 1962.

Lewis, Roy. *Sierra Leone.* London: Her Majesty's Stationery Office, 1954.

Macaulay, Zachary. Papers (1793–99), Henry E. Huntingdon Library, San Marino, CA.

Marrant, John. *A Narrative of the Lord's Wonderful Dealings with John Marrant,* 2d ed. London: Gilbert and Plummer, 1785.

McCrady, Edward. *The History of South Carolina in the Revolution 1780–1783.* New York: Macmillan, 1902.

McNeill, Ernest, ed. *Chesapeake Bay in the American Revolution.* Centreville, MD: Tidewater Publishers, 1981.

Meacham, Standish. *Henry Thornton of Clapham.* Cambridge: Harvard University Press, 1964.

Myers, Norma. *Reconstructing the Black Past: Blacks in Britain 1780–1830.* London: Frank Cass, 1996.

Norton, Mary Beth. "The Fate of Some Black Loyalists of the American Revolution," *Journal of Negro History* 58 (1973): 402–26.

Paine, Thomas. *The Writings of Thomas Paine.* New York: AMS Press, 1967, vol. 1.

Peterson, John. *Province of Freedom: A History of Sierra Leone.* Evanston, IL: Northwestern University Press, 1969.

Posey, John Thornton. *General Thomas Posey: Son of the American Revolution.* East Lansing: Michigan State University Press, 1992.

Raymond, W. O. "The Founding of Shelburne: Benjamin Marston at Halifax, Shelburne and Miramachi," *New Brunswick Historical Society Collections* 3 (1909).

Scobie, Edward. *Black Britannia: A History of Blacks in Britain.* Chicago: Johnson Publishing Company, 1972.

Sharp, Granville. *A Short Sketch of Temporary Regulations (Until Better Shall Be Proposed) for the Intended Settlement on the Grain Coast of Africa, Near Sierra Leona.* London: H. Baldwin, 1786.

———. *A Declaration of the People's Natural Right to a Share in the Legislature.*

———. Papers, New York Historical Society.

Sherrard, O. A. *Freedom from Fear.* New York: St. Martin's Press, 1959.

Shyllon, Folarin. *Black People in Britain 1555–1833.* London: Oxford University Press, 1977.

———. *Black Slaves in Britain.* London: Oxford University Press, 1974.

Smeathman, Henry. *Plan of a Settlement to Be Made Near Sierra Leona, on the Grain Coast of Africa.* London: T. Stockdale, 1786.

Smith, T. Watson. "The Slave in Canada," *Nova Scotia Historical Society Collections* 6 (1888).

Walker, W. St. G. *The Black Loyalists.* New York: Dalhousie University Press, 1976.

Wallace, David Duncan. *The Life of Henry Laurens with a Sketch of the Life of Lieutenant Colonel John Laurens.* New York: Putnam's, 1915.

Walvin, James. *Black and White: The Negro and English Society, 1555–1945.* London: Alvin Lane, Penguin Press, 1973.

———. *The Black Presence: A Documentary History of the Negro in England, 1555–1860.* New York: Schocken Books, 1972.

West, Richard. *Back to Africa: A History of Sierra Leone and Liberia.* New York: Holt, Rinehart and Winston, 1970.

Wilson, Ellen Gibson. *The Loyal Blacks.* New York: G. P. Putnam's Sons, 1976.

Wilson, Isaiah W. *A Geography and History of the County of Digby, Nova Scotia.* Halifax, 1900.

Winks, Robin W. *The Blacks in Canada, a History.* New Haven: Yale University Press, 1971.

Woodson, Carter G. *The History of the Negro Church.* Washington, DC: Associated Publishers, 1921.

Index